DRESS AND IDEOLOGY

DRESS AND IDEOLOGY

Fashioning Identity from Antiquity to the Present

EDITED BY SHOSHANA-ROSE MARZEL AND GUY D. STIEBEL

B L O O M S B U R Y

LONDON • NEW DELHI • NEW YORK • SYDNEY

Bloomsbury Academic

An imprint of Bloomsbury Publishing Plc

50 Bedford Square	1385 Broadway
London	New York
WC1B 3DP	NY 10018
UK	USA

www.bloomsbury.com

Bloomsbury is a registered trade mark of Bloomsbury Publishing Plc

First published 2015

© Shoshana-Rose Marzel and Guy D. Stiebel, 2015

Shoshana-Rose Marzel and Guy D. Stiebel have asserted their right under the Copyright, Designs and Patents Act, 1988, to be identified as editors of this work.

British Library Cataloguing-in-Publication Data

A catalogue record for this book is available from the British Library.

ISBN: HB: 978-1-4725-2549-9
PB: 978-1-4725-2934-3
ePDF: 978-1-4725-5808-4
ePub: 978-1-4725-5809-1

Library of Congress Cataloging-in-Publication Data

A catalog record for this book is available from the Library of Congress.

Typeset by Fakenham Prepress Solutions, Fakenham, Norfolk NR21 8NN
Printed and bound in India

CONTENTS

AUTHORS

Editors

Shoshana-Rose Marzel

Dr. Shoshana-Rose Marzel is lecturer at the History and Theory department, Bezalel, the Jerusalem Academy of Art and Design. Marzel specializes in fashion studies (theory and history), gender studies and nineteenth-century French novels. Her book on fashion in nineteenth-century French novels, *L'Esprit du chiffon: le vêtement dans le roman français du XIXème siècle*, was published by Peter Lang in 2005. She was invited editor of no. 39/2 (2006) of the academic French periodical *Archives Juives, revue d'histoire des Juifs de France*, on "Jews in the Clothes industry and commerce, in France," and of no. 24 (2013) of the online academic French periodical *Bulletin du CRFJ*, affiliated to the CNRS (with Gal Ventura), on XIXth Century French Visual Culture, France and International Convergences.

Guy D. Stiebel

Dr. Guy Stiebel is a lecturer in the Department of Archaeology and Near Eastern Cultures at Tel Aviv University. He specializes in military archaeology and history and themes of material cultures. In the past 17 years, Stiebel has co-directed the excavations at Masada on behalf of the Institute of Archaeology, The Hebrew University of Jerusalem. His study focuses upon material culture in Classical Palestine and mostly the encounter between material culture and literary sources. He earned his PhD at University College London (UCL) for the study *Armis et litteris: Roman military Equipment of Early Roman Palestine in Light of the Archaeological and historical Sources*. His four years' post-doc fellowship, at the Orion Center for the Study of the Dead Sea Scrolls and Associated Literature, was devoted to the study of the archaeology (*realia* aspects) of the War Scroll. Stiebel has published over 40 papers and co-edited six books. He serves as a co-editor of the series *New Studies in the*

Archaeology of Jerusalem and its Region of the Hebrew University and the Israel Antiquities Authority.

Contributors (in alphabetical order)

Lindsay Allason-Jones

Lindsay Allason-Jones was Director of the Centre for Interdisciplinary Artefact Studies and Reader in Roman Material Culture at Newcastle University until she retired in 2011. She was previously Director of Archaeological Museums for the university. An acknowledged authority on artefacts, particularly those from Hadrian's Wall, Roman Britain and Roman and Medieval Sudan, she is the author of 13 books, including *Women in Roman Britain* and *Daily Life in Roman Britain*. She is Trustee of many of the Hadrian's Wall museums, as well as the Hadrian's Art Trust.

Oz Almog

Oz Almog is Associate Professor (full tenure), Department of Land of Israel Studies, University of Haifa. He has published widely in scholarly journals and edited and authored books, including *The Sabra: The Creation of the New Jew* (University of California Press: Berkeley, 2000) and *Wielokulturowy Izrael* (Multicultural Israel) [Polish] (2011). Wydawnictwo Wyzszej Szkoly Pedagogicznej, TWP w Warszawie, Warszawa. His *Farewell to "Srulik": Changing Values among the Israeli Elite*, 2 vols (Zmora Bitan and Haifa University Press: 2004) was a bestseller in Israel and won two awards: the Bahat Award (University of Haifa Press and Zemora-Bitan Press) and the Rozen-Zvi Award (Faculty of Law, Tel Aviv University).

Ory Bartal

Dr. Ory Bartal is currently head of the History and Theory Department at Bezalel, the Jerusalem Academy of Arts and Design. His work focuses on Japanese Visual Culture and Contemporary Design. Bartal earned his Ph.D. in Cultural Studies from Tel Aviv University, and also holds an M.B.A. degree from Aoyama Gakuin University in Tokyo, Japan. In addition, Bartal is also an expert in Japanese marketing and business practices, with over 10 years of experience in senior positions at leading technology companies active in the Japanese market. Bartal contributes regularly to scientific journals.

Henriette Dahan-Kalev

Prof. Henriette Dahan-Kalev is a political scientist by training and specializes in gender and politics (theory and practice of political resistance). Dahan-Kalev is the founder of the Gender Studies Program at the Ben Gurion University and regularly contributes to scientific journals. Her article "You're so Pretty—You Don't Look Moroccan" (*Israeli Studies* 6 [2001], pp. 1–14) is considered ground-breaking. It is often reprinted and taught in introductory courses of postcolonial and critical studies in Israel and abroad.

Antonia Finnane

Antonia Finnane is Professor of History at the University of Melbourne with a research specialization in the social and cultural history of early modern and modern China. Her publications include *Speaking of Yangzhou: A Chinese City, 1550–1850* (Harvard East Asian Monographs 2004), winner of the 2006 Levenson award for a work on pre-twentieth-century China, and *Changing Clothes in China: Fashion, Nation, History* (New York: Columbia University Press, 2008). At present she serves as an associate editor (pre-1898 China) of the *Journal of Asian Studies*. Her current research concerns the impact of Maoism on small shops in Beijing during the periods of "socialist transformation" and the Cultural Revolution.

Beverly Lemire

Beverly Lemire received her D.Phil. from Oxford University and between 1987 and 2004 taught British History at the University of New Brunswick, Canada. In 2004 she moved to the University of Alberta, where she serves as Professor of History and Henry Marshall Tory Chair in the Department of History and Classics and the Department of Human Ecology. Her publications include *Fashion's Favourite: The Cotton Trade and the Consumer in Britain, 1660–1800* (1991); *Dress, Culture and Commerce: The English Clothing Trade before the Factory* (1997); *The Business of Everyday Life: Gender, Practice and Social Politics in Britain 1600–1800* (2005); and *Cotton* (2011), in the series *Textiles that Changed the World*. Recent edited works include a four-volume collection of documents *The British Cotton Trade* (2009) and *The Force of Fashion in Politics and Society: Global Perspectives from Early Modern to Contemporary Times* (2010).

Peter McNeil

Peter McNeil is Professor of Design History at the the University of Technology Sydney and Professor of Fashion Studies at Stockholm University. His work crosses chronologies and geographies from the eighteenth to the twentieth centuries; the focus is West Europe, North America, and Australia. He is currently an Investigator within *Fashioning the Early Modern: Innovation and Creativity in Europe, 1500–1800*, a Humanities in the European Research Area—Joint Research Programme (2010–13). He is editor and co-editor of eight works on fashion, including the four-volume work *Critical and Primary Sources in Fashion* (Berg, 2009). In 2014 he was appointed Distinguished Professor, University of Aalto, within the Academy of Finland 'FiDiPro' scheme.

Asher Salah

Dr. Asher Salah is senior lecturer at Bezalel, the Academy of Art and Design in Jerusalem. He is one of the leading specialists in the history and literature of Italian Jewry and a translator of Hebrew literature. He has written extensively on Jewish History in Italy, Cinema Studies, and contemporary Middle East politics. Amongst his numerous publications, his book *La République des Lettres: Rabbins, médecins et écrivains juifs en Italie au XVIIIème siècle*, was published by Brill, Leiden/Boston, in 2007.

Gal Ventura

Dr. Gal Ventura is senior lecturer at the Hebrew University of Jerusalem. She is an art historian and deals mainly with nineteenth-century art, the history of the family, maternity, breastfeeding, death, and Christian iconography in modern and contemporary art. She is co-editor of Bezalel History and Theory department's inter-disciplinary peer-reviewed e-journal, *Protocols*, in which she has published several articles. Her book, *Crying over Spilt Milk: Maternal Breastfeeding and its Substitutes in nineteenth-Century French Art*, was published in 2013 by Magnes Press.

LIST OF ILLUSTRATIONS

INTRODUCTION

During the French Revolution, one of the questions the revolutionaries struggled with was the new clothes of the new French citizen. In 10 Floréal an II (April 29, 1794) the newspaper *La Décade philosophique, littéraire et politique* published an article entitled "Considérations sur les avantages de changer le costume françois." Here's an extract of its content:

> Clothing presents physical and political considerations worthy of a reasonable republican's attention … Dressed in more sensible clothing than our own, men would become healthier, stronger, swifter, better able to defend liberty; women would give the state healthier children. A national costume would fulfill functions truly deserving of a free man's consideration, such as constantly proclaiming and recalling *la patrie*, and distinguishing French citizens from nationals of countries still stigmatized by the chains of servitude. It would make it easy to signal the age and public functions of citizens, without tampering with the sacred foundations of equality.[1]

As shown by this example, the concept that ideologies are expressed through what people wear is not a new one. However, although the relationship between ideas and their materialization in dress is an important issue in fashion research, paradoxically it is one of the least-researched themes. This book bridges this marked gap. To make the most of ideas, we stretched to ideologies; then, to demonstrate that the way people dress in order to promote ideologies is as old a notion as human culture, we included chapters that span a long duration of time, from the ancient world to the present; and last, in order to show that every (important) aspect of the relationships between ideology and clothing transcends location and time, we did not limit ourselves to the West, but integrated in each section chapters from a wide geographical and historical range.

Fashion *vs.* clothing

Clothing, dress, and fashion are not interchangeable terms. According to Joanne Eicher and Mary Ellen Roach-Higgins, the term "dress" refers to "an assemblage of modifications of the body and/or supplements to the body."[2] Joanne Entwistle defines dress as "an activity of clothing the body with an aesthetic element" while "[t]he term 'fashion' carries with it the more specific meaning of a system of dress that is found in Western modernity."[3] According to Barnard, "fashion is thus defined as modern, western, meaningful and communicative bodily adornments, or dress. It is also explained as a profoundly cultural phenomenon."[4]

The *Merriam-Webster Dictionary* defines the term fashion as "the prevailing style (as in dress) during a particular time."[5] Thus, according to Marilyn Revell DeLong,

> Fashion involves change, novelty, and the context of time, place, and wearer. Blumer (1969) describes fashion influence as a process of "collective selection" whereby the formation of taste derives from a group of people responding collectively to the *Zeitgeist* or "spirit of the times." The simultaneous introduction and display of many new styles, the selections made by the innovative consumer, and the notion of the expression of the spirit of the times provide impetus for fashion.[6]

To conclude so far, it may be said that fashion is the ability as well as the obligation to change one's dress style in accordance with the new collective one, even when clothes are still wearable. Already from these, fashion is spirit, while clothing, dress, garment, adornments, and so on are its material components.

But there is more to fashion.

Clothing-society *vs.* fashion-society

Most researchers consider that fashion first appeared during the fourteenth century.[7] For James Laver, "it was in the second half of the fourteenth century that clothes for both men and women took on a new form and something emerges which we can already call 'Fashion'."[8, 9]

In fact, fashion is the product as well as the expression of a new society: one which prizes novelty, which appreciates inventions and rewards inventors, and which encourages individuality, for in this new society individuality and individual initiatives are seen as beneficial for the collectivity; individual genius is comprehended as a contribution to all. Recognition of personal value goes hand in hand with body recognition and the will to embellish it—thus fashion. We'll term this society *fashion-society*. In Western history, the invention of fashion precedes and announces Renaissance Humanism. By definition, Humanism is a "system or mode of thought or action in which human interests, values, and dignity are taken to be of primary importance."[10] Thus, fashion that is centered on the body and its beautification is another concretization of Humanism: it is the visualization of humanity put at the center of all interests. To materialize these abstract concepts, from then on, clothes are designed to be close to the body, as opposed to the loose garments worn before that time.

Fashion-invention both expresses and symbolizes the break between medieval times and the Renaissance. Hence, fashion-society stands opposed to the one that preceded it, the one we term *clothing-society*. In clothing-society, innovations and, more so, inventions are perceived as dangerous to the collectivity, as threats to a way of life seen as the only true one. As the only true one, it needs no change. Hence, in this society, every member must erase his/her creative energies, to fit in the mold proposed to everyone. In this mold there is only one form of dress for everybody, it does not change; social status and/or positions are expressed through difference in clothing materials, not in forms. Thus, at its core, clothing-society prizes stability, tradition, and their endless repetition.[11]

Recently, researchers have argued that the idea of fashion as European is an outcome of Euro-centricity.[12] Although many researchers locate Fashion invention in the West, future studies, mainly concerning Japanese and Chinese history, could show otherwise.

Although grounded in history, these two terms—fashion-society and clothing-society—can also be used in order to apprehend societies, regardless of time and space. The properties of each of them have a profound impact on the lives, the thoughts, the ethos, and the lifestyles of their members.

Fashion, clothing and ideology

Some researchers address the question of ideology in its larger sense; for example, John Fiske considers that fashion magazines push young women to a particular prevailing ideology of femininity by means of fashion. Thus, young women are led to believe that they have to look stylish for men.[13]

However, in this book we are using the term *ideology* in a more limited sense. According to the *Random House Dictionary*, ideology is "[t]he body of doctrine, myth, symbol, etc., of a social movement, institution, class, or large group, [as well as] such a body of doctrine, myth, etc., with reference to some political and cultural plan along with the devices for putting it into operation."[14] Thus, each chapter in this book will address a distinctive ideology.

Our theoretical framework will be the distinction between clothing-societies *vs.* fashion-societies to understand the place of ideology in dress. While by definition fashion is about change, most often ideologies want to promote an eternal truth, one which also by definition cannot change. Hence, ideologist leaders often wish to establish societies based on everlasting values, the only true ones, thus bringing about the idea that a perfect society should not change. This position is often translated in a dress designed to embody those values, not ever to change as well. One such informative test case is communist China. One of the first steps taken by communist China's regime was to impose a unified look on all Chinese people, in the form of the simplest Mao suit (the Zhongshan suit), in grey or blue, with minimal hairdo. Through this the Party aimed at expressing values of simplicity, equality, and solidarity, according to the communist ethos. This kind of uniform was worn in China for more than 40 years, from the establishment of the People's Republic of China in 1949 until the suits fell into disuse during the 1990s, due to increasing Western influences.[15] In this example, uniform-like clothing is implemented with the imposition of the communist ideology on the Chinese. Moreover, as soon as the socio-political ideology changed, dress changed as well.[16]

The Communist choice of everlasting clothes can be understood as a will to be a clothing-society instead of a fashion-society. Consequently, to talk about fashion and ideology would be an oxymoron in this case.

Yet, some ideologies use the opposite (= fashion). In these cases, we are talking about ideological dress in a fashion-society. For example, feminism argues that freedom and civil rights equal the woman's right to wear whatever she wants. In this case, the ever-changing European fashion is used as a tool in the struggle for the promotion of the feminist agenda.

Using this book

This book is divided into four categories: Nationhood, Religion, Identity, and Politics. In order to show that the relationship between ideology and clothing transcends location and time, we carefully built each category in a non-chronological order, and integrated in each section chapters from a wide historical and geographical range.

Nationhood

The idea that nationhood expresses through clothing is a basic one, hence the universal concept of national costume, special clothes traditionally worn by a definite people. The creation of a national outfit responds to two requirements: the wish to materialize a particular national identity as well as the wish (and sometimes the need) to appear visually different from other peoples. Gradually, national costumes became folklore, and nowadays these special outfits are worn either by representatives of a definite location, such as folk dancers in international festivals, or at particular occasions—during national festivities, for instance.

Although the terms "ethnic dress" and "national costume" are quite close and sometimes overlap, national costume more often than not is attached to a distinct territory.[17] Ethnic dress is looser in meaning. Nowadays, with the intensification of both globalization and immigration processes, the term ethnic dress is used most often to describe an outfit or some elements of it that are connected to a person's ethnic origin. According to Jessica Strübel, this clothing carries social functions:

> [National] Clothing [...] indicates an aspect of one's own identity and demon-strates that group inclusion and exclusion are made apparent through modifying and supplementing the body. Ethnic dress is also worn by members of a group to distinguish themselves from the members of another group, especially in the face of powerful homogenizing forces.[18]

Moreover, these national outfits are also tied to national ideologies, in the sense that each ethnic group/nation also takes pride in an ideological legacy composed of particular values, such as courage, family values, patriotism, honesty, true justice, creativity, and so forth.

Yet, according to Benedict Anderson's *Imagined Communities*, a nation is a socially constructed community imagined by the people who perceive themselves as part of a distinctive group.[19] Consequently, the combination of imagination and common national values highlight the psychological dimension of national clothing.

The first chapter we present in this section recounts the evolution of Israeli national clothing. "Secular Fashion in Israel," by Oz Almog, describes how Jews coming back to their homeland tried to invent a new Jewish national look. At first, during the pre-state period and the early years of the State of Israel, the word "fashion" was associated with the unkempt pioneer, the *Sabra* look. It was mainly composed of khaki shorts and blue shirts characteristic of the socialist youth movements, biblical sandals, and dome-shaped caps known as *kova tembel*. In their simplicity, they materialized the national pioneering/socialist ideology and anti-diaspora *sabra* values.

However, Western influences gradually grew, thrusting aside the pioneering *Sabra* look. Individualism and eroticism, female independence and asser-tiveness, as well as youthful rebellion, found expression in new styles. Nowadays, elegance and beautification are legitimate; the notion of being "fashionable" is part of the cultural lingo. Hence, as Israeli society evolved from a Zionist socialist ideology to a Zionist bourgeois one, its looks changed from the simple *Sabra* to Western fashion. This evolution also expresses a movement from a clothing-society to a fashion-society.

The second chapter in this section, written by Antonia Finnane, entitled "Sartorial Boundaries on the Chinese Frontier," analyzes national clothing through Chinese art: despite China's history of shifting territorial borders and the corresponding changes over time in the country's ethnic composition, People's Republic of China territories, along with the residents thereof, are invariably described in textbooks, museums, and even in scholarly works as part of the Chinese nation. These claims are expressed in rather complex ways through vestimentary codes employed in the national arena, with 55 neatly packaged "national minorities" regularly being represented in national costume at major national and international spectacles. The ahistoricism of the packaging of "minority" (non-Han) cultures is exposed by frontier paintings from centuries past. For more than a millennium, Chinese artists have been turning for inspiration to ancient stories of cultural contact on China's inner Asian frontiers. Although usually anachronistic in their depictions of the non-Chinese subjects, these paintings are firmly grounded in actual relations between Chinese and Barbarian, Han and non-Han. Thus, the construction of a visible "other" was of fundamental importance to national identification.

In these case studies the imaginary/psychological factor is crucial. For Israelis, clothing was employed in order to concretize an imaginary new Jew in a reborn country, according to Zionist ideology, whereas in China, art continued to preserve an imaginary visual distinction between Chinese and Barbarian, Han and non-Han, according to a nationalist ideology.

Moreover, in both cases, nationhood through dress expresses a wish towards being a clothing-society: in China, ahistoricist art intended to maintain a stable national differentiation for centuries. First Israeli pioneers tried to establish a new society in which all its members would be mobilized for the benefit of a greater cause—socialist Zionism and a simple, uniform-like dress would fit everyone. However, as soon as Israelis left this communal ideology, they adopted Western fashion and its humanist agenda.

Religion

As religion often considers the body the territory of the sacred, rare are the religions that do not affect the body.[20] Religious body treatment includes clothing and is mostly divided into two categories: the clothing of observant ordinary believers *vs.* the clothing of the clergy. This division reflects different perspectives. The clergy often uses clothing both to concretize religious values as well and to make a neat visual distinction between ordinary believers and themselves, as well as to materialize hierarchies inside the religious order. According to Brian Turner:

> The religious hierarchy of grace largely reflects the division of the world into sacred and profane, which Durkheim (1961) thought was the axial distinction in the religious world-view. Lay people are, by definition, constantly involved

in routine, everyday activities in secular employments which are necessary to produce food and reproduce people. The superior status of religious charismatic depends on their clear detachment from that grinding reality of domestic labour and lifelong employment. This social detachment from the profane world may be denoted by a variety of social insignia—clerical dress, tonsures or rabbinical clothing—and by peculiarities of status, most notably seclusion and chastity.[21]

That said, how should the clergy be dressed? As Piponnier and Mane show in their *Dress in the Middle Ages*, Catholic clergy's outfit evolved from clothes used in the West from Classical times.[22] Monastic habits, in turn, retained a markedly medieval aspect until reformed by the Second Vatican Council (1962–5).[23] Moreover, clergy dress, either monastic or for priesthood, expresses different values:

> The salient characteristics of monastic dress have always been sobriety and conservatism. The orders proved even more retentive of archaic fashions than the hierarchy, and, in contrast to the deliberate splendour of ecclesiastical vestments, monastic dress was expressive of a renunciation of luxury. The contrast was functional in origin: the menial tasks of the monk related him sartorially to the peasant, […] rather than to the princes and prelates of the church, whose dress reflected the splendour of the ceremonies in which they engaged.[24]

Then, after being institutionalized, sacred clothing is expected to never change: "Sacred dress, conceived in all these different modalities, configures the body outside time, beyond 'fashion' perceived as the sartorial snares of Satan."[25] Codification of clerical clothing is not reserved for the West. Buddhist monks, for instance, have clothes institutionalized in a very characteristic manner: the monk's robe goes back to the Buddha's time. It is composed of the *triple robe* (*tricivara*), an inner garment or waistcloth, an upper robe, and an outer robe. Nuns can also add to these a vest or bodice.[26]

In our book, Asher Salah's chapter refers to the dress of clerics in Judaism. Contrary to many other religions, Judaism does not prescribe religious clothing, except for the *Tzitzit*, a male garment prescribed by the Bible.[27] There are also some clothes required during prayers, such as a masculine prayer shawl called a *tallith* and men's head covering. Thus, every Jewish community had/has to decide how clerics should be dressed. Asher Salah's "Rabbinical Dress in Italy" addresses this topic through the analysis of the evolution of rabbis' attire in Italy. From the sixteenth century onward, rabbis adopted a particular dress code that was conceived in imitation of the clothes of the Protestant clergy and the medical robe. Even though, the rabbi's attire was perceived among Italians as specifically Jewish attire for clergy, differing from the Catholic. A most interesting phenomenon can be seen here: the "Protestantization" of Italian Judaism, perceptible from the Counter-Reformation onwards, during the past three centuries of Italian Jewish history.

Ordinary believers also use clothing to express their religious belief. Some integrate its values into their clothing in everyday life (such as religious precepts of modesty, for example) in a minor way, while others can be extreme. For instance, the Judean sect of the Essenes, according to Joan E. Taylor,

> work (in white clothing) until the fifth hour and then assemble in one place, where they "gird their loins with linen cloths" and "bathe their bodies in cold water" […] It is wrong to think that white indicates linen as if a particular kind of material has the sole monopoly on the colour. The linen cloths worn by the Essenes are the wraps they wear in the baths and during their pure meals, not their everyday white clothing. […] But white was universally the colour of purity, cleanliness, freshness, and holiness. […] This dress worn beyond the Temple in everyday life would have advertised their high aims, distinctiveness, and identity to the world at large.[28]

The Essenes' ideology of purity was translated into thorough cleansing as well as white clothing. These choices show how completely abstract ideas can concretize in particular materialization. It also points to a harsh clothing-society.

Our second chapter in this section, Lindsay Allason-Jones's "Zoomorphic Brooches in Roman Britain: Decoration or Religious Ideology?" describes a much looser case of wearing religious ideology, by the pagans of Roman Britain. Groups of plate brooches in the form of animals have been found throughout the Northern provinces of the Roman Empire, but are particularly evident in Britain. These zoomorphic brooches have been found in ritual contexts to express the union between the worshipper and his/her deity. The Roman invaders brought to Britain the official state gods of Rome but did not attempt to convert the newly conquered to the Roman religion. Although this could suggest a harmonious religious atmosphere, there is some evidence that there were clashes of religious ideology between worshippers of different cults. Wearing a brooch or badge clearly declared the wearer's allegiance to a particular cult and may not have been without its dangers. In this way, people were standing up for their religious ideologies.

Our last chapter in this section is Oz Almog's "How Muslim Women Dress in Israel". Israel's Arab citizens live in a secular democratic state. Supervision of how women dress is informal and originates in common practices and negotiation between the individual and society. Like in the Arab world, Muslim society in Israel has undergone, over the last three decades, an Islamicist religious revival that has produced significantly stricter standards for how Muslim women should dress. An opposite trend is also evident today—a modern, Western, permissive look. These trends are in competition. Women's ways of dressing, and their fascinating maneuvering between these two poles, is evidence of their struggle.

All cases show that religious dress (and jewelry) tends toward an everlasting design, never to change. More than any other ideological category, religion tends toward clothing-society. The will to stay for ever the same, to never change, brought about, for example, Buddhist monastic dress that did not change for hundreds of years.

Having said that, we can also question whether religious ideologies do materialize in common clothing features. Actually, in light of the cases brought here (and others), we can deduce that some values do: for example, ideas of detachment from the ordinary world translate in very simple clothing (see monastic Catholic dress or that of the Essenes); ideals of religious purity concretize in cleanliness, whiteness, and utmost simplicity (Essenes and Buddhist monks, for instance). Moreover, most religious clothing tends to conceal the body through large clothes, as if religious ideology should always aspire to eliminate the presence of the human body (in Catholicism, Judaism, Buddhism, as well as in Islam). The (religious) clash between matter and spirit reaches here its climax. Moreover, this wish for elimination of the body is most noticeable concerning women; in that case, refers explicitly to sexuality and has to be liquidated. And finally, the dressing of clergy for the exercise of priesthood inclines towards differentiation from the common faithful, and often towards magnificence, such as evidenced by the clothes worn by Catholic clergy.

Identity

Identity in clothing is a well-researched topic in fashion studies, as clothing is often used by individuals to express components of their identity such as gender, social status, age, profession, and so forth. According to Susan Kaiser, "There are two important functions to clothes in nonverbal communication. First, they help us to negotiate identities, as we present our situated identities or roles, moods, values, and attitudes to one another. Second, they help us to define situations, that is, to socially construct the basis for our interactions."[29] In our book, we will emphasize some ideological aspects of clothes as identity markers.

Peter McNeil's chapter, "Ideology, Fashion and the Darlys' Macaroni Prints," the first chapter in this section, analyzes one genre of the printed satirical material of the eighteenth century: the Macaronis. "Macaroni" was a topical term connoting ultra-fashionable male dressing in England in c. 1760–80. By mocking Macaronis, these prints attacked their socio-political identity. For instance, one depicts the dress of an English aristocrat abroad. The mask of civility has slipped under the influence of alcohol; undone stockings and falling wigs, suggesting an uncivilized body, burst forth once the polite veneer of clothing is lost. The artificial performance of genteel or aristocratic "superiority" is exposed, and the class distinction undermined. What the Macaroni caricatures have in common is a recognition and exploitation of the power of dress. Underlying this insight is a self-conscious understanding of the performance of identity.

Ory Bartal's "Feminist Ideologies in Postmodern Japanese Fashion: Rei Kawakubo Meets Marie Antoinette in Downtown Tokyo" analyzes Japanese contemporary fashion via new styles in the late consumer culture that merged economics and aesthetics, creating a contemporary social ideology in Japan. These styles respond to social, economic, and technological changes, giving expression to globalization and establishing a new discourse regarding the bubble economic era. This fashion definitely has Japanese flavors not connected to the Orientalist image of the "Japanese Culture" but rather to the new socio-economic paradigm which expresses the triumph of the consumer culture as a central ideology of the postmodern *zeitgeist* in Japan.

Our third chapter in this section, Guy Stiebel's "Military Dress in Roman Palestine," explores military dress and fittings in Roman Palestine: those of the Roman soldier as well as those of the Judean warrior. These apparels functioned both as identity markers and as visualization of their antithetic ideologies: Roman apparel was the perfect materialization of an imperialist doctrine, while the look of the Judean warrior represented a rebellious independent Jewish ideology.

These examples show perfectly that whether in eighteenth-century England, present-day Japan or Roman Palestine, the use of clothing in order to express personal and social identity did not change. On an ideological level, either to express appraisal to the dominant capitalist ideology (in Japan), to satirize the socio-political pretensions of ultra-fashionable men in eighteenth-century England, or to express opposition to Roman imperialism, clothing's items serve as identity markers.

Politics

Political dress fulfills multiple functions: it can express and consolidate power, such as has been one of the purposes of Royal costume;[30] dress can express political affiliation as well as opposition to it. Furthermore, some historical periods are more prone than others to bring about political clothing. The afore-mentioned French Revolution provides an excellent example of such a period. In revolutionary France, items of dress stood for opposing political ideologies, and the clothes people wore could seal their fate.[31] Moreover, new revolutionary clothing items were designed, such as the liberty cap, the tri-colored cockade, the carmagnole, as well as entire new official dress and the *sans-culotte* attire, in order to materialize the new revolutionary ideology.

The four chapters proposed in this section demonstrate that, regardless of time and space, clothing and fashion are recognized as a powerful tool at the service of politics.

Our first chapter, "Fashion and Feminism," by Henriette Dahan-Kalev and Shoshana-Rose Marzel, tells how feminism uses fashion and particular clothing items in order to promote its agenda. Feminist demands concerning clothing occurred during the French Revolution, nineteenth-century political events, world wars, and continue nowadays regarding female Islamic dress in Europe. Feminists always understood the value of the inevitable bond between clothes and gender, and exploited it for the benefit of their political cause.

In her chapter "Fashion Politics and Practice in the Early Modern World: Indian Cottons in Japan and England," Beverly Lemire compares the reception of Indian cotton textiles in Japan and England in the seventeenth and eighteenth centuries. In both countries, cottons from India shattered stable socio-political hierarchies. The gradual acceptance of individual rights in dress took different routes, though these did not come readily in any community. The flourishing of *iki*-inspired styles in Tokugawa Japan reveals an oblique path, as middle-class Japanese employed these fabrics to push the legal limits of this material regime. The violence against calico-wearing English women reflects how ruthlessly traditional material precepts could be defended, particularly when innovations were symbolized by female agency. The battles over Indian cottons came to epitomize a fashionable collectivity, a growing individualism, and a new materiality.

Our third chapter, by Gal Ventura, "Breastfeeding, Ideology, and Clothing in nineteenth-Century France," depicts how the socio-political ambience towards breastfeeding that evolved during the nineteenth century impacted on maternity clothing and underwear. Through the analysis of French art, Ventura recalls how new clothing items were invented for hired wet-nurses and how the invention of a new corset enabled the bourgeois mother both to breast-feed and be fashionable.

This book closes with Shoshana-Rose Marzel's chapter "Dress as Political Ideology in Rabelais and Voltaire Utopias." Utopias translate ideologies through the inventions of imaginary socio-political worlds. While most English utopias advocate notions of frugality and austerity in dress, Rabelais's and Voltaire's advocate those in which egalitarian political regimes express through opulent, varied, and colorful dress, kept in the fashion of the day.

All these cases (and others) show that not only is politics a crucial factor in our lives, but it is also very influential concerning the way we dress: sometimes, it can seal people's destiny (such as during the French Revolution), be a tool in a struggle (gender struggle in feminism, class struggle in Japan and England in the seventeenth and eighteenth centuries, and more). Its symbolic aspects are no less important, as can be observed during the feminist struggle. Moreover, some political systems try to impose a clothing-society, such as did Communism and

Japanese monarchy in the seventeenth and eighteenth centuries, whereas other political systems integrate fashion-societies (such as seen in nineteenth-century France and the feminist combat).

Concluding remarks

The purpose of this book is to show that dress is an important tool at the service of ideology. Even in imaginary worlds such as utopias, clothing is used in order to express ideological aspirations. The will to express adherence to any ideology manifests best through what a person is ready to put on his/her own body.

Crossing time and space, people all over the world dress in order to carry out ideologies. Consequently, clothing expresses universal values. Nonetheless, despite their abstract similarities, some ideologies are not always manifested in the same clothing designs, while others are—for example, religious notions of simplicity and renunciation from the world expressed in simple clothes, such as those of Catholic monks, Buddhist monks, and Judean Essenes. On the contrary, political power does not always take the form of magnificence, as could be expected: visual splendor was the choice of the Catholic Church, but was rejected by the Communist party (in China as elsewhere). The same can be said concerning identity: it takes different clothing forms according to its goals and socio-historical contexts. And concerning nationhood: as every people claims its uniqueness, national costumes/ethnic dresses can vary greatly from each other.

This compilation of chapters showcases only a few case studies in order to highlight a much larger phenomenon. The same is said concerning its conclusions.

Notes

1   Quoted by Philippe Perrot, *Fashioning the Bourgeoisie: A History of Clothing in the Nineteenth Century*, Princeton, NJ: Princeton University Press, 1994, note 9, p. 204.

2   Mary Ellen Roach-Higgins and Joanne B. Eicher, *Dress and Identity*, Oxford: Berg, 1992, p. 7.

3   Joanne Entwistle, *The Fashioned Body: Fashion, Dress, and Modern Social Theory*, Cambridge: Polity, 2000, pp. 40–1.

4   Malcolm Barnard, *Fashion Theory: A Reader*, London and New York: Routledge, 2007, p. 3.

5   http://www.merriam-webster.com/dictionary/fashion

6   Marilyn Revell DeLong, "Theories of Fashion," Valerie Steele ed., *The Berg Companion to Fashion*, Oxford: Berg, 2010, p. 316.

7   Boucher, François, *Histoire du costume en occident des origines à nos jours*, Paris: Flammarion, 1996, p. 153; Lehnert, Gertrud. *Fashion: A Concise History*, London: Laurence King, 1999, pp. 11, 31; V. Steele, *Paris Fashion: A Cultural History*, New York and Oxford: Oxford University Press, 1988, p. 17.

8   James Laver, *Costume and Fashion: A Concise History of Costume*, London: Thames and Hudson, 1969, p. 62; Fernand Braudel, *Civilisation matérielle, économie et capitalisme, XVème–XVIIIème siècle. 1. Les structures du quotidien: le possible et l'impossible*, Paris: Armand Colin, 1979, p. 374.

9   Others, such as Sarah-Grace Heller, posit fashion invention two centuries earlier. See Sarah-Grace Heller, *Fashion in Medieval France*, Woodbridge: DS Brewer, 2007.

10 http://www.thefreedictionary.com/humanism

11 Shoshana-Rose Marzel, "La mode est un iconoclasme," Jean-Marie Marconot and Bernard Tabuce, eds, *Iconoclasme et Vandalisme: la violence de l'image*, Montpellier III: Université Paul-Valéry, 2005, pp. 271–84.

12 Jean Allman, *Fashioning Africa: Power and the Politics of Dress*, Bloomington: Indiana University Press, 2004, pp. 2–3.

13 John Fiske, *Introduction to Communication Studies*, London: Routledge, 1990, p. 180.

14 *Random House Dictionary*, 1973.

15 Antonia Finnane, "What should Chinese women wear?: a national problem," *Modern China* 22, 2 (April 1996): 99–131; Chen, Tina Mai, "Dressing for the Party: clothing, citizenship, and gender-formation in Mao's China," *Fashion Theory: The Journal of Dress, Body & Culture*, 5, 2 (May 2001): 143–71.

16 Jean Lock Kunz, "From Maoism to *ELLE*: the impact of political ideology on fashion trends in China," *International Sociology*, 11, 3 (September 1996): 317–35.

17 Manning Nash, *The Cauldron of Ethnicity in the Modern World*, Chicago: University of Chicago Press, 1989, p. 6.

18 Jessica Strübel, "Get your gele: Nigerian dress, diasporic identity, and translocalism," *The Journal of Pan African Studies*, 4, 9 (January 2012): 29–30.

19 Benedict Anderson, *Imagined Communities: Reflections on the Origin and Spread of Nationalism*, London and New York: Verso, 1991.

20 Lynne Hume and Joanne B. Eicher, *The Religious Life of Dress: Global Fashion and Faith*, London: Bloomsbury Academic, 2013, p. 1.

21 Brian Turner, *Religion and Social Theory*, London: SAGE, 1991, p. 87.

22 Françoise Piponnier, Perrine Mane, *Dress in the Middle Ages*, New Haven, CT: Yale University Press, 2000, p. 115.

23 *Encyclopedia Britannica*, Religious dress: http://www.britannica.com/EBchecked/topic/497306/religious-dress/66454/Roman-Catholic-religious-dress#ref538604

24 Ibid.

25 William J. F. Keenan, "*Sacre Bleu*: Faith, Fashion and Freedom: Marist Foundation

Garments, 1817–1862," in Elisabeth Arweck and William J. F. Keenan, *Materializing Religion: Expression, Performance and Ritual*, Aldershot: Ashgate, 2006, p. 119.

26 A. B. Griswold, "Prolegomena to the study of the Buddha's dress in Chinese sculpture: with particular reference to the Rietberg Museum's collection," *Artibus Asiae*, 26, 2 (1963): 85–131.

27 Esther Juhasz, "*Tzitzit*–Ritual Fringes," in Esther Juhasz (ed.), *The Jewish Wardrobe: From the Collection of the Israel Museum*, Jerusalem: 5 Continents Editions, 2012, pp. 44–51.

28 Joan E. Taylor, *The Essenes, the Scrolls, and the Dead Sea*, Oxford: Oxford University Press, 2012, pp. 84–5.

29 Susan Kaiser, *The Social Psychology of Clothing: Symbolic Appearances in Context*, New York: Fairchild Publications, 1997, p. 217.

30 Martine Kahane, "Pour bien gouverner, il faut bien paraître," in Martine Kahane, Noëlle Girte, and Marie Vacher, *Costumer le pouvoir: Opéra et cinéma*, Lyon: Fage éditions, 2013, pp. 13–18; Dominique et François Gaulme, *Les Habits du pouvoir*, Paris: Flammarion, 2012.

31 Richard Wrigley, *The Politics of Appearances: Representations of Dress in Revolutionary France*, Oxford: Berg 2002.

Bibliography

Allman, Jean, *Fashioning Africa: Power and the Politics of Dress*, Bloomington: Indiana University Press, 2004.

Anderson, Benedict, *Imagined Communities: Reflections on the Origin and Spread of Nationalism*, London and New York: Verso, 1991.

Barnard, Malcolm, *Fashion as Communication*, 2nd edn, London and New York: Routledge, 2002.

—*Fashion Theory: a Reader*, London and New York: Routledge, 2007.

Boucher, François, *Histoire du costume en occident des origines à nos jours*, Paris: Flammarion, 1996.

Braudel, Fernand, *Civilisation matérielle, économie et capitalisme, XVème–XVIIIème siècle. 1. Les structures du quotidien: le possible et l'impossible*, Paris: Armand Colin, 1979.

Chen, Tina Mai, "Dressing for the party: clothing, citizenship, and gender-formation in Mao's China," *Fashion Theory: The Journal of Dress, Body & Culture*, 5, 2 (May 2001): 143–71.

Encyclopedia Britannica, Religious dress: http://www.britannica.com/EBchecked/topic/497306/religious-dress/66454/Roman-Catholic-religious-dress#ref538604

Entwistle, Joanne, *The Fashioned Body: Fashion, Dress, and Modern Social Theory*, Cambridge: Polity Press, 2000.

Finnane, Antonia, "What should Chinese women wear? a national problem," *Modern China*, 22, 2 (April 1996): 99–131.

Fiske, John, *Introduction to Communication Studies*, London: Routledge, 1990.

Gaulme, Dominique et François, *Les Habits du pouvoir*, Paris: Flammarion, 2012.

Griswold, A. B., "Prolegomena to the study of the Buddha's dress in Chinese sculpture:

with particular reference to the Rietberg Museum's collection," *Artibus Asiae*, 26, 2 (1963): 85–131.

Heller, Sarah-Grace, *Fashion in Medieval France*, Woodbridge: DS Brewer, 2007.

Hume, Lynne and Joanne B. Eicher, *The Religious Life of Dress: Global Fashion and Faith*, London: Bloomsbury Academic, 2013.

Juhasz, Esther, "*Tzitzit*—Ritual Fringes," in Esther Juhasz ed., *The Jewish Wardrobe: From the Collection of the Israel Museum*, Jerusalem: 5 Continents Editions, 2012.

Kahane, Martine, "Pour bien gouverner, il faut bien paraitre," in Martine Kahane, Noëlle Girte et Marie Vacher, *Costumer le pouvoir: Opéra et cinéma*, Lyon: Fage éditions, 2013.

Kaiser, Susan, *The Social Psychology of Clothing: Symbolic Appearances in Context*, New York: Fairchild Publications, 1997.

Keenan, William J. F., "Sacre Bleu: Faith, Fashion and Freedom: Marist Foundation Garments, 1817–1862," in Elisabeth Arweck and William J. F. Keenan, *Materializing Religion: Expression, Performance and Ritual*, Aldershot: Ashgate, 2006.

Laver, James, *Costume and Fashion: A Concise History of Costume*, London: Thames and Hudson, 1969.

Lehnert, Gertrud, *Fashion: A Concise History*, London: Laurence King, 1999.

Lock Kunz, Jean, "From Maoism to *ELLE*: the impact of political ideology on fashion trends in China," *International Sociology*, 11, 3 (September 1996): 317–35.

Marzel, Shoshana-Rose, "La mode est un iconoclasme," in Jean-Marie Marconot and Bernard Tabuce, eds, *Iconoclasme et Vandalisme: la violence de l'image*, Montpellier III: Université Paul-Valéry, 2005, pp. 271–84.

Nash, Manning, *The Cauldron of Ethnicity in the Modern World*, Chicago: University of Chicago Press, 1989.

Perrot, Philippe, *Fashioning the Bourgeoisie: A History of Clothing in the Nineteenth Century*, Princeton: Princeton University Press, 1994.

Piponnier, Françoise and Perrine Mane, *Dress in the Middle Ages*, Yale University Press, 2000.

Random House Dictionary, 1973.

Revell DeLong, Marilyn, "Theories of Fashion," in Valerie Steele ed., *The Berg Companion to Fashion*, Oxford: Berg, 2010.

Roach-Higgins, Mary Ellen and Joanne B. Eicher, *Dress and Identity*, Oxford: Berg, 1992.

Steele, Valerie, *Paris Fashion: A Cultural History*, New York and Oxford: Oxford University Press, 1988.

Strübel, Jessica, "Get your gele: Nigerian dress, diasporic identity, and translocalism," The *Journal of Pan African Studies*, 4, 9 (January 2012): 29–30.

Taylor, Joan E., *The Essenes, the Scrolls, and the Dead Sea*, Oxford: Oxford University Press, 2012.

Turner, Brian, *Religion and Social Theory*, London: SAGE, 1991.

Wrigley, Richard, *The Politics of Appearances: Representations of Dress in Revolutionary France*, Oxford: Berg, 2002.

PART ONE

NATIONHOOD

1

SECULAR FASHION IN ISRAEL

OZ ALMOG

Pioneers *vs.* city dwellers

In national images depicting the early years of the State of Israel, the word "fashion" is deliberately associated with the unkempt pioneering *sabra* look: khaki shorts and blue shirts characteristic of the socialist youth movements, pinafores and *rubashka* shirts influenced by Eastern European style, Bedouin *kaffiyahs*, biblical sandals, and dome-shaped caps known as *kova tembel*. To a large extent, this look became Israel's national mode of dress, part of the mythological image created before the establishment of the state and continuing into its early years.[1]

Yet, in the introduction to *Changing Styles: 100 Years of Fashion in Eretz-Israel*, Ayala Raz's book (1996) on the history of fashion in Israel, the author notes that

> most of the Jewish population of pre-state Israel did not make do with blue shirts or even pinafores but rather wore clothes modeled after Paris fashions to the extent possible under the circumstances. The pioneers, whose shirts and worn-out shoes left an unforgotten impression on history, were a minority. While it is true that many appeared in public dressed in khaki and short pants during the period of austerity and rationing marking the state's early years, many others were seen dressed in tailored suits and fancy dresses in the latest styles.[2]

This discrepancy between the mythological *sabra* image and the way people actually dressed can be attributed to a number of factors. The first is the influence of the British Mandate government. The British meticulous style of dress may have had some impact on Jewish society. Secondly, most of the Jewish residents during the pre-state period lived in cities and therefore adopted urban rather than rural dress. Thirdly, most of the Jewish residents were European immigrants who brought with them patterns of dress and outward appearance from their countries of origin. Fourthly, many of the immigrants had worked in the clothing and fashion industry as tailors, leather workers, and milliners, or as owners of clothing stores or factories, and some tried to establish these businesses in their new country.

By the 1920s, Tel Aviv had already become the fashion capital of pre-state Israel. According to historian Yaacov Shavit, in 1931 Tel Aviv had no fewer than 17 textile factories, 16 small plants for embroidery and handicrafts, and 86 tailoring shops, serving a population of around 24,000.[3]

In *Changing Styles* Ayala Raz points out that

> the numbers show that in the 1920s and 1930s the clothing industry in pre-state Israel developed at an unprecedented rate, apart from short periods of crisis. In 1918 there were 166 small clothing factories. By 1928 another 647 had opened, with the total number reaching 1083 by the end of 1936. More people were employed in clothing and textile factories than in all other industries.[4]

Perhaps in contrast to the prevailing pioneering image, from its inception the Hebrew press offered regular sections on film and theater, literature and poetry, plastic arts, and fashion innovations. The first fashion column in pre-state Israel appeared as early as 1904. It was written by Hemda Ben-Yehuda, wife of Eliezer Ben Yehuda, and published in his newspaper, *Hashkafa*. Over time, the volume of fashion articles in the Hebrew press increased, and in the 1930s and 1940s almost all the newspapers ran articles and even entire sections on this topic.[5] Starting in 1941, professional fashion shows exhibiting readymade clothing held primarily in Tel Aviv attracted buyers from across the Middle East.

As more and more immigrant families became integrated into local life and as new generations of *sabras* joined the ranks of the local population, the trappings of European dress disappeared from the local scene and the proletarian–*kibbutz* style began dominating the Israeli fashion landscape. In the 1960s only a small minority comprising primarily older and more traditional men still sported felt homburg hats or Borsalino fedoras. Very few still wore vests or long chiffon dresses or stiffly starched shirts buttoned at the neck. Indeed, the local custom was to leave the top buttons unbuttoned. Ties also disappeared from the local fashion scene, and even the most prestigious officials, administrators, and state leaders avoided wearing ties, preferring open shirt collars even with suits or jackets.

The Ata takeover and products for everyone

The trend described above can be explained by the impact of the simple, straightforward, and frugal pioneering–*sabra* culture on the new immigrants. Other influencing factors include the hot Israeli climate, the water shortage, and the informal family atmosphere. The economic situation also prevented development of an opulent fashion culture modeled upon European trends.

In the 1950s, most apparel and footwear products were manufactured according to a uniform standard. Sale of these products was controlled by rationing through the Ministry of Rationing and Provision and by customs regulations put into effect to protect Israeli industry against competition with imported products. The textile factory that contributed more than any other factory to the Zionist fashion "standard" was the Ata plant. The factory was established on February 11, 1934 by Erich Moller, who was joined four years later by his cousin Hans. Both were Jewish immigrants whose family had owned prosperous textile factories in Czechoslovakia. The factory developed rapidly, and in its first year already had become the largest textile manufacturer in the Middle East. During the economic crisis in Europe prior to the outbreak of World War II, the factory's owners began producing uniforms, mainly for the British army, as well as clothing for civilians.[6] They were involved in all stages of production, from the threads through the finished products. Ata fabrics were sold in three main colors: khaki, blue, and white. In their simplicity they expressed the national pioneering/socialist ideology and the anti-Diaspora *sabra* values.

Ata's products, originally made from poplin, drill, and satin, were mainly heavy khaki trousers, coarse blue shirts, white underwear and thick woolen socks, and the popular *kova tembel*.[7] These items became the fashion trademark of Israel's working population, and indeed of the entire Zionist enterprise. Even the leader of the new nation, David Ben Gurion, often appeared in public dressed in khaki in an attempt to express identification with the Zionist enterprise and its ethos of sacrifice and simplicity—in short, leadership that spurned arrogance and was close to the people.

Meticulous care for one's outer appearance, like other refinements, was not a strong point of Zionist Israeli culture. It was a small, poor, anti-aristocratic, and partisan society lacking in codes and traditions of material beauty. This approach also dominated the period of austerity *(Tzena)*, during which most apparel and footwear were manufactured in standardized and low-priced styles known as "products for everyone" (*Totzeret Lakol*).

Appearance gains in importance

Starting in the mid-1950s, the textile and leather industries began to develop rapidly. According to the government yearbooks, in 1956 Israel had around 1,150 textile factories that employed 12,000 people and manufactured clothing, coats, socks, hats, and other apparel items in thousands of different models. That same year, there were no fewer than 350 shoe factories, around 20 shoe salons, 100 workshops manufacturing shoes by hand, and 2,000 shoemakers; 1956 was also the first year in which crepe soles and synthetic heels were produced, initiating a revolution in the shoe industry.

Preoccupation with outward appearance was found mainly among the affluent population of the larger cities. In fact, there was a small province of glamour and fashion consciousness in Tel Aviv. During the austerity period Lola Bar was considered the most outstanding fashion designer for society women and designed formal attire for the wives of several national leaders. In 1950 Miriam Yaron was crowned Miss Israel, the nation's first beauty queen, in a contest that was to become an annual event. La'Isha journal, the beauty pageant's sponsor, was the most important player on the Israeli fashion scene.

Maskit, Israel's first fashion house, was founded in 1954. The company's products were produced by artisans from the mass waves of immigrants. Maskit had three objectives: to provide employment and a livelihood for the immigrants, to preserve material and cultural traditions of the immigrants, and to show Israeli society that the immigrants from Arabic-speaking countries were not deprived but rather people with a rich cultural and aesthetic heritage. Ruth Dayan, wife of Moshe Dayan, was Maskit's founder, leader, and guiding spirit.[8] Dayan hired Finy Leitersdorf, a Hungarian-born fashion designer, as Maskit's head designer. Her spouse, artist Yohanan Simon, also designed prints for the company's fabrics. Combining the artists' authentic contributions with her classic/cosmopolitan education, Leitersdorf put together an original style that merged biblical themes, the ingathering of the exiles, and the special lighting and landscapes of Israel into a modern line that was the epitome of "Israeliness." Among Leitersdorf's most outstanding designs are her Desert Coat and her Ein Gedi dress.

In the large cities, and particularly in Tel Aviv, small pockets of post-sabra salon culture cropped up, where people danced to the anti-establishment sounds of rock 'n' roll and wore young American fashions. Young men traded their khaki shorts, biblical sandals, and unruly forelocks for tight-fitting shirts and trousers, high-heeled patent leather shoes, and Elvis hairdos. For the first time young women sported pumps and full skirts. The gatekeepers of pioneering sabra society considered salon culture a form of treason or heresy, and some "defiant" youngsters were even unceremoniously kicked out of the youth movements simply for daring to wear clothes that were modern, erotic, or individualistic.

Then, as now, Tel Aviv was the nation's fashion capital and trendsetter. In the late 1950s and early 1960s, the social code of beauty enhancement gained ground among women, influenced by Hollywood and its glamour girl stars.[9]

Boutique and Batik

The first major turnaround in Israeli fashion and beauty culture took place toward the end of the 1960s. Israel's stirring victory in the Six-Day War motivated people to celebrate and open up. Furthermore, the flower children revolution in the West had an impact on Israeli style, as did the debut of television broadcasts in Hebrew and the influx of foreign volunteers to the *kibbutzim*. The press began featuring more fashion columns and more pictures, and advertisements became more professional. A second generation of fashion manufacturers and merchants emerged, and new department stores featured apparel and shoe departments. The Israel Export Institute opened a Fashion Center, and Israeli Fashion Week was launched for buyers from abroad. The Shenkar College of Textile Technology and Fashion was founded in 1970.

Boutiques—a term new to the Israeli lexicon—began sprouting in Tel Aviv.[10] These boutiques sold mainly beatnik clothes inspired by the flower child fashion trends, and their foreign-sounding names added to their exotic flavor. Israelis also began to frequent Palestinian stores in the territories conquered in the Six-Day War, particularly in East Jerusalem. The clothes they found there together with the hippie/shanti influence produced a new ethnic and somewhat bedraggled style.

Western influences grew, thrusting aside the pioneering *sabra* look. Individualism and eroticism, female independence and assertiveness, and youthful rebellion found expression in the new styles: tight-fitting clothing, miniskirts and tights, knee-high boots, and matching plastic accessories. For the first time elegance and beautification gained legitimacy, the notion of being "fashionable" became part of the cultural lingo, and fashion trends changed at a dizzying pace.

Nonetheless, until the 1990s most Israelis continued to dress conservatively and did not comply with changing fashion trends. The average Israeli went on wearing clothes that ranged from casual to downright sloppy, and was much less concerned about outward appearance than his middle-class counterpart in the West. Most *sabra* women avoided clothing and shoes that attracted too much attention, and very few wore high heels. They also shunned lipstick, makeup, manicures and pedicures, and sophisticated or provocative hairdos.

The culture of beauty

In the 1970s the fashion industry in Israel began to become more professional. One of the first indications of this change emerged in the language.
The fashion terminology of the 1960s—"fashion artist," "fashion planner," and
even "fashionist"—was replaced by a patently more prestigious term—"fashion
designer." Indeed, during that time a new generation of fashion designers and
fashion photographers came of age, among these were designers Gideon
Oberson, Riki Ben-Ari, Shuki Levy, and Doreen Frankfurt, and photographers
Peter Herzog and Mila Haramati.[11]

Fashion in Israel reached its zenith between 1968 and 1973. At Fashion
Weeks, Israeli manufacturers introduced their newest styles to leading buyers
and fashion journalists from around the world. Manufacturers such as Beged Or,
Polgat, and Gottex gained international fame, penetrating exclusive chain stores
and outlets in Europe and the United States.

Fashion models such as Karin Dunsky, Hani Peri, and Tami Ben-Ami were
turning into media heroines, particularly in women's magazines. The use of
cosmetics increased as well, particularly after the Revlon Israel plant opened in
1962. Indeed, many a young Israeli man breathed in the fragrance of Revlon's
popular Charlie perfume when kissing his sweetheart for the first time.

Toward the end of the 1970s, fashions from abroad gradually began to exert
more and more influence on Israeli styles of dress. During this new era, the
glory of the sabra-pioneering khaki style began to wane, as did the conservative
Eastern European fashions.

Sabras in American jeans

The outward trappings of the sabra style did not disappear completely during
the 1970s. Indeed, the sabra style actually absorbed a number of new items
expressing old values, among them checkered woolen bedroom slippers
manufactured by HaMegaper, military parkas, and Ray-Ban sunglasses, whose
popularity was inspired by Israeli pilots. Nevertheless, khaki—the ultimate
symbol of the sabra—disappeared from the scene, along with the kova tembel.

The fact that during this period American influences began to infiltrate the
fashions of the younger generation is of particular importance from the sociological perspective. Three articles of clothing adopted by the sabras in the 1970s
contributed to the gradual shift from the image of "bedraggled" *Palmachnik/
kibbutznik* to that of sloppy American hippie chic: t-shirts, sweatshirts, and jeans.

T-shirts became extremely popular in Israel. They were very suitable for the
hot climate, gradually supplanting white Ata undershirts, and they offered an

opportunity to look somewhat American at an affordable price. In the early 1970s, most t-shirts were solid-colored, and the batik tie-dyeing technique, easily done at home, was used to jazz them up a bit.

Like t-shirts, sweatshirts also eventually became a way for individuals and groups to express themselves. Both t-shirts and sweatshirts played a part in supplanting the *sabra* style because they easily competed with the flannel shirts of the youth movements and added English-language logos to the Israeli landscape.

Jeans

One of the most important symbols of American democracy made its debut in 1860, when a 26-year-old Jewish man named Levi Strauss came from Bavaria to the West Coast of the United States with a roll of canvas in order to sell tents to the gold miners. But the miners, whose knees were bruised from kneeling in the rocky streams, needed durable trousers, and Levi was quick to fill this market gap. From then on, jeans have been associated with cowboys, independence, class equality, youth culture, free sex, and feminism, just to name a few. It was not until the 1950s that jeans were worn in Israel, and even then only by a few, mainly those serving in the merchant marines or lucky individuals who received them as gifts from relatives in America.

More jeans began to be seen in Israel toward the end of the 1960s, when volunteers began flocking to the *kibbutzim* and tourism from abroad increased. Indeed, for young people there was no more treasured gift than a pair of jeans. Yet, for parents and teachers, jeans were a symbol of the hippie rebellion that seemed to be threatening the social order. Moreover, by wearing jeans young-sters managed to circumvent school uniform directives, for while most schools required blue trousers, no one pair of blue jeans is ever identical to another.

In the mid-1970s, authentic Lee and Levi's stonewashed jeans began to be imported to Israel. It is interesting, and perhaps not coincidental, that in 1978 the person instrumental for obtaining the Levi's franchise for Ata was none other than Ata CEO Amos Ben Gurion, son of David Ben Gurion.

A coalition of pomp and circumstance

The melting-pot steamroller activated by the Labor movement in the name of Zionist/socialist values elicited a heavy price among those who did not share these ideologies. Indeed, values, traditions, and cultural perspectives on food, housing, family, religion, and dress that were different did not flourish in the "Labor State." When the Likud came to power in 1977, all this began to change.

Those responsible for the Likud's victory were later referred to as the "coalition of the deprived": members of the Beitar party and right-wing organizations, religious people, members of the urban lower-middle class, and immigrants from Arabic-speaking countries. In addition to their common political "enemy," these groups had three main common denominators: positive ties to religion and Jewish tradition, a hawkish political orientation, and a fondness for pomp and circumstance. The new leader, Menachem Begin, was the ultimate antithesis of the prevailing unkempt look, and this too contributed to his appeal among his supporters and admirers.

For the religious population, pressed suits and dresses, ties, and felt hats represented the discipline of true believers as well as respect for supreme authority. Among immigrants from Arabic-speaking countries, fondness for the button-down, tailored, and elegant *"Firangi"* look had begun in their cities of origin—among them Baghdad, Cairo, Tripoli, and Marrakesh—under the influence of the Italian, British, and French colonial regimes.

The shift toward a more elegant style of dress reflected the movement of those on the margins of society toward the center and the closing of social gaps.[12]

The Israeli-born children of the immigrants from Arabic-speaking countries, who until then had felt deprived and marginal, sought a style of their own, and like the minorities in the United States found it in the rock 'n' roll culture. Thus emerged the Israeli version of the punk, referred to as the *pushtak* and later the *chahchah*, who modeled himself on the bombastic braggart "look at me" style of dress of John Travolta and gangster movies: tight trousers and close-fitting flowered shirts, along with pointy shoes and heavy gold neck chains. The female counterpart, known as a *fre'ha* and equivalent to a bimbo, sported tight low-cut trousers or super-short miniskirts and high and bulky platform shoes.

The words *chahchah* and *fre'ha* were derogatory terms when used by members of the old-time Ashkenazi elite to express contempt for this segment of the population. Paradoxically, however, from the historical perspective those dubbed *chahchah* and *fre'ha* actually were ahead of their times, and their daring, individualistic and creative form of dress paved the way for a new aesthetic, creative, and festive era in Israeli society.

Brand names take over

During the 1980s, fashion and appearance became even more important to Israelis. One primary reason was that for the first time many Israelis were able not only to go on vacation abroad but also to purchase clothes abroad. During that time, counterfeit consumer goods, commonly called knock-offs, began being manufactured in countries like China, India, and Africa, making many clothes less expensive and more accessible to vast populations worldwide. This new abundance virtually eradicated the sewing and knitting tradition that had been so popular among women in the first two decades of the Israeli state.

For the first time as well, competition developed between new local brands such as Rosh Indiani or Pilpel and imported brands, leading to a marked improvement in the local products. The term "fashion brand" began to be adopted by the media and the younger generation and became an important consideration when choosing clothing.

A particularly revolutionary and symbolic change took place in the shoe industry. Shoes, an expensive product usually only purchased once every several years, became in the 1980s something consumable and fashionable bought twice a year or even more frequently. The selection increased as well. Once upon a time most people had two pairs of sandals—one for everyday wear and another for festive occasions. But in the 1980s a typical wardrobe included shoes for the beach, for sports, for work, for going out, and even more. This revolution caused many a shoemaker to retire and the profession to virtually disappear. The shoe stores on Neve Shaanan Street near the Tel Aviv Central Bus Station and Hehalutz Street in Haifa drew shoe shoppers from across the country.

Not only did these shoe stores feature the latest brands of foreign shoes, they also sold locally made shoes of a quality never before seen in Israel. For example, Hamegaper, one of Israel's oldest shoe manufacturers, changed its name to the more foreign-sounding Mega. This change was more than symbolic, for its uniform line of black, gray, white, or brown shoes gave way to a rainbow of colors, including new metallic shades.

For the first time children's shoes and sandals meeting European specifications appeared on the shelf, followed by shoes for adults, generating a new standard of quality and comfort. The Teva Naot plant at Kibbutz Naot Mordechai in the Upper Galilee, one of Israel's first shoe factories, also played a role in this revolution. In the mid-1980s, the German Birkenstock company began exporting its popular orthopedic clogs and sandals to Israel. The success of these imported sandals led Teva Naot to manufacture its own line of comfortable and anatomically correct footwear. In fact, Naot was given the rights to use the Birkenstock patent, and even improved on the German version. Their sandals gained in popularity, stealing the stage from the biblical sandals that had been one of the most familiar marks of the *sabra*.

Opening the export tap

The first time an imported brand of clothing provoked mass demand was in the early 1980s, when Lacoste polo shirts began being imported from France to Israel. These high-quality shirts with their crocodile emblem were considered quite prestigious. The Lacoste craze was a promo for the obsession with brand names that began taking over Israel in the 1990s, heralding a major change in how Israelis relate to outward appearance. Indeed, all the landmarks in the development of Israeli fashion and fashion consciousness mentioned above were merely the forerunners of the fashion revolution of the 1990s that emerged along with economic prosperity.

In 1993, in the wake of the Israel–European Union Free Trade Agreement and the emergence of shopping malls, marketing chains, and import companies such as Hamashbir Lazarchan, European and American fashion brands began to flood the Israeli market, among them Calvin Klein, Zara, GAP, and Banana Republic. What had once been considered something only the wealthy could even dream of became overnight within reach of the average Israeli, with an immediate impact on outward appearance.

At first the fashion revolution made its mark mainly among the wealthy and in the center of the country. Within a short time Tel Aviv boasted a huge supply of popular brands as well as mono-brand and multi-brand shops selling the most *au courant* and high-quality fashion items from such top designers as Donna Karan and Yves St. Laurent, to name just a few. Not all these brand names survived and not all the shops were able to make a go of it, but the fashion revolution did not lose momentum and gradually shifted to the lower socioeconomic groups, creating an extremely broad middle class.

The era of the models

In the 1990s, fashion was no longer merely a topic for the lifestyle sections of newspapers or for women's magazines. It had become an important news topic in all the Western media. The launching of the World Fashion Channel—broadcast in Israel since 1999—is one indicator of the growing importance of fashion worldwide. In the 1990s as well, the Israeli media began devoting countless columns and special sections to fashion topics. In April 1990, *Burda Style*, one of the world's most popular fashion magazines, began appearing in Hebrew, signifying a new momentum in professional fashion publications in Israel.

The growing demand for models in the late 1980s led to the opening of modeling schools and modeling agencies, which in turn held beauty contests.

Image Models, managed by Betty Rockaway, opened in 1985. The agency was associated with the *Olam Ha'isha* fashion magazine and in the 1990s began running the Face of the Nineties and Super Model competitions. The Look agency, established in 1988, collaborated with the *Yedioth Aharonot* daily newspaper and the *La'Isha* and *Rosh Ehad* magazines in launching and organizing the Beauty Queen and Discovery of the Year competitions. Michaela Bercu was Israelis first international model. Leah Fletcher and Karin Dunsky founded the first modeling schools in Israel.

In the early 1990s, the big bucks involved in the international fashion scene led to the emergence of global supermodels such as Claudia Schiffer and Naomi Campbell, who earned extremely high salaries. In many ways these models were heirs to the media halo of Hollywood starlets from the 1940s and 1950s.[13] As modeling began to be linked to getting rich, the stereotype of models began to change. Models were now thought of as independent career men and women determined to succeed against all odds. Tami Ben-Ami, the house model for Gottex and for years informally considered Israel's queen model, played a pioneering role in this image change. After she retired, Ben-Ami launched her own cosmetics line, helping create the new model/businesswoman status. Local fashion designers such as Aviva Pivko and Yuval Caspin also began to climb the ladder of prestige and success and be included in the list of local culture heroes. One designer in particular stood out above the rest—the eccentric boutique owner Tova (Tovaleh) Hasin, star of Tel Aviv's gossip columns.

Influenced by this new global trend, Israel began exporting a respectable number of models. Moreover, a class of local supermodels, among them Galit Gutman and Yaron Fink, began being photographed for prestigious fashion magazines and modeling for world-renowned agencies. They also became popular interviewees in the Israeli media and the idols of admiring youth. Indeed, it is no wonder that a modeling career has since then become the dream of many Israeli young people. For example, early in 1998 *Elite* announced it was seeking a poster girl for its Mekupelet chocolate bar. Within weeks, the company received no fewer than 13,000 applications.

The revenge of the blazers

The growing importance of personal grooming to Israelis derived not only from the developments in the media and the world of advertising mentioned above, but also from technological advancements in the manufacture of popular merchandise and products. How a product looks is one of the secrets of marketing, and constant improvements in appearance generate what can be referred to as an "aesthetic environment," which has an impact on those working in the manufacturing plant as well. Cutthroat competition for jobs in

Israel also helped increase the value of personal appearance. Beauty is an economic asset that many people intuitively sense is a factor in who is hired and who is promoted.

Growing contact with other countries, through tourism and business, is another influential factor. The typical *sabra* of the 1940s, 1950s and 1960s did not know how to knot a tie and considered a tailored blazer to look ridiculous. In Israel today more and more suits and ties can be seen, even among groups and professions that formerly dressed more casually, for example coaches of professional sports teams. Indeed, one of the signs of the changing times can be seen in the final project assigned in 1996 to students at the advertising and marketing school run by the Israel Advertising Association and the Technion. The students were asked to propose ideas to convince young and ambitious administrators and businessmen aged 25–35 that wearing a tie to work would benefit their career advancement.

My body and me

The growing importance of outer appearance also gave rise to a major industry concerned with self-enhancement and self-care, ranging from products for more youthful looking skin and for concealing age marks to plastic surgery clinics offering face lifts, breast enhancements and reductions, hair removal, and the like.

Naturally, those most influenced by this fashion and grooming craze were the young people who grew up in its midst. They were also the group most exposed to the new cult of beauty, promoted mainly through American television series in which outward appearance is the main focus: *The Bold and the Beautiful*, *Baywatch*, *Beverly Hills 90210*, and their various spinoffs. From the outset, Channel Two, Israel's most popular television station, placed emphasis on beauty. In 1995, Erez Tal announced a contest to select a female host to replace Meirav Levin on Israel's version of *Wheel of Fortune*. The competition, a quasi-reality show culminating in a choice among six competitors, kept millions of viewers glued to their TV screens. While the competition was merely a humorous advertising gimmick, it marked not only the vast influence of Channel Two, but also the worship of beauty characterizing Israeli secular society as a whole.

Beauty and fashion consciousness now begins in preschool. Today's parents get dressed up for parties, family celebrations, or official ceremonies. For their children, getting dressed up is second nature and part of their daily routine. Indeed, many Israeli children wear the latest Western fashions even at school, and the morning routine in many Israeli homes has begun to resemble that of a theatrical actor. Many Israeli teens do not dare leave the house unless they are wearing the latest and coolest clothes and shoes, whose purchase places a major burden on the family budget and is the source of many a vocal argument with their parents.

Another indication of the growing importance of fashion is the fact that girls are putting on makeup, coloring their hair and wearing high heels at a younger and younger age. Generally speaking, outward appearance has become a primary standard, if not the uppermost standard, among young secular society in Israel, causing a rise in the prevalence of a number of serious side effects, among them depression, anorexia nervosa, and low self-esteem. The media have lowered the age for beauty worship, to the outrage of many.

Summary of current social trends affecting Israeli fashion

Marketing consciousness in a hyper-capitalistic world

To borrow the words of anthropologist Erving Goffman (1959), "the presentation of the self in everyday life" has become extremely important today due to rising free market competition.[14] Cutthroat competition on the global market nurtures new initiatives in the fashion industry, making it one of the most dynamic and creative industries in the world today.[15]

Local identities in place of traditional identities

In today's global and capitalistic environment, in which traditional identities of race, ethnicity, nationality, and religion are gradually weakening, fashion is gaining importance.[16] Through their style of dress people can sustain alternative and local niche identities, for example based upon employment or hobbies.

A global collage

Globalization has made people increasingly aware of fashion trends and genres around the world, as seen in the carnival-like fashion culture of the younger generation. This culture draws upon different ethnic, occupational, and other sources, and combines articles of clothing that once would never have been worn together. Perhaps the most fitting motif would be "anything goes," provided that it is the result of self-awareness and the need to put forward some sort of image or persona.

A tailored world

The telecommunications revolution has created a world of visual expressions, making younger generations extremely sensitive to shapes and colors.[17] Because people tend to adapt themselves to their physical surroundings, today's tailored, stylized, and colorful fashions conform to their tailored environment.

The democratization of tastes

The West is becoming more democratic—more tolerant and accepting of what is irregular, different, and new. Global fashion breaks down frameworks and traditions and expresses tolerance of a wide array of visual expressions. The right to dress according to one's personal taste and style is in some respects an extension of the basic rights to liberty and freedom of expression.

The new dandy

Radical individualism can lead to narcissism, expressed among other things by dandyism and an addiction to self-cultivation. Today's meticulous care for outward appearance—and sloppiness can also be a meticulously nurtured look—also expresses a form of ego worship that has developed in freedom-loving Western society.

Testing boundaries and breaking down norms

The global fashion code is subject to the broader cultural code of maximum flexibility and adventurousness. This code aims at examining possibilities, extending limits, and transforming the impossible and inacceptable into the likely and conventional. Every fashion has its antithesis, and every style has its anti-style, which is a style unto itself. Global fashion involves refinement and prestige, which goes hand in hand with the consciously sloppy, the shanti look. High technology lives in peace with individualism ("I'll wear what I feel like wearing"), and all of this has merged with the brand name herd mentality that makes sure we fall in line with the latest offerings on the shelves.

Western democracy has broken down hierarchies of age, status, race, and gender, and this too is reflected in what we wear.[18] One example is the unisex style, which has blurred distinctions between masculinity and femininity. Another example is the breakdown in officewear conventions. Not only have white-collar workers abandoned their starched white shirts, but they have replaced their suits with jeans and t-shirts.

Normalization of eroticism and sexuality

Western liberalism is also expressed in the normalization of eroticism and sexuality, seen in how both men and women dress today. Prominent examples include low-rise tights and trousers, low-cut blouses and tank tops, and spiked hairdos.

Constant change

In today's global, pluralistic, technological, and competitive environment, the most stable thing is change. In fashion as well, the name of the game is to change clothes as often as theatrical actors change costumes. One solution is to create a simple, minimalistic, and less-expensive style, such as the fashion of wearing harem pants or patched trousers.

This changing style also expresses the growing urge in post-modern society for something new that will generate enjoyment, curiosity, content, and meaning in a world that has become emptied of content. This has led to ravenous hunger to buy new articles of clothing and social pressure to vary one's appearance, indeed to a frenetic vicious circle in which the new and cool fashion item one purchases in no time at all becomes *passé*.

Profession defines lifestyle

People, and particularly careerists, today spend more and more time at work, and this leaves its mark on how they dress. The need to move quickly from one place to another also has an impact. The trend, therefore, is toward less formal and more comfortable styles—jeans, t-shirts, lightweight sweaters, and sneakers. In general, the distinction between clothes worn at work and clothes worn at home is disappearing, as is the difference between fancy and casual dress. Indeed, the casual style has become the most predominant, for it emphasizes body shapes and curves and conveys a youthful and competitive look.[19]

Ambivalent speech

The secular elite in the Western world, including in Israel, has developed an ambivalent attitude toward fashion and outward appearance, similar to its ambivalent attitude toward practically every social phenomenon.[20] On the one hand, it encourages the fashion cult and places major emphasis on outward appearance, particularly through the media. On the other hand, it criticizes the culture of materialism and exterior appearance in that it exalts the container and not the content, and it decries the narcissism and irrational pursuit of new fashion products as the result of capitalist brainwashing.

32

DRESS AND IDEOLOGY

Notes

1 Almog, Oz, *The Sabra: The Creation of the New Jew*, Berkeley: University of California Press, 2000, pp. 1–9.

2 Ayala Raz, *Changing Styles: 100 Years of Fashion in Eretz-Israel*, Tel Aviv: Yediott Ahronoth Press, 1996, p. 134.

3 Yaacov Shavit, *The Textile Industry in Eretz Israel 1854–1956*, Tel Aviv: The Israeli Association for Textile, 1992, pp. 40–51.

4 Raz, *Changing Styles*, p. 85.

5 Dayla Bar-Or, *Between the Little Black Dress and the Sarafan*, MA thesis, University of Haifa, 2004.

6 Dayla Bar-Or, *The ATA Textiles Enterprise and the Israeli Society, 1934–1986*, PhD Thesis, University of Haifa, 2010.

7 O. Almog and M. Livne, "Clothing and Appearence Patterns in the Kibbutz," *Anashim Israel* www.peopleil.org, 2009.

8 Raz, Ayala, *Changing Styles*, pp. 154–6.

9 George Sproles and Leslie Davis Burns, *Changing Appearances: Understanding Dress in Contemporary Society*, New York: Fairchild, 1994.

10 Maoz Azaryahu, *Tel Aviv: Mythography of a City*, New York: Syracuse University Press, 2007, pp. 109–15.

11 Raz, *Changing Styles*; Nurit Bat-Yaar, *Israel Fashion Art 1948–2008*, Tel Aviv: Resling Publishing, 2010.

12 Oz Almog, "One middle class—three different lifestyles: the Israeli case," *Geography Research Forum*, 24, (2004): 37–58.

13 David Mansour, *From Abba to Zoom: A Pop Culture Encyclopedia of the Late 20th Century*, Walnut, Kansas City, MO: Andrews McMeel Publishing, 2005, p. 470.

14 Erving Goffman, *The Presentation of Self in Everyday Life*, Garden City, New York: Doubleday Anchor Books, 1959.

15 Stella Bruzzi and Pamela Church Gibson, "Introduction," in Stella Bruzzi and Pamela Church Gibson eds, *Fashion Cultures: Theories, Explorations and Analysis*, London: Routledge, 2005, pp. 1–5.

16 B. J. McVeigh, *Wearing Ideology: State, Schooling and Self-presentation in Japan*, Oxford: Berg, 2000, pp. 23–7.

17 David Kunzle, *Fashion and Fetishism: Corsets, Tight-Lacing and Other Forms of Body-Sculpture*, Stroud: Sutton Publishing, 2004, pp. 277–8.

18 Paul Jobling, *Fashion Spreads: Word and Image in Fashion Photography Since 1980*, Oxford: Berg, 1999, p. 75.

19 S. Heathfield, "Dress for Work Success: A Business Casual Dress Code," *About.com Guide*, 2011.

20 Malcolm Barnard, *Fashion as Communication*. London and New York: Routledge, 1996, p. 3.

Bibliography

Almog, Oz, *The Sabra: The Creation of the New Jew*, Berkeley: University of California Press, 2000.

—*Farewell to "Srulik": Changing Values Among the Israeli Elite*, Yehuda: Zmora Bitan and Haifa University Press, 2004 (2 vols), in Hebrew.

—"One middle class—three different lifestyles: the Israeli case," *Geography Research Forum*, 2004, 24 [Special Issue: Spatial and Socio-Economic Aspects], 37–58.

Almog, Oz and Livne, M., "Clothing and Appearence Patterns in the Kibbutz," *Anashim Israel*, www.peopleil.org, 2009, in Hebrew.

Azaryahu, Maoz, *Tel Aviv: Mythography of a City*, New York: Syracuse University Press, 2007.

Barnard, Malcolm, *Fashion as Communication*, New York and London: Routledge, 1996.

Bar-Or, Dalya, *The ATA Textiles Enterprise and the Israeli Society, 1934–1986*, PhD Thesis, University of Haifa, 2010, in Hebrew.

Bar-Or, Dalya, *Between the Little Black Dress and the Sarafan*, MA thesis, University of Haifa, 2004, in Hebrew.

Bat-Yaar, Nurit, *Israel Fashion Art 1948–2008*, Tel Aviv: Resling Publishing 2010, in Hebrew.

Bruzzi, Stella and Pamela Church Gibson, "Introduction," in Stella Bruzzi and Pamela Church Gibson eds, *Fashion Cultures: Theories, Explorations and Analysis*, London: Routledge, 2005.

Goffman, Erving, *The Presentation of Self in Everyday Life*, Garden City, New York: Doubleday Anchor Books, 1959.

Heathfield, S., "Dress for Work Success: A Business Casual Dress Code," About.com Guide, 2011.

Jobling, Paul, *Fashion Spreads: Word and Image in Fashion Photography since 1980*, Oxford: Berg, 1999.

Kunzle, David, *Fashion and Fetishism, Corsets, Tight-Lacing and other Forms of Body-Sculpture*, Stroud: Sutton Publishing, 2004.

Mansour, David, *From Abba to Zoom: A Pop Culture Encyclopedia of the Late 20th Century*, Walnut, Kansas City, MO: Andrews McMeel Publishing, 2005.

McVeigh, B. J., *Wearing Ideology: State, Schooling and Self-presentation in Japan*, Oxford: Berg, 2000.

Raz, Ayala, *Changing Styles: 100 Years of Fashion in Eretz-Israel*, Tel Aviv: Yedioth Ahronoth Press, 1996, in Hebrew.

Shavit, Yaacov, *The Textile Industry in Eretz Israel 1854–1956*, Tel Aviv: The Israeli Association for Textile, 1992, in Hebrew.

Sproles, George and Leslie Davis Burns, *Changing Appearances: Understanding Dress in Contemporary Society*, New York: Fairchild, 1994.

2

SARTORIAL BOUNDARIES ON THE CHINESE FRONTIER

ANTONIA FINNANE

The daily dress of people in China's cities and towns does not at first glance suggest any ideological influences at work other than those related to modern consumer lifestyles: consumerism, materialism, individualism, elegance. In this, contemporary Chinese dress differs markedly from that of half a century ago, when the Sun Yatsen suit, the Lenin suit and the cadre suit—usually lumped together by Westerners as "the Mao suit"—competed with each other for status within the highly political vestimentary order of Maoist China. The ruling ideology of those decades, socialism, faded away after Mao's death, leaving a vacuum that has been filled by nationalism.

Compared to other societies in Asia, and perhaps to earlier incarnations of itself, China does not now seem to set much store even by national dress. Nonetheless, nationalist ideologies do find expression in the vestimentary domain. A state ideology of national unity, powerfully promoted through museums, textbooks, and television, is expressed at national and international events through the deployment of national costume worn by the "national minority" peoples, as representatives of China. Members of these minorities— Hui Muslims, for instance—can themselves bring strong ideological interests to bear on clothing worn within their communities, while within the Han majority, potentially divisive ethno-cultural nationalism is evident in the *hanfu* (Han dress) movement, directed at reviving ancient forms of Han Chinese dress.[1]

The politics of national unity have in fact made the issue of national dress a vexed one in China. Concerned to maintain the territorial integrity of the multi-ethnic empire bequeathed by the Qing dynasty (1644–1911), the country's rulers, mostly Han, have been anxious to avoid too close an overlap of the categories "Chinese" (*Zhongguo, Zhonghua*) and Han, so have avoided adopting obvious garments such as the *tangzhuang* (Chinese-style jacket) and *qipao* (mandarin-collar dress) as national costume. The Han majority is occasionally represented at public events by people wearing such garments, but on the whole, national costume is left to the national minorities. Han people wear modern dress. Ye Qianyu's 1953 painting of *The Great Unification of the Nationalities* (*Minzu da tuanjie*) showing Mao Zedong and Zhou Enlai in sober, modern dress while the nationalist minorities cavort around them in many-colored dress-ups is a depiction applicable to the present day.[2]

In this particular realm of nationalist iconography, i.e. national costume, Han cultural claims are thus usually left unstated, except insofar as modern dress is consistent with a historical self-view of the Han as more cultured or civilized than other peoples in East Asia. In this self-view, however, can be found the cracks in the foundations of the official story. In tension with the myth of pre-destined national unity in contemporary China is a body of work central to China's cultural heritage—literary, folk, the graphic arts—in which the Han people of the central plains and the *hu* or barbarian peoples of the neighboring steppes, mountains, and deserts are seen as inhabiting quite different lands. In a long tradition of representations of the frontier in Chinese history, clothing was one of the means used by graphic artists to depict difference.

Frederick Turner's description of the frontier as "the meeting ground between savagery and civilization"[3] is applicable to the frontier in the Chinese historical worldview. It was a shifting zone in geographical terms but one where "this culture of ours"[4] always met its opposite, a way of life and a set of rituals that distinguished "barbarians" (*hu*, *fan*) from Chinese. Around the beginning of the Common Era, the frontier was essentially a meeting ground between Xiongnu and Han, terms which to the Chinese signified savagery and civilization respectively. In contemporary Chinese society, "Han" denotes the major ethnic group, accounting for more than 90 percent of the population of China, but at that time it was a reference to subjects of the Han dynasty. "Xiongnu" (literally "ferocious slave") was its antonym, and referred to the mainly nomadic subjects of a great but unstable empire.

From the graphically depicted differences between the Han and the Xiongnu in narrative paintings of the frontier, it can be surmised that the Chinese sense of self was strongly informed by a consciousness of the alien, horse-riding, warlike peoples who populated the frontier. Mark Edward Lewis has neatly summarized the early Han dynasty view of material life in the contrasting cultural spheres which constituted the known world: "the nomads ate meat and drank milk; the Chinese ate grain. The Xiongnu wore skins and furs; the Chinese wore hemp and silk. The Chinese had walled towns, fields, and houses; the Xiongnu [supposedly] … had none."[5] Virtually all of these paired opposites are graphically represented in one of the most famous treatments of the Han–Xiongnu encounter, the Song Dynasty (960–1279) illustrations to an eighth-century song cycle known as *Eighteen Songs of a Nomad Flute: The Tale of Lady Wenji*.[6]

Figure 2.1   Unidentified artist (active early 15ᵗʰ century). Eighteen Songs of a Nomad Flute: The Story of Lady Wenji, Episode 5: Encampment by a Stream. © Metropolitan Museum of Art. Accession no. 1973.120.3. Image source: Art Resource NY.

The Xiongnu are thought by some to be identical with the Huns who appeared in Europe in the fourth century. Although the evidence is not strong, the parallel is analytically suggestive. The idea of Attila the Hun in Europe is comparable to the idea of the Xiongnu in China, and indeed there are similar stories about the Hun and the Xiongnu, barbarians in the West and East respectively. In Europe, the legend of St Ursula tells of the martyrdom of a princess who refused to marry a Hun chieftain, putatively in the fourth century. In China the legend of Cai Wenji (b. 177 CE) tells of a well-born woman's return to her parents after 12 years of enforced marriage to a Xiongnu prince. In both cases, an encounter with the barbarians provides a way of articulating a value central to the civilized or cultured society: virginity in Christendom, filial piety in Confuciandom.

Both legends have inspired numerous paintings, which again are worth comparing. The illustrations to *Eighteen Songs of a Nomad Flute: The Tale of Lady Wenji* exist in various forms, of which the most complete (although by no means the finest) is a late version owned by the Metropolitan Museum of Art. This handscroll, copy of an original tentatively attributed to Li Tang (c. 1050–1130),[7] is in most respects quite unlike the legend of St Ursula as depicted by Hans Memling (c. 1430–94) on the shrine in St John's Hospital in Bruges.[8] Yet each of these works is a series of illustrations of a legend featuring a barbarian prince, the one Hun and the other Xiongnu. The artists came to comparable conclusions as to how to represent this figure. Memling, painting at a time that the Ottoman Empire was rapidly expanding, depicted the Hun as a Turk, or at least in a turban. The Chinese handscroll shows the Xiongnu prince dressed in the style of the Khitans (Kitan, Qidan), founders of the Liao Dynasty (916–1125). This dynasty, presiding over an empire on China's northern frontier in the tenth century, coexisted with the Northern Song Dynasty (960–1127), which controlled the greater part of the terrain occupied by Han Chinese. The Khitans developed a written language that looked like Chinese[9]), and left a rich visual record of themselves. Like the Ottomans in Europe, they were long visible on the horizon of the known, cultured world, posing both a threat and a puzzle to the Song Chinese.

The capacity of each of these legends to delineate contrasting "cultural spheres" is also evident from paintings. Two paintings of St Ursula in the Hotel de Clûny impressed Anna Brownwell Jameson for just this reason. "The artist," she observed, "has taken great pains to distinguish the heathen and barbarous court of England from the civilized and Christian court of Brittany."[10] Correspondingly, the opening and closing scenes of *Eighteen Songs* provide a sharp contrast between the warlike barbarians engaged in sacking the city, and the peaceable Chinese going about their business in the same city after the cessation of conflict. The barbarians wear armor and carry weapons. The Chinese wear long garments or short, according to their social status, and pay their respects to each other with hands folded beneath sleeves, all in accordance with sentiments articulated in the concluding stanza of the poem:

> *I return home and see my kin …*
> *As I hold towel and comb, I rediscover the good rituals and etiquette.*
> *Touching the qin again enables me to live or die without regret.*[11]

Here we reach the limits of comparison. The chivalric code and martial values of European societies were not entirely alien to China, but they were normatively suppressed in favor of civil, literary values, especially during the Song Dynasty.[12] To the extent that the frontier was a "meeting ground between savagery and civilization," it was best represented by horse-riding, armed barbarians confronting gown-wearing Chinese.

Variations in this configuration show that the frontier was also a place of cultural negotiation, "a place of reversal," as Jean Franco writes, "where the civilized may become barbarian and the barbarian civilized."[13] In the fourth century BCE, King Wu Ling of Zhao attained ascendancy over the Xiongnu by "changing into barbarian dress, and shooting from horseback."[14] In the twelfth century, a commentary on barbarian people entering into the Chinese orbit described them as "unfastening the silk cap-strings [on their armor], submitting and paying respects [to the emperor]; putting away their weapons, and receiving the calendar."[15] Such accommodations illustrate the norm, which was a juxtaposition of barbarian and Chinese as hunter and farmer, warrior and scribe, the one dressed in skins and the other in silks.

What is the relationship between clothes in works of art and the actual garments worn by people in history? In *Seeing Through Clothes*, Anne Hollander investigated "how clothes in works of art are connected with clothes in real life," concluding that a systematic relationship existed between painting and fashion in European history.[16] A similar relationship pertained in China: that is, fashion burgeoned in Chinese cities synchronously with the proliferation of illustrated books for women and the expansion of the art market in the sixteenth and early seventeenth centuries.[17] But this is to consider the relationship from the perspective of people who wore clothes. How painters decided to depict clothes in the first instance is another matter, particularly if their subject was historical.

One source of information for painters working on frontier themes was descriptions in historical works. In the case of the Xiongnu, educated people in imperial China must have had some impression of what clothing was worn because standard reading matter included works such as the official histories of the Han dynasty, and the *Historical Records* (*Shi ji*) by Sima Qian (c. 145–86 BCE). From these it could be ascertained that the barbarians "wore their hair down and fastened their clothing on the left," and "dressed in clothes made of skins, and used furs as quilts."[18] Furs, skins, and a left-hand fastening accordingly feature in barbarian dress as depicted in Chinese painting. Of these features, the left-hand fastening had canonical status. Confucius himself said: "But for Guan Zhong, we should now be wearing our hair unbound, and the lappets of our coats buttoning on the left side."[19]

These classical references were echoed in later texts. Liu Shang (fl. 773 CE) drew on them in *Eighteen Songs of a Nomad Flute*, in which he told the story of Lady Wenji. Forced into a barbarian marriage, living in a tent on the steppe far from kith and kin, the disconsolate Wenji laments:

I clean my hair with mutton fat, but it is seldom combed
The collar of my lambskin robe is buttoned on the left;
The fox lapels and badger sleeves are rank-smelling
By day I wear these clothes, by night I sleep in them.[20]

The Song Dynasty illustrations to the songs accordingly show Xiongnu men in fur-trimmed hats, as well as carrying quivers of leopard skin and wearing gowns fastened on the left-hand side. For some reason the artist chose to depict the women, including Lady Wenji, in right-fastening gowns. This may have been an assertion on his part of Wenji's cultural influence on barbarian society.

Another resource for the painter of historical events was other paintings. In the Palace Museum's *Zhuo xie tu* (Respite), a handscroll painting of a Khitan hunting party taking a break, Khitan artist Hu Gui (fl. tenth century) portrays figures which, taken individually, are almost identical to those depicted in the *Eighteen Songs* scroll, right down to the leopard-skin quivers. The distinctive hairstyles of Khitan men, featuring two pigtails hanging from the temples and sometimes a shaven head, are well known from tomb murals and appear in both these paintings. Likewise, every Khitan (or Xiongnu) man is shown wearing boots, in pointed contrast to the Chinese men in *Eighteen Songs*, all of whom wear shoes. The one significant difference in terms of costume is that the women in Hu Gui's painting wear their gowns fastened on the left. The men in both paintings have the elongated torso and slender hips that Angela Falco Howard finds characteristic of Liao (Khitan) statuary.[21] In brief, there is little to distinguish the Khitan painting of contemporary Khitans from the presumably Han Chinese painting of the ancient Xiongnu.

Given this similarity, the question of how the Xiongnu of ancient times were to be depicted by the painter of *Eighteen Songs* might perhaps be rephrased as a question about how the *Khitan* were to be depicted. In other words, the narrative theme of the painting, centered on the Xiongnu, may well have been secondary to the subject matter, which is for the most part Khitan land, Khitan material culture, Khitan people. In the analysis of Robert Rorex and Wen Fong, "to the early Southern Song viewer the [painting] *Eighteen Songs* represented no mere historical romance but a real, all-pervading national trauma,"[22] a reference to the constant threat of actual invasions by peoples who were referred to as *hu* or *fan*, i.e. barbarian. According to Irene Leung the painters were respectfully recognizing the culture of their non-Chinese neighbors — or at least of the Khitan, and coming to terms with it in a way consistent with the Song's status as a lesser empire. Comparing this handscroll and its lookalike predecessors with a sixteenth-century handscroll painting by You Qiu (fl. 1553–1591+) lends weight to Leung's conclusion. The subject of You Qiu's painting is not Lady Wenji but a slightly earlier historical figure, Wang Zhaojun (fl. first century BCE), but the two have much in common.

Wang Zhaojun was a palace lady in the court of Emperor Han Yuandi (r. 48–33 BCE) and was offered in marriage to the Xiongnu Khan (*shanyu*) as part of a peace settlement. Unlike Cai Wenji, she never returned to Han territory, but like them she became a legendary figure.[23] Painting history shows that to some degree her legend became entwined and confused with Wenji's. "The Return of Wenji" (*Wenji gui Han*) and "Zhaozhun's Departure for the Frontier" (*Zhaojun chusai*)[24] are titles that could be indiscriminately applied to a number of frontier paintings, as demonstrated by two almost identical works held by the Jilin Provincial Museum and the Osaka Municipal museum respectively. The former depicts Wenji's return, the latter Zhaojun's departure.[25] The major difference between the two is the addition in the latter of a maid carrying a *pipa*, or Chinese lute. The *pipa* is steadily associated with the legend of Wang Zhaojun, who is said to have played it to "soothe her longing for home."[26] Wenji's instrument, as indicated in the verse cited above, is the *qin*, or Chinese zither.

The legend of Wang Zhaojun has taken various forms over time. A ninth-century version associated with Dunhuang presents a sympathetic picture of the Khan and includes detailed descriptions of Zhaojun's life "among the barbarians."[27] This version brings to mind Irene Leung's reading of the *Eighteen Songs* and is consistent with the marriage alliance policy that characterized frontier relations during the Tang Dynasty (618–907). By contrast, the early seventeenth-century edition of the play *Autumn in the Han Palace* fails even to get Zhaojun across the border. Instead of proceeding to married life among the Xiongnu, she flings herself into the river demarcating Chinese and barbarian territory.[28]

You Qiu does not portray a suicide, but his is a grim painting. The date of its execution, 1554, suggests a response on his part to contemporary border problems posed by pirates on the coast and Mongols on the northern frontier. You Qiu is known as a painter of "fair ladies" (*meiren*),[29] but in 1554 he produced a painting full of movement and violence. The beginning of the handscroll shows the wintry scene of a river that the party has already crossed. The men depicted riding on the further side appear to be Mongols. With facial hair, hooked noses, heavy faces, wearing trousers and boots, they present a forbidding appearance. Two timid-looking women are riding in their midst. They wear what appear to be barbarian hats (*hu mao*), but their gowns, worn over pleated skirts and tied with knotted girdles, are in the Chinese style familiar from Ming figure paintings, and provide a striking contrast to the clothes of the barbarians.

Rendered in black and white "outline style" (*baimiao*), this unusually dark painting projects a view of frontier relations consistent with the actual history of Ming–Mongol contact, which was marked by the conspicuous absence of marriage alliances.[30] The contrast between the barbarian men and the Chinese women is in keeping with the lines of the play *Autumn in the Han Palace*, where aspects of Han and *hu* culture are constantly juxtaposed.[31] The contrary is the case in *Eighteen Songs*, where the painter's treatment of the contrast is gentler than the lines of the poem he purports to illustrate: the fur hats are few, skins are not apparent in actual clothing, and the mien of the barbarians is gentle. In commenting on the clothing depicted in the earlier scroll, Rorex and Fong in fact found it difficult to distinguish between Chinese and Khitan.[32]

How might these frontier tales have been viewed on the other side of the border? Surprisingly, there does exist a painting that enables us to reflect on a "barbarian" view of these encounters: Zhang Yu's *Return of Wenji*, executed in the Jin Dynasty (1115–1234). The Jin was founded by the Jurchen people and was effectively a successor to the Liao although eventually extending over a much greater area of China. Unlike the Khitans, the Jurchen left few reminders of how they looked. For this reason, Zhang Yu's painting is frequently published in books of costume history. By comparing textual evidence with the painting, costume historians have identified the following items of Wenji's dress as characteristic of Jin Dynasty clothing: the marten-fur hat, long-legged boots with pointed toes, and cloud cape, as well as her hairstyle, consisting of long pigtails at the side of the face.[33] A Chinese envoy accompanies the party, distinguished by his official hat and fan. The remaining horsemen are all "barbarian," although it is worth noting that the Jin Dynasty forbade the use of this term (fan, not hu) in 1191.[34]

The painting is difficult to read in terms of the cultural politics of Jin–Song relations, but clearly the artist has made decisions different from those of the *Eighteen Songs* painter. The painting is of the return rather than the forward journey. Wenji looks steadfast, rather than timid, unhappy, or irresolute. The clothing of Wenji is rendered with extraordinary attention to detail, the overall effect being of a rather assertive display of Jurchen culture. It can be concluded that if tribute was being paid to the Southern Song, as suggested by the focus on the return among other things, it was being offered by an equal.

In the seventeenth and eighteenth centuries, the frontier was tamed and incorporated into a vast empire ruled by the Manchus in association with their Chinese servants—the scholar–officials of the empire. The Manchus liked to think of themselves as descendants of the Jurchen. They cultivated a strong historical genealogy to legitimate their possession of the throne. They endeavored to retain a martial ethos, manifest in their dress, with its close-fitting gown, narrow sleeves, horse-shoe cuffs, horse-riding jacket—all markedly different from the extravagant robes of the Ming gentleman. Chinese scholar–officials were forced to adopt both the Manchu gown and Manchu hairstyle, which they saw as barbarian and by which they were initially appalled.

The Manchus hated talk of "barbarians" and were watchful of any references to the border peoples. From this perspective, Hua Yan's eighteenth-century portrayal of Zhaojun's departure for the frontier poses a slight conundrum except insofar as Zhaojun may have lost some of her Ming-dynasty intransigence in the course of the dynastic transition. Hua Yan (1682–1756) was a southern painter, born in the southern province of Fujian but active in Hangzhou and occasionally Yangzhou, leading to his occasional inclusion among the so-called "eccentric" (*guai*) artists of Yangzhou. He was widely travelled, including in the north-east, and his oeuvre is marked by an interest in the frontier uncommon in his circle.[35] At least three paintings of Zhaojun are attributed to Hua Yan, along with one of Wenji, all of them showing a rather fragile-looking young woman holding a *pipa* as she is led away on either a horse or a camel by her captor. She wears a "sleeping rabbit" (*wotu*) fur cap of the sort frequently depicted in winter scenes of this period and a fur-lined jacket. The folds of her clothing and the delicacy of the figure bring to mind the sing-song girls of places like Suzhou and Yangzhou. Indeed, we know that these girls posed for artists. The version held by the Shanghai Museum, along with one established forgery, carries a poem by Shi Chong (249–300), the first of many written about Zhaojun in the course of China's literary history. The opening lines establish the captive's identification with her Han origins, and the trauma of going into exile:

I am a child of the Han, deemed suitable for the household of the Khan.
Before the farewells are over, the advance carriage raises the banner.
High and low, all are weeping; the horse in harness whinnies in sorrow.
My belly is knotted in grief, my tears are ribbons of pearls.[36]

Another of these paintings carries a poem by Du Fu (712–770), which concludes with lines even more challenging: *For a thousand years the lute speaks a Tartar*[hu] *tongue | We make out grief and hatred expressed within the tune.*[37]

While the poems place these paintings unambiguously in the tradition of Han–*hu* confrontations, a number of factors suggest they should be considered as part of a rapidly expanding genre of "fair lady" or "beauty" (*meiren*) paintings, which existed in the Ming but experienced a boom in the Qing.[38] These factors include Hua Yan's social position as a professional painter, the simple composition and modest dimensions of the paintings (around 125 centimeters long), together with their hanging-scroll format, suitable for middle-range buyers in the art market, and the existence of numerous other decorative hanging-scroll paintings of Zhaojun, all of which show her as elegantly dressed, sometimes strikingly so. It should be noted that comparable portrayals exist of Wenji, although she did not have quite Zhaojun's status as a "beauty."

Commenting on the somewhat later frontier paintings executed by Ren Bonian (1840–96), Yu-chih Lai remarked on this artist's attention to sartorial detail: he "adorns his Su Wu in a fur-trimmed coat and a robe with long, elegant sleeves and an ornamental blue ribbon hanging almost to the ground," presenting a figure of "unprecedented youthfulness and handsome charm."[39] Su Wu (140–60 BCE), a male counterpart to Wenji in the Chinese captivity narratives, was an emissary of the Han court to the Xiongnu. Taken captive and forced to live among the barbarians for 19 years, he became a symbol of steadfastness in the face of adversity, and of loyalty to "this culture of ours." During the Cultural Revolution a popular folk-song about him, *Su Wu tends the sheep* (*Su Wu muyang*), fell out of favor due to its emphasis on the distinction between the Han and the Xiongnu, and the "two lands" to which they separately belonged.

Lai explains Ren's novel approach to the depiction of Su Wu in terms of the art market in Shanghai. As a Treaty Port and a rapidly expanding center of international trade, Shanghai was home to an increasingly materialist society with a concern for appearances. In brief, people in Shanghai liked pretty pictures, also fine clothes. Yet Hua Yan, in the preceding century, was painting for a market that has been described in comparable terms.[40] Considered alongside earlier paintings of frontier subjects such as Zhaojun and Wenji as "beauties," Ren Bonian's painting of Su Wu looking resplendent rather than tattered seems consistent with developments in the art market and trends in taste before that time.

The most striking aspect of Ren Bonian's frontier paintings arguably lies not in Su Wu's sartorial splendor, but rather in the barbarians, who are conspicuous by their absence. This leaves the impression that the north-west frontier had ceased to loom large in the Chinese imagination, and indeed Lai analyzes Ren's frontier paintings in terms of a "new frontier": the coast. The barbarians whom Ren Bonian chose not to paint were thus not the Manchus (whom he could not anyway have painted for political reasons), or even the Xiongnu, but rather the Westerners, who like the Khitan, the Jurchen, and the Mongols for some earlier painters were very much part of Ren's present.

In the early twentieth century, Chinese dress styles began to change in response both to the cosmopolitanism of the Treaty Ports and to political change, which finally resulted in the collapse of the Qing empire in 1911 and a corresponding collapse of Manchu dress codes. Curiously, Chinese men were left with a choice of barbarian clothes to wear: on the one side was the Western suit, strongly favored in the early years of the Republic; on the other side was the Manchu gown. The gown won out in the short term: it was seen, for want of anything better, as more Chinese than the suit.[41] Just as curiously, Chinese women ended up wearing a garment that evolved from various elements in Chinese, Western, and Manchu dress, but that came to be known as the *qipao*, which in effect means the Manchu gown. This has survived as the main form of Han Chinese ethnic dress, replacing the loose jacket and pleated skirt (*aoqun*) that defined Han women's dress under Manchu rule.

In recent years, as noted at the beginning of this chapter, there has been a movement in China to revive an indigenous form of dress for Han Chinese. Adherents of this movement are seeking to popularize ancient forms of dress for ceremonial occasions. Avoiding the fusion styles of the Tang dynasty onwards, *hanfu* activists have gone back to a time when the difference between Han and Xiongnu, Chinese and barbarian, was supposedly unambiguous.

The Chinese government likes the patriotism evinced by this sort of movement, but has to counter the implications of the thinking behind it, particularly in light of troublesome ethnic relations in Tibet and Xinjiang. In the summer of 2009, as the country prepared to celebrate 60 years of rule by the Communist Party, the frontier was the subject of massive propaganda campaigns in which Han and non-Han were pictured shoulder to shoulder, cheek to cheek, in demonstrations of ethnic harmony, national unity, and a spirit of economic development. Myths that used to be about separation, suffering, and longing for home had long since been rewritten as myths about inter-cultural marriage and the merging of cultures to form the Chinese nation.

Su Wu and Wenji have a relatively modest place in this new frontier, but Zhaojun, brought to the stage in 1978 and to the television screen in 2008, has a prominent position, somewhat comparable to that of Princess Wencheng (d.680) in the Tibetan context.[42] Visitors to Zhaojun's tomb in Inner Mongolia can contemplate an entirely new set of images of her, most notably a bronze statue showing her riding companionably alongside the Khan, and a large bas-relief sculpture, showing her face alongside his in a style familiar from revolutionary posters of workers, soldiers, and peasants. Unlike in earlier centuries, when both Han bride and barbarian groom were usually shown in the dress styles of the time, these figures are presented in the gowns and cloaks of a rather unspecific past. They gesture only in a generic way to a difference that is no longer supposed to matter.

Notes

1 On Muslim dress, see Maris Gillette, "What's in a Dress? Brides in the Hui Quarter of Xi'an," in Deborah Davis ed., *The Consumer Revolution in Urban China*, Berkeley: University of California Press, 2000, pp. 80–106. On the *hanfu*, see Juanjuan Wu, *Chinese Fashion From Mao to Now*, London: Berg, 2009, pp. 124–6.

2 For a good reproduction see Zhang Tianman, *Ye Qianyu* Shijiazhuang: Hebei Jiaoyu Chubanshe, 2002, 112–13.

3 Frederick Turner, *The Frontier in American History*, Books on Demand, 2010, p. 2.

4 A reference to the translation of *si wen* in Peter Bol, *This Culture of Ours: Intellectual Transitions in T'ang and Sung China*, Stanford: Stanford University Press, 1994.

5 Mark Edward Lewis, *The Early Chinese Empires: Qing and Han*, Cambridge, MA: The Belknap Press, 2007, p. 133.

6 Robert A. Rorex and Wen Fong, *Eighteen Songs of a Nomad Flute: The Story of Lady Wen-chi*, New York: The Metropolitan Museum of Art, 1974.

7 Julia K. Murray, *Mirror of Morality: Chinese Narrative Illustration and Confucian Ideology*, Honolulu: University of Hawai'i Press, 2007, p. 81.

8 This is one of a series of miniatures rendered for the Shrine of St Ursula, held in the Memling Museum, in St John's Hospital in Bruges. According to Mrs [Anna] Jameson (*Sacred and Legendary Art*, vol. 2, London: Longman, Brown, Green, Longmans, & Roberts, 1857, p. 516), "There is a good set of engravings (coloured after the originals) in the British Museum."

9 Daniel Kane, *The Kitan Language and Script*, Leiden: Brill, 2009.

10 Jameson, *Sacred and Legendary Art*, p. 516.

11 Rorex and Fong, *Eighteen Songs*, verse 18, n.p. Romanization adapted. On this "happily-ever-after" conclusion, see Dore J. Levy, "Transforming Archetypes in Chinese Poetry and Painting: The Case of Ts'ai Yen," *Asia Major*, Third Series, VI, 2 (1993), pp. 147–68. My thanks to Freda Murck for this reference.

12 See John King Fairbank's discussion of "the symbiosis of wen and wu" in Fairbank and Merle Goldman, *China: A New History*, Cambridge, MA: Harvard University Press, 2006, pp. 108–12.

13 Jean Franco, *Critical Passions: Selected Essays*, Mary Louise Pratt and Katherine Elizabeth Newman eds, Durham, NC: Duke University Press, 1999, p. 330.

14 Dai Ping, *Zhongguo minzu fushi wenhua yanjiu* (*Studies in the Clothing Culture of the Peoples of China*), Shanghai: Shanghai renmin chubanshe, 2000, p. 182.

15 Adapted from Irene S. Leung, "The Frontier Imaginary in the Song Dynasty: Revisiting Cai Yan's 'Barbarian Captivity' and Return," Ph.D. thesis, University of Michigan, Ann Arbor, 2001, p. 10.

16 Anne Hollander, *Seeing Through Clothes*, Berkeley: University of California, 1993, p. xi.

17 See Antonia Finnane, *Changing Clothes in China*, London: Hurst, 2007, pp. 44–56.

18 Zhang Ruili and Zhao Bin, "Qin Han Xiongnu fuzhuang xingzhi tanxi" ("Exploratory Analysis of the Design of Xiongnu Clothing in the Qin and Han Dynasties"), *Xiyu yanjiu (Research on Western China)* 2 (2008): 62–7.

19 James Legge, *Confucian Analects: The Great Learning and the Doctrine of the Mean*, New York: Dover Publications, 1971, p. 282. Book 14, Hsien Wan, Chapter XVIII, 2. Guan Zhong (725–645 BCE) was a statesman in the state of Qi.

20 Rorex and Fong, *Eighteen Songs*, verse 5, n.p.

21 Angela Falco Howard, "Buddhist sculptures of the Liao Dynasty: a reassessment of Osvald Siren's study," *Bulletin of the Museum of Far Eastern Antiquities*, 56 (1984): 6.

22 Rorex and Fong, *Eighteen Songs*, Introduction, n.p. Romanization adapted.

23 See Hing Foon Kwong, *Wang Zhaojun: Une Héroine Chinoise de l'Histoire à la Légende*, Paris: Collège de France, Institut des Hautes Etudes Chinoises, 1986.

24 I follow here the translation of the title of You Qiu's painting used by Shanghai Museum. *Shimao fengqing: Zhongguo gudai renwu huajing pinji* (*Highlights of Ancient Chinese Figure Painting from the Liaoning Provincial Museum and the Shanghai Museum*), Shanghai: Shanghai guji chubanshe, 2008, vol. 2 (Exhibit 60), p. 410.

25 Susan Bush, "Five Paintings of Animal Subjects or Narrative Themes and Their Relevance to Chin Culture," in Hoyt Cleveland Tilleman and Stephen H. West eds, *China Under Jurchen Rule: Essays on Chin Intellectual and Cultural History,* Albany, NY: SUNY Press, 1995, pp. 195–6.

26 John Myers, *The Way of the Pipa*, Kent, OH: Kent State University Press, 1992, p. 8.

27 Eugene Eoyang, "The Wang Chao-chun legend: configurations of the classis," *Chinese Literature: Essays, Articles, Reviews*, 4, 1 (January 1982): 4.

28 Kimberley Besio, "Gender, loyalty, and the reproduction of the Wang Zhaojun legend: some social ramifications of drama in the Late Ming," *Journal of the Economic and Social History of the Orient*, 40, 2 (1997): 263.

29 Ren Daobin, "Mingdai Jiangnan shinütu mianxiang moshihua tan wei" ("The routinization of painting of female faces in Ming Jiangnan"), *Meishu shilun* (Fine Arts History) (2009), p. 9.

30 Ning Chia, "Women in China's Frontier Politics: Heqin," in Sherry J. Mou ed., *Presence and Presentation: Women in the Chinese Literati Tradition*, Honolulu: University of Hawai'i Press, 2003, p. 44.

31 Besio, "Gender, Loyalty, and the Reproduction of the Wang Zhaojun," p. 263.

32 See Rorex and Fong, *Eighteen Songs*, commentary on verse 13.

33 Hua Mei, *Fushi yu Zhongguo wenhua* (*Dress and Chinese Culture*), Beijing: Renmin chubanshe, 2001, pp. 290–1; Zhou Xidai, *Zhongguo gudai fushi shi* (*History of Chinese Clothing before Modern Times*) Taibei: Nantian shuju, 1989, p. 369.

34 Bush, "Five Paintings of Animal Subjects," p. 195.

35 See Ginger Cheng-chi Hsü, "Traveling to the Frontier: Hua Yan's *Camel in the Snow*," in *Lifestyle and Entertainment in Yangzhou*, Lucie Olivová and Vibeke Børdahl eds, Copenhagen: NIAS Press, 2009, pp. 345–75.

36 Han Xin, "Hua Yan zhi Liang fu 'Zhaojun chusai tu'" ("A Study of the Two Hua Yan Paintings of 'Zhaojun Departs for the Frontier'"), in *Hua Yan yanjiu* (*Studies of Hua Yan*), Shanghai: Shanghai shuhua chubanshe, 2003, pp. 256–9.

37 See Paul F. Rouzer, *Articulated Ladies: Gender and the Male Community in Early Chinese Texts* Cambridge, MA: Harvard University Asia Center, 2001, p. 194.

38 Shen Yizheng, "Lidai meiren huaxuan: xu" (Preface to "Selected Paintings of Fair Ladies"), in He Gongshang ed., *Lidai meiren huaxuan* (*Selected Paintings of Beauties Through the Ages*), Taibei: Yishu tushu gongsi, 1999, p. 7.

39 Yu-chih Lai, "Remapping Borders," p. 565.

40 See Ginger Cheng-chi Hsü, *A Bushel of Pearls: Painting for Sale in Eighteenth-Century Yangchow*, Stanford: Stanford University Press, 2001.

41 See Lin Yutang, "The Inhumanity of Western Dress," in Lin Yutang, *The Importance of Living*, London: Heinemann, 1938, pp. 257–62.

42 Historically, Princess Wencheng was a more important figure in Tibetan than in Chinese lore, but in contemporary times she serves the PRC as a symbol of Tibetan-Han.

Bibliography

Besio, Kimberley, "Gender, loyalty, and the reproduction of the Wang Zhaojun legend: some social ramifications of Drama in the Late Ming," *Journal of the Economic and Social History of the Orient*, 40, 2 (1997): 251–82.

Bol, Peter, *This Culture of Ours: Intellectual Transitions in T'ang and Sung China*, Stanford: Stanford University Press, 1994.

Bush, Susan, "Five Paintings of Animal Subjects or Narrative Themes and Their Relevance to Chin Culture," in Hoyt Cleveland Tilleman and Stephen H. West eds, *China Under Jurchen Rule: Essays on Chin Intellectual and Cultural History*, Albany, NY: SUNY Press, 1995.

Chia, Ning, "Women in China's Frontier Politics: Heqin," in Sherry J. Mou ed., *Presence and Presentation: Women in the Chinese Literati Tradition*, Honolulu: University of Hawai'i Press, 2003, pp. 39–108.

Dai Ping, *Zhongguo minzu fushi wenhua yanjiu* (Studies in the Clothing Culture of the Peoples of China), Shanghai: Shanghai renmin chubanshe, 2000.

Eoyang, Eugene, "The Wang Chao-chun legend: configurations of the classis," *Chinese Literature: Essays, Articles, Reviews*, 4, 1 (January 1982): 3–22.

Fairbank, John King and Merle Goldman, *China: A New History*, Cambridge, MA: Harvard University Press, 2006.

Finnane, Antonia, *Changing Clothes in China*, London: Hurst, 2007.

Franco, Jean, *Critical Passions: Selected Essays*, Mary Louise Pratt and Katherine Elizabeth Newman eds, Durham, NC: Duke University Press, 1999.

Gillette, Maris, "What's in a Dress? Brides in the Hui Quarter of Xi'an," in Deborah Davis ed., *The Consumer Revolution in Urban China*, Berkeley: University of California Press, 2000, pp. 80–106.

Han Xin, "Hua Yan zhi Liang fu 'Zhaojun chusai tu'" ("A Study of the Two Hua Yan Paintings of 'Zhaojun Departs for the Frontier'), in *Hua Yan yanjiu* (*Studies of Hua Yan*), Shanghai: Shanghai shuhua chubanshe, 2003, pp. 256–9.

Howard, Angela Falco, "Buddhist sculptures of the liao dynasty: a reassessment of Osvald Siren's study," *Bulletin of the Museum of Far Eastern Antiquities*, 56 (1984): 1–95.

Hsü, Ginger Cheng-chi, *A Bushel of Pearls: Painting for Sale in Eighteenth-Century Yangchow*, Stanford: Stanford University Press, 2001.

—"Traveling to the Frontier: Hua Yan's *Camel in the Snow*," in Lucie Olivová and Vibeke Børdahl eds, *Lifestyle and Entertainment in Yangzhou*, Copenhagen: NIAS Press, 2009, pp. 347–75.

Hua Mei, *Fushi yu Zhongguo wenhua* (*Dress and Chinese Culture*), Beijing: Renmin chubanshe, 2001.

Jameson, Mrs [Anna], *Sacred and Legendary Art*, vol. 2, London: Longman, Brown, Green, Longmans, & Roberts, 1857.

Kane, Daniel, *The Kitan Language and Script*, Leiden: Brill, 2009.

Kwong, Hing Foon, *Wang Zhaojun: Une Héroïne Chinoise de l'Histoire à la Légende*, Paris: Collège de France, Institut des Hautes Etudes Chinoises, 1986.

Legge, James, *Confucian Analects, The Great Learning and the Doctrine of the Mean*, New York: Dover Publications, 1971.

Leung, Irene S. "The Frontier Imaginary in the Song Dynasty: Revisiting Cai Yan's 'Barbarian Captivity' and Return," Ph.D. thesis, University of Michigan, Ann Arbor, 2001.

Levy, Dore J., "Transforming archetypes in Chinese poetry and painting: the case of Ts'ai Yen," *Asia Major*, Third Series, VI, 2 (1993): 147–68.

Lewis, Mark Edward, *The Early Chinese Empires: Qing and Han*. Cambridge, MA: The Belknap Press, 2007.

Lin Yutang, "The Inhumanity of Western Dress," in Lin Yutang, *The Importance of Living*, London: Heinemann, 1938, pp. 257–62.

Murray, Julia K., *Mirror of Morality: Chinese Narrative Illustration and Confucian Ideology*. Honolulu: University of Hawai'i Press, 2007.

Myers, John, *The Way of the Pipa*, Kent, OH: Kent State University Press, 1992.

Ren Daobin, "Mingdai Jiangnan shinütu mianxiang moshihua tan wei" ("The Routinization of Painting of Female Faces in Ming Jiangnan"), *Meishu shilun* (*Fine Arts History*) (2009): 9–?

Rorex, Robert A. and Wen Fong, *Eighteen Songs of a Nomad Flute: The Story of Lady Wen-chi*, New York: The Metropolitan Museum of Art, 1974.

Rouzer, Paul F., *Articulated Ladies: Gender and the Male Community in Early Chinese Texts*. Cambridge, MA: Harvard University Asia Center, 2001.

Shanghai Museum, *Shimao fengqing: Zhongguo gudai renwu huajing pinji* (*Highlights of Ancient Chinese Figure Painting from the Liaoning Provincial Museum and the Shanghai Museum*), Shanghai: Shanghai guji chubanshe, 2008.

Shen Yizheng, "Lidai meiren huaxuan: xu" (Preface to "Selected Paintings of Fair

Ladies"), in He Gongshang ed., *Lidai meiren huaxuan* (*Selected Paintings of Beauties Through the Ages*), Taibei: Yishu tushu gongsi, 1999.

Turner, Frederick, *The Frontier in American History*, Books on Demand, 2010.

Wu, Juanjuan, *Chinese Fashion from Mao to Now*. London: Berg, 2009.

Zhang Ruili and Zhao Bin, "Qin Han Xiongnu fuzhuang xingzhi tanxi" (*Exploratory Analysis of the Design of Xiongnu Clothing in the Qin and Han Dynasties*), *Xiyu yanjiu* (*Research on Western China*) 2 (2008), pp. 62–7.

Zhou Xidai, *Zhongguo gudai fushi shi* (*History of Chinese Clothing before Modern Times*), Taibei: Nantian shuju, 1989.

PART TWO
RELIGION

3
RABBINICAL DRESS IN ITALY[1]

ASHER SALAH

The question of rabbinical dress, an important aspect of material culture of the Jews in Italy, has not been the object of deep scrutiny by scholars and historians of early modern and modern Italian Judaism.[2] This chapter deals with this question through the analysis of visual evidence provided by portraits of Italian Jews and rabbis from Renaissance to the twentieth century. It will show that, contrary to what have been often asserted, the institutionalization of rabbinical dress occurred before the Reformation (i.e. before the nineteenth century), and secondly that rabbinical dress evolved in Italy bearing strong similarities to the dress of the clergy in Protestant lands and the medical garb worn in Italy.

Jewish iconographic sources

The promulgation of sumptuary laws, regulating specific items of dress that might be worn by various individuals on certain occasions, is a well-known chapter of European social history from the late Middle Ages to the eighteenth century.[3] Within the Jewish communities these decrees were often issued by the rabbis or by the communal authorities and have been used by scholars in order to study different aspects of the material culture of the Jews in early modern Europe.

From these sources two general conclusions have been drawn, as far as Italy is concerned: Firstly, that the Jews in Italy imitated in their clothes the fashion of the upper classes of the Christian society;[4] secondly that "Jewish clothing is uniform and reflects a social homogeneity that is a prime characteristic of Jewish life."[5]

Should we hence infer that rabbis dressed like all the other Jews in their communities? Whatever answer we could be tempted to give to this question, one thing is sure: no sumptuary law known to us stipulates how a rabbi was supposed to be dressed.

In the past decade, while dealing with the intellectual history of Italian Judaism in the early modern period, not once did I run into portraits of rabbis and Jewish physicians that constitute an invaluable, yet still largely unexplored, source of information about clothes and fashion. This material has been somehow overlooked by previous scholarship that was perhaps not fully aware of the relatively large number of depictions of Italian Jewry.

My collection includes some 40 portraits, from the seventeenth to the nineteenth century, spanning over a period of some 300 years. Forty portraits are not much compared to the 1,100 names of rabbis and physicians catalogued in my bio-bibliographical dictionary of eighteenth-century Jews,[6] but still they offer a sufficiently broad basis from which to make some general considerations about Jewish clothing of the time.

Material of this kind lends itself to different sorts of inquiries related to questions of fashion and Jews, from the custom of covering one's head[7] to the use, or should we rather say disuse, of the beard among Italian Jews in early modern period;[8] from the social functions of clothes to issues pertaining to the esthetic values of the Jews in the past. From all the questions raised by this material, I am interested in a more particular one, namely rabbinical clothing. I will try to pinpoint the problem as follows: did the rabbis in Italy in the exercise of their functions make use of specific garments that distinguished them both from the rest of their congregation and from other religions' clergy? And in the affirmative, from which moment is it possible to ascertain the use of a distinctive cassock? Under which circumstances? And what forms and shapes did it take?

But before getting to the heart of the matter, some preliminary methodological comments concerning the use of iconographic sources are necessary.

Firstly, we should be suspicious of the apparent immediacy of the visual image and of its documentary value. Art is always about representation and imagination. As such it can be an extremely fruitful field for the historian of mentalities, of prejudices, and of stereotypes, but it can also be misleading and fallacious for the scrutiny of material culture. Early modern portraits belong to a pictorial genre subject to rigid conventions, from the pose of the figure depicted to the objects that surround it. The simple fact of being portrayed with a certain dress does not tell us by itself that it was worn daily or on every occasion.[9] Moreover, we must be very careful and remember that many rabbinical portraits in our collection were realized without the knowledge or the consent of the person portrayed and therefore they correspond more to the artist's image of how a rabbi should be dressed than how he actually dressed. An interesting instance of the fallacious nature of the image can be found in the portrait of rabbi Mosheh Gentili (1663–1711) that appears in the frontispiece of the second edition of his book *Melekhet Mahashevet* (or *Intentful Work*), printed in Königsberg in 1819, where a black *kippah* has been placed on his head in order to make him look more like an Eastern European Hassid than an Italian scholar of the late seventeenth century.

Secondly, our information derives from a wide range of different iconographic sources, belonging to disparate stylistic registers, realized with different techniques, whose degree of precision and realism can vary considerably from one portrait to another. Some of them are lavish paintings on canvasses commissioned by the portrayed persons; others are extremely stylized engravings appearing on book title pages, such as the portrait of Leon Da Modena (1571–1648). Other are depicted on wedding contracts (*Ketubot*)—where a portrait of the groom and the bride can be seen in richly decorated prenuptial agreements and was sometimes reused for different couples—on medallions, or in lithographs distributed *post mortem* for celebratory purposes, such as the one depicting rabbi Abraham de Cologna from Mantua (1755–1832). In one case, we have also a caricature by Pier Leone Ghezzi (1674–1755) of a famous Roman Rabbi, Tranquillo Corcos (1660–1730).[10] The Corcos portrait can be read as one of the earliest instances of the formation in Europe of a new kind of anti-Semitism, where a racial stereotype (the hooked nose) replaces the religious one.[11] Therefore, not every testimony has the same degree of reliability, especially when stereotypes related to the mostly non-Jewish artists' backgrounds can interfere with the representation of clothes used by Jews.

This should induce us to be prudent, since in the representation of Jewish scenes there could be at work two contrasting but equally deforming principles. On the one hand, there could be an attempt to transform foreignness into something more familiar and, subsequently, less threatening[12] (as happens in the paintings by Alessandro Magnasco [1667–1749], where the only detail indicating the fact that we are assisting to a Jewish prayer is the ritual shawl, the *tallith*, over the head of the preacher. No one amongst the other congregants wears any distinctively Jewish dress, such as the red hat that Jews were obliged to wear, as can be seen in the more realistic depiction of a Jewish funeral in Venice by Marco Marcuola [1740–93]). On the other hand, we have the drive to exaggerate the depiction of the exotic, of the uncanny, and of curious detail (as can be seen in this image, where the anonymous artist has introduced several Jews in Oriental dress, a quite unexpected sight in a small Italian Jewish community such as Reggio Emilia, where no local Jew went around with this kind of accoutrement).

Lastly, portraits become fashionable among Italian Jews only in the late seventeenth century.[13] It is true that we have earlier evidence of pictures hanging on the walls of Jewish homes', such as Leone da Modena's (1571–1648), when, in his *Historia de Riti Hebraici*, he writes that "*in Italia molti* [Jews] *si fanno lecito tener ritratti e pitture in casa, massime non essendo di rilievo ne di corpo compito*" [in Italy many Jews allow themselves to keep in their homes portraits and pictures, especially if they are not in relief nor represent the full body].[14] We know of at least one case of a Jewish woman sending her portrait to a Christian writer,[15] and it is highly probable that some rabbinic figures had in their studies images of their masters as early as the sixteenth century, though none of these portraits have survived.[16] In any case, in the Jewish world, even in the much acculturated Italian communities, these are still isolated occurrences attested with a considerable delay compared to other social categories in the Christian environment, where the birth of portraiture is considered a definitive feature of the early fifteenth century.[17] After the first and few attested instances in the seventeenth century—such as the portrait of the cabalist Menahem Azariah da Fano (1548–1620)[18] and Leon da Modena's, which appears in the frontispiece of his book devoted to Jewish ritual, *Historia de riti Hebraici* (Venice, 1638)—it is only during the eighteenth century that it is possible to speak about a Jewish widespread patronage of arts and of prominent Italian Jews asking renowned artists to paint their portraits, as was the case in the Northern European Sephardic communities, with paintings commissioned to renowned artists such as Rembrandt, Reynolds, or Gainsborough.[19]

From what precedes it should be clear that in order to benefit as much as possible from the analysis of this kind of iconographical source much prudence is needed and that we must use this material by comparing it to other forms of documentary evidence, such as the communities *takanot*, rabbinical responsa, the "prammatiche," i.e. dispositions regulating the life of the community and its institutions, being attentive to what happens in other cultural and religious contexts, in a perspective both diachronic and synchronic.

Yet, it is not possible to do without the visual evidence for at least two reasons. The first is linked to the high degree of precision and realism usually found in the depictions of Jewish life by Christian artists from the early sixteenth century,[20] notwithstanding the aforementioned anti-Semitic biases. Secondly, the written testimonies through which we can get an idea of how rabbis dressed in the crucial period of Jewish history in which traditional society was being overrun by modern tendencies are surprisingly scant.

Rabbinical dress

Rabbinical dress in Italy has not been the object of deep scrutiny by scholars and historians. As far as Italy is concerned, we can rely almost exclusively on Alfred Rubens' classical contribution, though much outdated, which refers to Italian Jews' clothing habits.[21] Rubens summarizes the issue as follows:

> There is no traditional rabbinical robe and the robes worn at the present time are derived from the black Geneva gown and white bands of the Calvinist or Reformed Church, while the round black hat which was adopted during the nineteenth century in Austria and Germany must be derived ultimately from the similar headgear of the Greek Orthodox clergy.[22]

Rubens does not say anything about the reasons for the appropriation of the Protestant cassock by rabbis, an even more surprising appropriation considering that it concerns not only the Jews living in areas inhabited mainly by Protestants, but also, as in the case of the Italian peninsula, in states where the official religion is Catholicism. Moreover, he seems to have been led astray by the still-widespread but inexact assumption that the adoption of a specific dress by rabbis was a nineteenth-century innovation done under the auspices of the Jewish reform movement in Central Europe.

In fact, there is substantial evidence that the thrust to create a distinctive dress for rabbis emerges already in the late Renaissance and mainly in the communities of Italy and the Netherlands. Before that time, rabbis apparently dressed as the rest of the Jews in their congregations. This is the conclusion reached by the Israeli Roberto Bonfil in his essential work on rabbis and Jewish communities in Renaissance Italy:

> For the XVI Century I have not found that the ordained Rabbis in Italy wore special garments unique to their status.[23]

Nevertheless, it seems, from a disposition of Verona's community in 1557, that cantors and all those who led the prayer, except the rabbi, had to wear a special mantle.[24] On the nature of this mantle little is known, but to judge from sixteenth-century Ashkenazi legal sources it seems to have been either a particularly sumptuous *tallith*, the ritual shawl, of silk or a garment similar to the "cappa," the mantle worn by university doctors. The main halakhic authorities of the time were critical of this use, considered to be a sign of haughtiness and presumption to be avoided,[25] but the thrust to establish a vestimentary difference between the rabbis and the congregation is evidently in action in the way of wearing the *tallith*.[26] Concerning the *tallith*, Paolo Medici (1671–1738), a Florentine apostate, writes that "the rabbis keep it over their heads in order to distinguish themselves from the rest of their congregation and act in this way more for lavishness than for religious zeal."[27] Finally, in the second half of the seventeenth century, this desire for distinctiveness has become a reality: most of the rabbinical portraits in Italy show the rabbis wearing a characteristic dress, with the clerical bands and the black gown.

The portraits of Moshe Gentili and David Nieto (1654–1728) are among the most remarkable and earliest examples of this phenomenon. Since we are dealing with rabbis from Venice and Leghorn, cities with strong ties with the Jewish communities of England and the Netherlands, it is quite likely that the adoption of such a garment was made under a Northern European Sephardi influence, where we have several examples of rabbis dressed likewise at least a decade before Italy and where Protestantism was the majority's religion. Is this to be considered a dress specifically conceived for rabbis? Certainly not.

Yet, although it is not common to every category of Jews and bears a strong resemblance to academic and medical costumes of the time, professional categories in Italy used to wear a similar collar to the one of the reformed clergy in Protestant countries, though a little bit longer and not necessarily white. The influence of the medical garb on the rabbinical cassock is even more plausible, since rabbis were assimilated with physicians as far as their social status was concerned in the edicts of many Northern Italian Jewish communities.[28]

Nevertheless, in the eighteenth century this kind of garb has become exclusively rabbinical, since physicians and other classes of people discontinued its wearing. In 1775 Pope Pius VI (1775–99), in his *Editto sopra gli Ebrei*, forbids the rabbis to use a distinctive cassock and obliges them to wear the same clothes as the rest of the community members.[29] This can be read as evidence that rabbis were indeed wearing a special dress, not dissimilar from the one which appears in many portraits of the time. For instance, Cecil Roth presents evidence that at about the same time of the edict, in 1777, a rabbi from Modena, Zecharia Padova, "after a quarrel with the leaders of his community, caricatured them in an etching, in which he depicted himself seated in his study and his elegantly-dressed opponents advancing on him, one of them—his bitterest enemy—having a dog's body."[30] The dress by itself suffices to identify the rabbi from the lay community leaders.

Rabbinical dress institutionalization

From the second half of the nineteenth century the dress of rabbis and ministers in Italian synagogues, with the adoption of the square hat with the addition of a small pompon and belt, has remained almost unchanged to today.[31] At this point we can legitimately speak of a uniform, and as such it was conceived in the circles of Reformed Judaism in Germany around 1840.

Attilio Milano, in the last paragraphs of his *History of the Jews in Italy*, dedicated to rabbinical dress, records the aforementioned transformation and writes:

> Since nineteenth century, the different needs that appeared in Italian and also foreign communities significantly altered the profile of the rabbi, who becomes a communal clerk, a preacher and a minister of the offices in the synagogue while losing the prerogatives of the judge, the master and the spiritual guide ... We could almost say that a visible sign of this change is the cassock that the rabbi begins using for the religious ceremonies under the prayer shawl (tallith).[32]

Milano is perfectly right to correlate the transformations in the role and the functions exerted by the rabbi, in the sense of an increasing subordination to the lay authorities of the community and his shrinking prerogatives from leader and judge to simple religious clerk—what in the Habsburg area was called *Geistliche Beamter*—and of a stronger striving to a more formal and distinctive dress code (called in many German documents of the nineteenth century *Amtstracht*). Insofar as the formation of the rabbis is progressively attributed to special institutions, such as the rabbinical seminaries, the increasing distinctiveness of their apparel is not necessarily the result of a thorough reform of Judaism explicitly formulated by particular sectors of the community, but can be read as the simple effect of a widespread change in the sense of decorum related to the new role the rabbi is called to assume. Although it resembled the clerical dress of the reformed churches, a rabbi's attire, as attested in most of the portraits, was most certainly perceived among Italians as specifically Jewish attire for clergy, in all ways differing from the Catholic.

We can trace the different development stages of a distinctive rabbinical cassock among Italian Jews from a cloth that was initially shared by various professional categories in the seventeenth century to its official adoption by Italian rabbis in the nineteenth century, after it had fallen into disuse among all other segments of the population. This process of specialization corresponds to a phenomenon that has been already observed among the clergy of other religions.[33] As a matter of fact, clergy dress tends to be more conservative and therefore to anachronistically transform clothes, once widely used among the general population, into a distinctive sign of their religious status. This is true at least for the Catholics with the *pallium*, as well as for the Reformed churches, where even the Geneva collar is a relic of the ancient amice, a square linen band wrapped around the priest's neck during the celebration of the mass, which was quite in fashion among lay people in different parts of Europe in the Middle Ages long before the Reformation.

This particular conservatism is not peculiar to the clergy, but it is possible to find examples and analogies to it in the survival of the wig among British barristers, of the top hat for the high Jewish festivals in the Spanish and Portuguese congregations in London and in Amsterdam, and in the so-called "Jewish caftan," which according to some opinions derives from the way Polish nobles once dressed.

Three important deductions can be extracted from the above material on the development of the rabbinical cassock in Italy:

1   First of all, that the adoption of a specific clerical uniform for rabbis predates the emancipation of the Jews in Western Europe in the nineteenth century, and therefore it cannot be attributed to the Reform movement that was born only subsequently to the French Revolution. The progressive acceptance and diffusion of the rabbinical cassock is not only the expression of an assimilatory drive of the Jews toward the mores of the surrounding societies. On the contrary, we know that there has been strong resistance from the authorities of the State, for instance in Prussia, to allow Jewish services to resemble Christian ones and to give clerical status to the rabbinate, as far as the mid-nineteenth century.[34]

2   Secondly, though rabbinical dress was not only conceived in imitation of the clothes of the Protestant clergy—it was also molded after the example of the physician's garb—I think that through its historical development we can follow what I deem to be one of the most interesting phenomena in the past three centuries of Italian Jewish history. Tentatively, I would be tempted to call this phenomenon a more or less unconscious "Protestantization" of Italian Judaism, perceptible from the Counter-Reformation onwards, and which culminated in an intense dialogue and rapprochement between Jews and Protestants on Italian soil in the past two centuries.

Most of those Italian Jews who today refer to the synagogue as the "temple," to the prayer book as the "hymnary," to the rabbinical assemblies as "Synods," and who call the rabbis "reverends" may have forgotten the origin of such a lexicon. There is little doubt that these terms belong to the religious sphere of the Reformed Churches and not that of Catholicism.

3   Thirdly, and lastly, rabbinical garments show us a European Judaism that follows the same fashion continent-wide, notwithstanding local national and religious differences. Italian, German, French, and British rabbis dress alike, with slight and insignificant local particularities such as the round clerical hat in France (*chapeau clerical*) as opposed to the hexagonal one in Italy (*toque*).

Therefore we should not be surprised that the topic of rabbis' dress was not a central issue in the debates concerning reform of Judaism that otherwise torn European Jews, at least in the first half of the nineteenth century. Clerical garb had long been an established custom among rabbis in most Western European synagogues.[35] Champions of the Orthodox camp, from David Sintzheim (1745–1812) to Samson Raphael Hirsch (1808–88), are dressed in the same way as their opponents among the reformers, from Abraham Cologna (1755–1832) to Abraham Geiger (1810–74). In fact, in a Württemberg document of 1847, the white collar bands of the rabbinic garb are called "Moses Tablets," including them in a specifically Jewish semantic field of reference rather than stressing their dependence on a foreign religious model.[36] An attack condemning the by-then-traditional canonical robes of rabbis' dress will come only later, in the second half of the nineteenth century, from elements inside Jewish society that reacted to modernity *in toto*, reinventing a supposedly original tradition through a vehement opposition toward anything that was considered an effect of emancipation even when, such as was the case of the cassock, it did not constitute a divide between liberal and conservative milieus.[37]

Perhaps we should introduce a distinction between a programmatic reform (which actively fights for a change in liturgy, its musical accompaniment, and the structure of the synagogue—whether the *Bimah*, the altar, should be in the center or not—and on the compulsory character of the traditional Jewish Law) and an underground and unconscious reform linked to a deep and therefore imperceptible change in mentalities.[38]

Conclusion

According to the Jewish tradition, there are no particular vestments for rabbis. However, in Italy, from the sixteenth century onwards, some rabbis and other ministers chose special ways of dressing, and from the second half of the seventeenth century this desire for distinctiveness has become a general reality: most rabbis wore a characteristic dress, with the clerical bands and the black gown. This evolution happened with virtually no discussion: the rabbinical cassock was not debated since nobody deemed it debatable and no one considered, at least in Italy, its use as an instance of a dangerous imitation of the mores of the Gentiles— quite the opposite, since no Catholic priest ever dressed like an Italian rabbi.

This particular Jewish dress is still in use nowadays, as the following will show: during the Pope's visit to Rome's synagogue in 1986, even the choir members were dressed with the rabbinical cassock, something absolutely unusual in normal occasions, but this was done precisely with the purpose of affirming the distinctiveness of the Jewish attire from the Catholic one. This is a most striking example of how Protestant clerical dress has been definitively Judaized by Jews living in a Catholic environment. Ironically enough, sometimes common patterns of civilizations and of cultures emerge when we scrutinize what each one of them claims to be their distinctive characteristics.

Notes

1   Another version of this chapter was published as "How Should a Rabbi Be Dressed? The Question of Rabbinical Attire in Italy from Renaissance to Emancipation (Sixteenth–Nineteenth Centuries)", in Fashioning Jews: Clothing, Culture, and Commerce (Leonard Greenspoon ed.), Creighton University Published by Purdue University Press, (2013), pp. 49–66.

2   Among the first, and to date the very few, who devoted themselves to this subject we should mention Leopold Löw, "Die Amstracht der Rabbinen," in *Gesammelte Schriften*, IV (Szegedin, 1889), pp. 217–34.

3   On Jewish sumptuary legislation in general see: Salo Wittmayer Baron, *The Jewish Community: Its History and Structure to the American Revolution*, 3 vols, Philadelphia: Jewish Publication Society, 1942; Louis Finkelstein, *Jewish Self-Government in the Middle Ages*, New York: JTSA, 1924. For Eastern Europe, see Elliott Horowitz, "Sumptuary Legislation," in *YIVO Encyclopedia of Jews in Eastern Europe*, http://www.yivoencyclopedia.org/article.aspx/Sumptuary_ Legislation; for Italy Roberto Bonfil, *Jewish Life in Renaissance Italy*, Berkeley: University of California Press, 1994, p. 104ff.; Ariel Toaff, "La vita materiale," in *Storia d'Italia: Annali 11/1*, Corrado Vivanti ed., Torino: Einaudi, 1996, pp. 239–67; Maria Giuseppina Muzzarelli, "Il vestito degli ebrei," *Zakhor*, 4 (2000), pp. 161–8. On Italy but without much information on Jews, Catherine Kovesi Killerby, *Sumptuary Law in Italy: 1200–1500*, Oxford: Clarendon Press, 2002.

4   Thérèse Metzger, *Jewish Life in the Middle Ages: Illuminated Hebrew Manuscripts of the Thirteenth to the Sixteenth Centuries*, Secaucus, NJ: Chartwell Books, 1982), p. 138 and Ariel Toaff, "La vita materiale," p. 257.

5   Kenneth Stow, *Theater of Acculturation: Roman Ghetto in the Sixteenth Century*, Seattle: University of Washington Press, 2001, p. 184.

6   Asher Salah, *La République des Lettres: Rabbins, médecins et écrivains juifs en Italie au XVIIIè*, Leiden/Boston: Brill, 2007.

7   Raphael Straus, "The Jewish hat as an aspect of social history," *Jewish Social Studies*, 4 (1942): 59–72.

8   Elliott Horowitz, "The early eighteenth century confronts the beard: Kabbalah and Jewish self-fashioning," *Jewish History*, 8 (1994): 95–112; idem., "Visages du judaisme: De la barbe en monde juif et de l'élaboration de ses significations," *Annales: Histoire, Sciences Sociales*, 49 (1994): 1065–90.

9   A striking example of the discrepancies between visual documents and reality is the beard. In Christian iconography in the Middle Ages, Jews were depicted almost invariably wearing a beard, for the symbolic purpose of underscoring the obsolescence of their faith, while it is known from other sources that the vast majority of the Jews in Christian lands were barefaced and clean-shaven. Cf. Bernard Blumenkranz, *Le juif medieval au miroir de l'art chrétien*, Paris, 1966, pp. 18–20.

10 Reproduced in Attilio Milano, *Il ghetto di Roma*, Roma: Carucci, 1988. Other satirical portraits of Jews from Italy in A. Rubens, *A Jewish Iconography*, London: The Jewish Museum, 1954, p. 59.

11 Isaiah Shachar, "The Emergence of the Modern Pictorial Stereotype of 'The Jews' in England," in *Studies in the Cultural Life of the Jews in England presented to Avraham Harman*, Jerusalem: Magnes, 1975, pp. 331–66, situates in the mid-eighteenth century the emergence of a new stereotype of the Jew, which is economic (the Jew as a peddler), cultural (the bearded Jew with a turban-like hat in a strange garb and speaking a broken English), and racial (hooked nose, dark complexion with a peculiar cast of eyes) more than religious.

12 Samantha Baskind, "Bernard Picart's etchings of Amsterdam's Jews," *Jewish Social Studies*, 13, (2007): 40–64.

13 On the background of this phenomenon see Richard Yerachmiel Cohen, *Jewish Icons*, Berkeley: University of California Press, 1998 (especially chapters 1 and 3

that are based on two articles originally published in Hebrew in *Zion*, 57 (1992), pp. 275–340 and 58 (1993), pp. 407–52.

14 Leon Da Modena, *Historia de Riti Hebraici* (Paris, 1637), p. 10.

15 The Venetian Sarra Coppia Sulam to the Genoese Ansaldo Ceba. Cf. Don Harran, *Sarra Coppia Sulam: Jewish Poet and Intellectual in 17th Century Venice*, Chicago: University of Chicago Press, 2010, pp. 23–4.

16 Moses A. Shulvass, *The Jews in the World of Renaissance*, Leiden: Brill, 1973, p. 235 mentions portraits of Meir ben Isaac Katzenellenbogen, the Maharam of Padua and his son, a lost medaillon of Leon da Modena, and even a statue of Judah Minz. Yet Elliott Horowitz's remarks induce to more prudence about the possibility of the Maharam of Padua having being portrayed: "Speaking of the Dead: the Emergence of the Eulogy among Italian Jewry of the 16th Century," in D. Ruderman ed., *Preachers of the Italian Ghetto*, Berkeley: University of California Press, 1992, p. 157. In any case, these are rare and exceptional instances in the 17th century, as rightly stressed by Aviad Hacohen, "Diuqanaot Hakhamim: Bein Halakhah UMaaseh" ("Images of Scholars: Between Halakhah and Reality"), in *Mahanayim*, 2 (1995), pp. 100–21.

17 Andrew Martindale, *Heroes, Ancestors, Relatives and the Birth of the Portrait*, Maarssen and The Hague: SDU, 1988; Joanna Woodall, *Portraiture: Facing the Subject*, Manchester: Manchester University Press, 1997.

18 David Kaufmann, "Menahem Azarya da Fano et sa famille," *Revue d'Etudes Juives*, 35 (1897), pp. 84–90.

19 For England see Alfred Rubens, *Anglo-Jewish Portraits*, London: The Jewish Museum, 1935. For Altona-Hamburg see Peter Freimark, "Portraets von Rabbinern der Dreigemeinde Altona-Hamburg-Wandsbek aus dem 18. Jahrhundert," in P. Freimark, A. Jankowski, and I. S. Lorenz eds, *Juden in Deutschland: Emanzipation, Integration, Verfolgung und Vernichtung*, Hamburg: Hans Christians, 1991, pp. 36–57.

20 Richard Cohen, *Jewish Icons: Art and Society in Modern Europe*, Berkeley: University of California Press, 1998, p. 67.

21 Alfred Rubens, *A History of Jewish Costume*, New York: 1967. The same critic addressed the more recent work by Richard Cohen, *Jewish Icons*, focused on the history of Northern and Central European Judaism.

22 Rubens, *A History of Jewish Costume*, p. 190.

23 Roberto Bonfil, *Rabbis and Jewish Communities in Renaissance Italy*, Oxford: Oxford University Press, 1990, p. 76, quotes a Mantua pragmatic from the year 1599 that reads: "the excellent ordained rabbis, by the agreement of the Committee, are allowed to dress as they please, as are the honorable physicians."

24 Ibid., p. 118.

25 Mordechai Breuer, "Ha-Semikhah Ha-Ashkenazit," in *Zion*, 33 (1968), p. 42. The Italian rabbi from the Renaissance, Messer David Leon, also opposes the use of this dress, which he calls "sudar shel begged," worn by some Sephardi rabbis and their disciples in Constantinople in a responsum published by Salomon Schechter, "Notes sur Messer David Leon," *Revue d'Etudes Juives*, 24 (1892), p. 137. An ambivalent, though lenient, attitude toward the "cappa" characterizes rabbi Joseph Colon's reponsa, a contemporary of Messer Leon, due apparently to his ignorance of the exact shape of this dress, see Moses Avigdor Shulvass, "Mahlokotav Shel Messer Leon Im Rabbanei Doro Ve-Nisiono Lehatil Maruto Al Yehudei Italia," *Zion*, 12 (1946): 17.

26 In the Middle Ages only the beard could have been a distinctive sign of piety worn by certain cantors and rabbis, and even this quite seldom. Cf. Elliott Horowitz, "Visages du judaisme: De la barbe en monde juif et de l'élaboration de ses significations," *Annales. Histoire, Sciences Sociales*, 49 (1994), p. 1082. In the eighteenth century beards ceased almost completely to function as a sign of the rabbinical class. Cf. Horowitz, "The Early Eighteenth Century Confronts the Beard," p. 103.

27 Paolo Medici, *Riti e costumi degli ebrei*, Venezia: 1801, p. 58. A similar statement, though limited to the sole cantors, can be read in Leon Da Modena, *Historia de riti ebraici*, Venezia: 1638, p. 29.

28 Bonfil, *op. cit.*, p. 76 quotes a Mantua pragmatic from the year 1599 that reads: "the excellent ordained rabbis, by the agreement of the Committee, are allowed to dress as they please, as are the honorable physicians."

29 Attilio Milano, "L'editto sopra gli ebrei," *Rassegna Mensile di Israel*, 19 (1955), pp. 118–25.

30 Cecil Roth, *Jewish Art: An Illustrated History* (New York: McGraw-Hill, 1961), p. 521. The picture was in Cecil Roth's personal collection and today is located at the Brotherton Library at the University of Leeds, UK.

31 The rabbinical dress was therefore codified in the community's statutes. See an example of late nineteenth-century Rome in Gianfranco Di Segni, "Innovazioni nel culto religioso a Roma nella seconda meta' dell'Ottocento," *Zakhor*, 8 (2005), p. 72 where it is written that "Art. 5: Tutti gli ufficanti e i sagrestani dovranno presenziare la celebrazione di tutte le funzioni religiose, indossando sempre l'abito talare. Art 20: I sefarim saranno sempre portati dai Celebranti vestiti dell'abito talare". Di Segni remarks that "è interessante notare che la sollecitazione affinché i chazannim indossino l'abito talare viene dal presidente della comunità non dal rabbino (a cui probabilmente la questione non interessava molto)."

32 Attilio Milano, *Storia degli ebrei in Italia*, Torino: Einaudi, 1963, p. 442.

33 Daniel Roche, *The Culture of Clothing: Dress and Fashion in the* Ancien Regime, Cambridge: Cambridge University Press, 1999, p. 454 writes: "The progress from lay clothes to the clothes of the modern clergy can be seen as part of the history of the widening gap which increasingly separated ecclesiastics from everybody else. The role of the councils, especially Trent, has to be emphasized in order to express the trend toward differentiation, accentuated in the 17th century."

34 Michael A. Mayer, *Response to Modernity: a History of the Reform Movement in Judaism*, Oxford: Oxford University Press, 1988, p. 110.

35 The differences between the dress of the cantors, the rabbis, and in some places also of other communities' officials, should be further investigated, as well as the codes of dressing in particular circumstances of the liturgical calendar.

36 Michael Mayer, *Response to Modernity*, p. 103.

37 Michael Silber, "The Emergence of Ultra-Orthodoxy: The Invention of a Tradition," in Jack Wertheimer ed., *The Uses of Tradition,* New York: JTS Press, 1992, pp. 23–84. In the *psak* of Michalowce in 1865 the canonical robes for the cantor were included among the innovations that were severely forbidden, p. 40.

38 In Gianfranco Di Segni, "Innovazioni nel culto religioso a Roma nella seconda meta' dell'Ottocento," *Zakhor*, 8 (2005): 72 we can read about a detailed dress code for rabbis and cantors in late nineteenth-century Rome.

Bibliography

Balletti, Andrea, *Gli ebrei e gli estensi*, Reggio Emilia: 1930.

Baron, Salo Wittmayer, *The Jewish Community: Its History and Structure to the American Revolution*, 3 vols, Philadelphia: Jewish Publication Society, 1942.

Baskind, Samantha, "Bernard Picart's etchings of Amsterdam's Jews," *Jewish Social Studies*, 13, (2007): 40–64.

Bemporad, Dora Liscia, *Maggino di Gabriello hebreo venetiano: i Dialoghi sopra l'utili sue inventioni circa la seta*, Firenze: Edifir, 2010.

Blumenkranz, Bernard, *Le juif medieval au miroir de l'art chrétien*, Paris: 1966.

Bonfil, Roberto, *Rabbis and Jewish Communities in Renaissance Italy*, Oxford: Oxford University Press, 1990.

—*Jewish Life in Renaissance Italy*, Berkeley: University of California Press, 1994.

Breuer, Mordechai, "Ha-Semikhah Ha-Ashkenazit," in *Zion*, 33 (1968): 15–46.

Cohen, Richard, *Jewish Icons: Art and Society in Modern Europe*, Berkeley: University of California Press, 1998.

Da Modena, Leon, *Historia de Riti Hebraici*, Paris: 1637.

—*Ziqnei Yehudah*, S. Simonsohn ed., Jerusalem: 1956.

Di Segni, Gianfranco, "Innovazioni nel culto religioso a Roma nella seconda metà dell'Ottocento," *Zakhor*, 8 (2005), pp. 43–75.

Finkelstein, Louis, *Jewish Self-Government in the Middle Ages*, New York: JTSA, 1924.

Freimark, Peter, "Portraets von Rabbinern der Dreigemeinde Altona-Hamburg-Wandsbek aus dem 18. Jahrhundert," in P. Freimark, A. Jankowski, and I. S. Lorenz eds, *Juden in Deutschland: Emanzipation, Integration, Verfolgung und Vernichtung*, Hamburg: Hans Christians, 1991, pp. 36–57.

Giannoccolo, Laura, *Samuele Jesi (1788–1853) incisore*, Areastampa: Correggio, 2007.

Hacohen, Aviad, "Diuqanaot Hakhamim: Bein Halakhah UMaaseh ("Images of Scholars: Between Halakhah and Reality"), in *Mahanayim*, 2 (1995): 100–21.

Harran, Don, *Sarra Coppia Sulam: Jewish Poet and Intellectual in 17th Century Venice*, Chicago: University of Chicago Press, 2010.

Heiman Ganz, Mozes, *Memorbook: History of Dutch Jewry from the Renaissance to 1940*, Baarn: Bosch & Keuning, 1977.

Horowitz, Elliott, "Speaking of the Dead: The Emergence of the Eulogy among Italian Jewry of the 16th Century," in D. Ruderman ed., *Preachers of the Italian Ghetto*, Berkeley: University of California Press, 1992, pp. 129–62.

—"Sumptuary Legislation," in *YIVO Encyclopedia of Jews in Eastern Europe*, http://www.yivoencyclopedia.org/article.aspx/Sumptuary_Legislation

—"The Early Eighteenth Century Confronts the Beard: Kabbalah and Jewish Self-fashioning," *Jewish History*, 8 (1994): 95–112.

—"Visages du judaisme: De la barbe en monde juif et de l'élaboration de ses significations," *Annales: Histoire, Sciences Sociales*, 49 (1994): 1065–90.

Katz, Dana, *The Jew in the Art of the Italian Renaissance*, Philadelphia: University of Pennsylvania Press, 2008.

Kaufmann, David, "Menaham Azarya da Fano et sa familie," *Revue d'Etudes Juives*, 35 (1897): 84–90.

Kovesi Killerby, Catherine, *Sumptuary Law in Italy: 1200–1500*, Oxford: Clarendon Press, 2002.

Löw, Leopold, "Die Amstracht der Rabbinen," in *Gesammelte Schriften*, IV (Szegedin, 1889), pp. 217–34.

Mann, Vivian B. ed., *Gardens and Ghettos: The Art of Jewish Life in Italy*, New York: The Jewish Museum, 1989.

Martindale, Andrew, *Heroes, Ancestors, Relatives and the Birth of the Portrait*, Maarssen & The Hague: SDU, 1988.

Mayer, Michael A., *Response to Modernity: A History of the Reform Movement in Judaism*, Oxford: Oxford University Press, 1988.

Medici, Paolo, *Riti e costumi degli ebrei*, Venezia, 1801.

Metzger, Thérèse, *Jewish Life in the Middle Ages: Illuminated Hebrew Manuscripts of the Thirteenth to the Sixteenth Centuries* Secaucus, NJ: Chartwell Books, 1982.

Milano, Attilio, "L'editto sopra gli ebrei," *Rassegna Mensile di Israel*, 19 (1955), pp. 118–25.

—*Il ghetto di Roma*, Roma: Carucci, 1988.

—*Storia degli ebrei in Italia*, Torino: Einaudi, 1963.

Morosini, Giulio, *Via della fede mostrata agli ebrei*, Roma, 1683.

Muzzarelli, Maria Giuseppina, "Il vestito degli ebrei," *Zakhor*, 4 (2000): 161–8.

Roche, Daniel, *The Culture of Clothing: Dress and Fashion in the Ancien Regime* Cambridge: Cambridge University Press, 1999.

Roth, Cecil, *Jewish Art: An Illustrated History*, New York: McGraw-Hill, 1961.

—"Portraits of Jews," in *Encyclopedia Judaica*, 1971.

Rubens, Alfred, *Anglo-Jewish Portraits*, London: The Jewish Museum, 1935.

—*A Jewish Iconography*, London: The Jewish Museum, 1954.

—*A History of Jewish Costume*, New York: Valentine Mitchell, 1967.

Salah, Asher, *La République des Lettres: Rabbins, médecins et écrivains juifs en Italie au XVIIIème*, Leiden/Boston: Brill, 2007.

Schechter, Salomon, "Notes sur Messer David Leon," *Revue d'Etudes Juives*, 24 (1892): 137.

Shachar, Isaiah, "The Emergence of the Modern Pictorial Stereotype of 'The Jews' in England," in Issachar Ben-Ami and Dov Noy eds, *Studies in the Cultural Life of the Jews in England presented to Avraham Harman*, Jerusalem: Magnes, 1975, pp. 331–66.

Shulvass, Moses A., *The Jews in the World of Renaissance*, Leiden: Brill, 1973.

—"Mahlokotav Shel Messer Leon Im Rabbanei Doro Ve-Nisiono Lehatil Maruto Al Yehudei Italia," *Zion*, 12 (1946): 17–23.

Silber, Michael, "The Emergence of Ultra-Orthodoxy: The Invention of a Tradition," in Jack Wertheimer ed., *The Uses of Tradition*, New York: JTSA, 1992, pp. 23–84.

Stow, Kenneth, *Theater of Acculturation: Roman Ghetto in the Sixteenth Century*, Seattle: University of Washington Press, 2001.

Straus, Raphael, "The Jewish Hat as an Aspect of Social History," *Jewish Social Studies*, 4 (1942), pp. 59–72.

Toaff, Ariel, "La vita materiale," in Corrado Vivanti ed., *Storia d'Italia: Annali 11/1*, Torino: Einaudi, 1996, pp. 239–67.

Woodall, Joanna, *Portraiture: Facing the Subject*, Manchester: Manchester University Press, 1997.

4

ZOOMORPHIC BROOCHES IN ROMAN BRITAIN: DECORATION OR RELIGIOUS IDEOLOGY?

LINDSAY ALLASON-JONES

Evidence for the appearance of the people who lived in Roman Britain between the first and fifth centuries CE comes from sculptural representations, fragments of textiles, and accessories found in excavations, as well as tantalizing snippets of information from literary texts. The latter, however, usually refer to the people living around the Mediterranean, with little reference to Roman Britain or the other provinces in north-west Europe, and it is important to realize that a description of an article of clothing or jewelry worn in Rome or Egypt may have been relevant only to the dress of a very small minority of the inhabitants of Britannia.

The word "fashion," in the modern sense, can be seen in hairstyles throughout the Empire. According to Ovid it was easier to count the acorns on an oak tree than to list the varieties of hairstyle to be seen in Rome in the first century CE.[1] Women in Britain would have kept up to date with the latest styles by studying portraits on recently minted coins of empresses, or by questioning those who had recently arrived from the Continent, although Ovid advised women to avoid these changes and stick to a style that suited the shape of their face.[2]

In the north-west provinces, there were few other concessions to fashion; one wore what one's tribe wore, and this was invariably slow to change.[3] Even in Rome itself, men from all walks of life wore a tunic, with decorative stripes indicating rank rather than acting as a fashion statement; the toga was usually only worn on formal, ceremonial occasions and was not a practical day-to-day garment. The equivalent iconic item of clothing for women was the *stola*, although this was worn only by matrons in Rome and fell out of use in the second century CE, to be replaced by a simple tunic.[4] In the provinces the tunic varied in shape, particularly the shape of the sleeves, and in the way the garments were fastened, making women from the individual provinces identifiable wherever they went. It was only in the third century CE that the women of the Imperial family began to wear a new style of tunic and women across the Empire followed suit.[5] Throughout the period the length of the tunic was rarely dictated by fashion, as the shorter tunics were mostly worn by slaves.

As far as can be discerned from the archaeological evidence, colors were also unaffected by changes in taste; only the wealthy could afford to wear brightly dyed cloth. Some colors also had social significance; purple, for example, was symbolic of the Emperor, whilst snow white was worn by politicians wishing to stress their suitability for office.[6] Many people were limited to the natural colors of wool and linen, unless they could dye their own clothes with naturally available dyestuffs.[7]

In the wearing of accessories, tribal affiliations were stronger than the whims of taste. The women of the Treveri, for example, wore close-fitting bonnets while those of the Ubii wore very large, spherical bonnets; women from some of the other tribes of North-west Europe are not known to have worn head coverings at all.[8] Even the wearing of jewelry, which one might presume to have been purely a matter of taste, with jewelers continually producing new styles in order to attract new customers, has been found to have been dictated by tribal norms, albeit with more chronological nuances than textile garments.[9]

Studies of jewelry from Roman Britain have indicated that brooches were mostly utilitarian, worn by both women and men to fasten clothing.[10] This presumption may be true of the brooches whose bows permit enough fabric to be grasped firmly, but falters with small plate brooches, when the space between the pin and the back of the plate is often less than five millimeters, whilst the space between the catchplate and the hinge may be as little as ten millimeters. In these cases, insufficient cloth can be caught to secure a heavy tweed, such as would be used for a cloak, or even the woolen cloth used for the Gallic costume worn by many women in the province.[11] The conclusion might be that these small plate brooches were not utilitarian fasteners but were simply decorative, particularly as most are decorated with multi-coloured champlevé or millifiori enameling, or repoussé decoration, were it not for the evidence that fashion played little part in the type of jewelry worn in the province. In particular, there is a group of plate brooches in the form of animals, some enameled, some not, which can be found throughout the northern provinces of the Roman Empire, but which are particularly evident in Britain.[12] Many of these have been found in ritual contexts and their distribution indicates unusual patterns of use, leading to the conclusion that they had significance beyond the merely aesthetic for their wearers.

Modern archaeologists have tended to call all objects that have a moveable pin and a catchplate "brooches" and thus considered them to be jewelry,

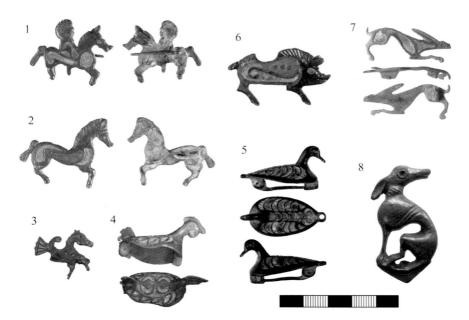

Figure 4.1 Examples of zoomorphic brooches from Roman Britain. © The Portable Antiques Scheme/Trustees of the British Museum.

whether practical at confining clothing or not. However, observation of modern populations will remind us that the differences between a brooch, worn purely as a decorative fastening, and a badge, worn to represent an aspect of its wearer's life, may be very subtle and this may lead to the proposition that the zoomorphic brooches were intended as badges. If this is so, then what was the symbolism the images intended to convey, and does this symbolism link the wearer to particular ideologies?

A brooch from South Shields Roman fort at the mouth of the River Tyne in north-east England, showing a boar, the symbol of the Twentieth Legion, running to the right, might point to these brooches having been worn by military men, their relatives, or retired veterans as symbols of a particular unit.[13] However, the known symbols of the Roman legions in Britain—the boar (Twentieth Legion Valeria Victrix) and the bull (Sixth Legion Victrix and Ninth Legion Hispana)—are noticeably rare in brooch form, whilst the capricorn, the symbol of Second Legion Adiutrix and Second Legion Augusta, is completely missing. The universal symbol of the Roman military, the eagle, is also rarely seen as a brooch, although it appears many times in stone reliefs, three-dimensional stone sculpture, and bronze statuettes, as well as in intaglio on finger rings.[14]

In Britain the Roman army was not solely made up of legions; there were also as many as 63 or 64 auxiliary units serving in the province at any one time.[15] These units were not made up of Roman citizens, but were recruited from Rome's neighbors and allies, and thus brought exotic beliefs from beyond the Mediterranean world to British shores. It is not clear if symbols were painted on shields or embroidered on pennants to differentiate these auxiliary units from each other, or if particular animals were of special significance to any of them. It is possible that animal symbols were used, based on traditional beliefs that different animals had attributes that made them suitable for adoption by military troops. The distribution of the zoomorphic badges as a whole, however, would appear to preclude them having a solely military significance, as examples are largely confined to the area south and east of the Humber–Severn rivers line, an area which had a predominately civilian population throughout the Roman period. The alternative suggestion that these zoomorphic images refer to deities appears to be more convincing, although this then leaves the question: which deities?

The most comprehensive catalogue of zoomorphic brooches in Britain can be found in the Portable Antiquities Scheme (PAS) database and this has been used to create the distribution maps published in this chapter. The scheme was initiated in 1997 and extended to cover the whole of England and Wales during 2003. Under the scheme, a team of locally based Finds Liaison Officers record discoveries reported by members of the public on an online database (www.finds.org.uk). As a high proportion of the objects included in the database have been found by metal detectorists, there is a bias towards rural sites not scheduled under the British Ancient Monument Acts. To counter this, a range of published archaeological site reports have also been trawled through to find further examples, but this has simply confirmed the impression that zoomorphic badges are rarely to be found on purely military sites; they are unusual finds on the military frontier of Hadrian's Wall, completely missing from the Antonine Wall further north, and only a few have been found in Southern Scotland or Wales.

The animals favored by brooch manufacturers were hares and horses as well as horses with riders, with only occasional dogs, boars, lions, leopardesses, stags, and bulls. There are also a number of birds, of which cockerels and ducks are the most identifiable and most frequently occurring, with very few eagles. The hippocamp appears on a few brooches and a turtle (or tortoise) is known on two, but increasing numbers of fish are being found, six alone in recent excavations at Caerleon in south Wales (Peter Guest pers. comm).

Horses on their own [Fig. 4.1, no. 2] are often linked to the Gallic deity Epona, an Indo-European horse deity associated with mares and fertility.[16] She became popular amongst the Roman cavalry in Gaul and Germany, but dedications to her are rarely found in Britain, and then only in military contexts.[17] Irby-Massie has concluded of Epona that "she was an appropriate protectress of mounted units"[18] and it is noticeable that the horse badges have a more military distribution [Fig. 4.3a] than the horse-and-rider brooches [Fig. 4.3b] or even the

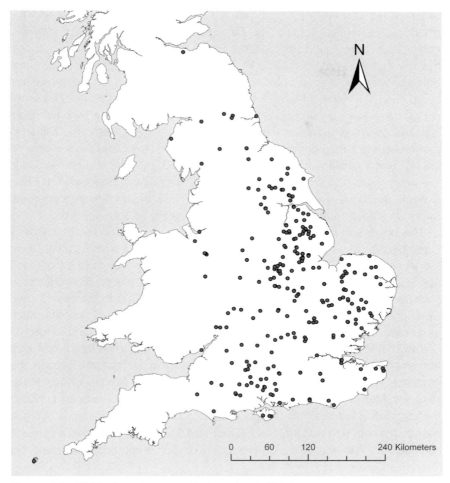

Figure 4.2   Distribution of zoomorphic brooches in Britain.

other zoomorphic badges. In this context it is particularly interesting that one of the horse brooches was found in Cumbria, close to Maryport Roman fort (*Alauna*), where a stone relief of Epona has been found showing the goddess in her tradition pose, sitting sideways on her horse.[19] However, it can be said that the Maryport connection is an exception, as sites that have produced inscriptions or sculpture of Epona do not otherwise produce either horse brooches or horse-and-rider brooches, suggesting that the brooches do not have a strong link with the deity.

On the horse-and-rider brooches the rider is always male and sits astride, which would also appear to rule out any link between the brooches and the goddess Epona (Fig. 4.1, no. 1). Through his research, Ferris has identified two types of horse-and-rider brooches: the first is a very stylized "cut-out" that has little detail and merges the rider with his horse; the second is much more detailed, with the legs and arms of the rider clearly visible, as is his hair and beard, and the horse's mane.[20] On the second type the rider is sometimes shown carrying a sword[21] or a baton,[22] but lacks the helmet or shield that might distinguish him as a warrior. These brooches are more common in Britain in the third century than on the Continent and, indeed, the Continental examples are noticeably different in appearance.[23] Ferris (1986) suggested that the British examples were concentrated mostly in East Anglia; the Portable Antiquities Scheme database has extended this significantly, although the distribution still favors sites south of the Humber–Severn line [see Fig. 4.3b].

The horse-and-rider brooches are more often to be found on Romano-Celtic temple sites—eight from Hockwold-cum-Wilton, five from Lamyatt Down (Somerset), three from Hayling Island (Hampshire), two each from Woodeaton (Oxfordshire) and Cold Kitchen Hill (Wiltshire), and one each from Nettleton (Wiltshire), Nor'Nour (Isles of Scilly), Haddenham (Buckinghamshire), and Corbridge (Northumberland)—or from sites with known ritual deposits, such as Lode and March in Cambridgeshire, Brampton in Norfolk, and Undley in Suffolk.[24] This evidence Toynbee,[25] Johns,[26] and Ferris[27] interpreted as linking the brooches with a Romano-Celtic rider god, but at Lamyatt Beacon the brooches were originally associated with the classical Roman deities Mars, Hercules, Mercury, and Minerva,[28] although the final excavation report confined the association to Mars.[29] At Brigstock in Northamptonshire, the center of a cult based on a rider god was identified, which was flourishing in the third and fourth centuries CE. This site, although producing no horse-and-rider brooches, did

Figure 4.3 **A** Distribution of horse brooches; **B** Distribution of horse-and-rider brooches.

produce a number of bronze statuettes of mounted riders, and Henig took this as evidence that the deity was "certainly to be equated with Mars."[30] Green was of the opinion that depictions of horsemen always had cult significance and were linked "to some aspect of Mars."[31] Mars, as a god of war, was a deity with a strong connection with the Roman army, and dedications to him and depictions of him in stone and metal tend to be distributed in military areas; this contrasts with the predominately civilian distribution of the horse-and-rider brooches and may support the idea that the brooches relate to a native deity worshipped by the tribes inhabiting the distribution area, rather than Mars.

The hare badges can be divided into hares that are running [Fig. 4.1 no. 7] and those that are crouching, with a few, such as an example from Baldock (Hertfordshire), showing the hare being seized by a predator, usually a dog.[32] Small figurines of hares have been found in Britain in Romano-Celtic shrines, such as Thistleton.[33] Green has suggested a link between hares and Celtic society,[34] although Johns considered this tenuous; however, it should be recalled that Boudicca released a hare whilst evoking the goddess Andraste (Dio Cassius LXII.7.3), and Julius Caesar included hares with geese and cockerels as important beasts for Celtic religion (Dio Cassius LXII.2). Traditionally, hares have been associated with lunar and hunting deities, particularly Diana, as well as being recognized as messengers of Mercury. The distribution of both types of the hare brooches shows a curious pattern, with one example on Hadrian's Wall and a scattering across Norfolk, Suffolk, Essex, and Kent, but with distinct concentrations in Hampshire and Lincolnshire. This may suggest a link to otherwise unidentified cult centers.

It can be difficult, on occasions, to tell the difference between a running dog and a running hare if a brooch is damaged, but there are fewer running dog brooches from Britain than horses or hares. This is unexpected, as dogs have been identified as the attributes of both Silvanus and Diana, both deities worshipped in Britain, whilst they are also linked to healing shrines, such as that of Nodens at Lydney.[35] Ross specifically linked dogs to the deities Sucellos, Nehalennia, and Nodens,[36] whilst Toynbee noted that Epona often carries a dog.[37] The distribution of dog brooches is mostly in the Lincolnshire area, with little overlap with the distribution pattern of the hares.

Plotting the distribution of brooches depicting other animals has produced some surprises. The stag, which was not a common military symbol, has a very clear military distribution, even though the number of examples is few. Crummy linked the stag to the worship of the Celtic deities Silvanus and Cernunnos,[38] but the popularity of stag hunting amongst Roman army officers should not be ignored, and it is possible that the stag brooches had a secular significance. The boar [Fig. 4.1, no. 6], which was also an animal hunted for sport, was a known symbol of the Twentieth Legion. There is the one un-enameled boar badge from South Shields (Tyne and Wear) previously mentioned, but otherwise the type avoids military sites. This lack of a military distribution may reflect the animal's importance to the native population, as can be seen by its appearance on Iron Age coins and helmet crests.[39] The bull, which is associated with two of the legions in Britain (Second Adiutrix and Second Augusta), might be expected to be common in the military zone in the north, but only one example is included in the Portable Antiquities database, and that in the extreme south. In Celtic mythology the bull was associated with solar cults,[40] an association that can also be seen through the bull's importance to the worshippers of the eastern mystery cult of Mithras.[41] None of the bull brooches from Britain show the animal with the three horns of Celtic tradition, nor have any of the Mithraea excavated in Britain produced any bull brooches.

Lion brooches are to be found in a line up the center of the country in very rural contexts, where it is unlikely the inhabitants had any first-hand knowledge of the live animal. Throughout the Roman Empire the lion was a well-known symbol "of the ravening power of death and man's victory over it"[42] and is a common image in funerary contexts throughout Roman Britain. The lion was also linked to Hercules through the legend of his First Labour, the victory over the Nemean Lion. Hercules was considered merely a hero in most provinces of the Roman Empire, but in Britain he was venerated as a god and there are many images of him in stone or bronze, easily identified by the lionskin cloak worn over his shoulder. No major cult center dedicated purely to Hercules has been discovered in Britain as yet, but the artefactual evidence indicates that he was very popular with the military. The distribution of the lion brooches along the rural spine of the country, largely avoiding the military zone, would suggest that the brooches are not linked to the official cult of Hercules.

The leopard/leopardess, whose association with the cult of Bacchus is discussed by Hutchinson (1986), has a limited southern distribution in brooch form, at odds with Hutchinson's findings of Bacchic imagery over the rest of the country: 37 percent of her data is from military sites, 28 percent from towns, and 18 percent from minor settlements. Excavations of the Roman fort of Camelon in Scotland produced several artefacts which could be linked to the cult of Bacchus, including a stud and a pin depicting panthers or leopardesses, but no leopard or leopardess brooches were amongst the assemblage (Maxfield, forthcoming).

Whilst Pickard[43] was of the opinion that the enameled zoomorphic brooches were made in Britain between CE 50 and 150, the three-dimensional chicken and duck brooches may have been the products of the Rhineland.[44] They are so distinctive in appearance and share so many common details that wherever the source was it may be confidently asserted that the brooches came from the same or associated workshops. This makes their distribution pattern in Britain very interesting. If they shared a manufacturing center and were simply worn as attractive items of jewelry, one would have expected them to share a distribution

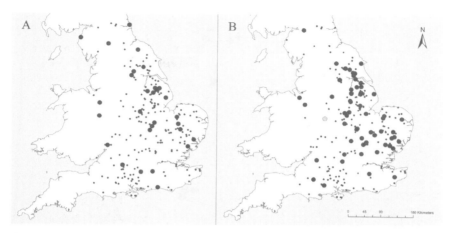

Figure 4.4   **A** Distribution of cockerel brooches; **B** Distribution of duck brooches.

pattern. The maps shown as Figures 4.4a and b reveal the ducks to have been considerably more popular than the chickens but with a tighter distribution, from Yorkshire down to Suffolk, whilst the chickens show a distinct military spread. It is rare for a site to produce both chickens and ducks, which, again, one might expect if the brooches had the same distributors.

The cockerel [Figure 4.4] appears regularly in sculpture as an attribute of the Roman god Mercury and the cockerel brooches have been firmly linked to the worship of Mercury by Crummy.[45] In apparent confirmation of this, a cockerel brooch was found in association with cockerel bones in the temple at Lancing Down.[46] However, whilst Crummy also associated enameled shoe brooches and purse brooches with Mercury as the god of travel, it is noticeable that Mercury's other attributes, the goat and the tortoise, are not obviously represented by brooches; no goat brooches at all are recorded in the Portable Antiquities Scheme database and only two in the shape of tortoises, although they are more convincing as turtles (YORYMM392 and BERK-28DDA1).

The popularity of ducks [Fig. 4.4b; 4.1, no. 5] defies explanation at the moment. A range of birds has been identified as having religious significance for both the Roman and Celtic populations (see below), yet ducks do not feature at all. If it is accepted that the other zoomorphic brooches can be linked to recognized deities, this is curious, and may indicate the worship of a native British water deity whose existence has not yet been revealed by sculpture or illustrated inscriptions.

The number of bird brooches that cannot be identified as chickens or ducks is limited and can be divided into eagles, swans, parrots, and peacocks, although with only a few of each. They reflect the distribution of zoomorphic brooches in general. The limited number of eagle brooches has been remarked upon earlier;

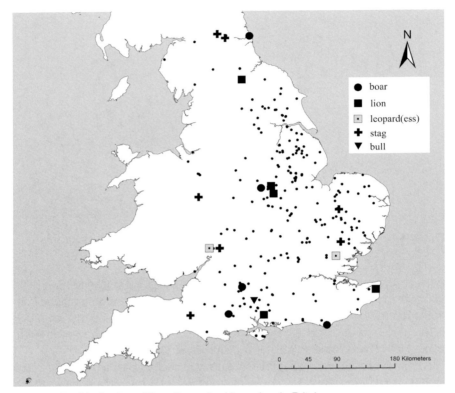

Figure 4.5   Distribution of the other animal brooches in Britain.

as a symbol of the military, the Roman Empire and of Jupiter, more might have been expected if the brooches were worn generally to declare political or military allegiance. The lack of eagles may confirm that the wearing of such brooches was a Celtic trait and not one common in the Mediterranean heartlands of the Empire. Swans were linked to Jupiter as, in legend, he appeared to Leda in the form of a swan, but were also associated with Celtic solar cults.[47] Peacocks were sacred to Juno in Roman religion and in the first century CE became linked to Christian beliefs,[48] but were already considered to be symbols of immortality before their adoption by the early Christians.[49]

Fish were also Christian symbols from the first century due to the first letters of the Greek for 'Jesus Christ, God's son, savior' making the word for fish, *ichthys*. The Christian symbol was simply two curved crossing lines, which represented a swimming fish, and some of the enameled brooches show a similar form. However, a number of the brooches depict leaping salmon, an image which Ross has linked to the worship of Nodens at Lydney.[50] Their British distribution, except in only a few instances on the Isle of Wight, perversely avoids coastal areas, suggesting perhaps that the wearers had riverine fish in mind.

The other sea creatures are more mythological in that they depict *hippocampi*, creatures with the head and foreparts of a horse and the hindquarters of a fish [Fig. 4.1, no. 3]. Again, these are not particularly associated with coastal sites. They are usually to be found in Roman iconography linked with the water deity Neptune, whose chariot was drawn by *hippocampi*. In Celtic mythology it is possible that they were water spirits, who later became the waterhorses with evil intent, known as kelpies.

This is not a comprehensive survey of all the zoomorphic brooches to be found in Britain; there will be examples in museum collections or in publications that have eluded the author. However, there is enough evidence to indicate that the brooches were not linked to military units, with the possible exception of the horse and stag examples, but could be symbols associating the wearer with a particular deity. Brooches, by their very nature, are easily transportable, so the discovery of apparent geographic groupings of some types, for example the horse-and-rider brooches, at shrines and in ritual deposits may support Johns' suggestion that the brooches were the Roman equivalent of pilgrim badges or decorative souvenirs.[51] She concluded that the objects were bought at the shrines and either dedicated to the deity at the shrine or taken away and worn proudly as proof that the wearer had visited that shrine, in a similar manner to medieval pilgrim badges.[52]

The dating of the badges indicates that while the horse-and-rider brooches can be dated to the late second or third centuries and appear to have continued into the fourth century CE,[53] the other zoomorphic brooches are more closely associated in date with the general run of enameled brooches, that is in the second century CE. The disappearance of enameled objects in general from dated contexts after the early third century suggests that they ceased to be fashionable, making the horse-and-rider brooches of particular interest.

Religious observance in Roman Britain can be divided into public and private. Public worship included veneration of the deities of the Roman pantheon, particularly Jupiter, Roma and the Deified Emperors, and members of the public were expected to turn up at the calendared ceremonies to pay due respect, whether they believed in that deity or not. This was one of the mechanisms through which the Roman government attempted to unite the disparate peoples under their rule.[54] Public worship also included the rituals and ceremonies carried out by military units when seeking the favor of a deity or thanking that deity for benefits received. This ritual activity could be dedicated to one or more of the gods of Rome but could also be directed at a deity from an auxiliary unit's homeland, as can be seen from dedications to the Alaisiagae, Baudihillia, and Friagabis by "the unit of Hnaudifridus" at Housesteads (*RIB* 1567; see also *RIB* 1593 and 1594). Military units might also adopt a deity native to the region in which they were stationed, such as the god Antenociticus, who was worshipped by the First Cohort of Vangiones, which was originally raised in Germany, at Benwell on Hadrian's Wall (*RIB* 1328). Private worship included paying respect to the gods of hearth and home, the Lares and Penates, if the worshipper followed the beliefs of the city of Rome, but in Britain private worship mostly reflected the belief of individuals in their native deities or those brought from other provinces by Roman soldiers or merchants, the latter including Mithraism and Christianity and covered by the catch-all description of "mystery religions." The Roman government was not averse to the people under their rule worshipping any deity they wished, as long as they paid public respect to the official deities. The only exceptions were those cults which practiced human sacrifice, or religions such as Christianity and Judaism that are monotheistic. Both exceptions were because human sacrifice and a lack of veneration to the Deified Emperors were seen as potential threats to the stability of the Empire, and these were thus political, rather than theological, objections.

Most religions practiced in Roman Britain were centered on the use of a stone altar and it is through the inscriptions on such altars that we can build up a picture of the religious life of the province. The altars vary greatly in size, from the large examples dedicated by whole units, such as the group of altars to Jupiter Best and Greatest at Maryport (*RIB* 814–831), all of which are well over a meter in height, to personal dedications that might be as small as 12 centimeters (see, for example, an altar to Diana from Corbridge: *RIB* 1126). Stone altars were, however, expensive, requiring access to a sufficient amount of the raw material and a skilled mason to carve it, and would have been beyond the means of many people. For those with limited funds, alternative ways of declaring allegiance would have been required.

Intaglios worn in finger-rings are regularly regarded as indicators of personal ideologies worn openly to signify particular allegiance.[55] Intaglios were, however, expensive and had to be observed closely before the device could be recognized. The zoomorphic brooches would not only have been cheaper to buy but would have been very conspicuous when worn; the metal would gleam as brightly as gold whilst the enamel, in primary colors, would be very evident. We can presume that the wearers were making a statement, a statement they expected other people to be able to recognize and also a statement they were willing, even proud, to make in public. There are many modern parallels: Ban the Bomb badges, lapel and tie pins worn to indicate the support of a political party or charity, colored ribbons expressing solidarity with people with Aids or breast cancer—all these symbols are clearly understood by contemporary observers and important to their wearers. Today we may be uncertain as to the deities indicated by each zoomorphic brooch, but we can conclude that they represented a symbol of a heartfelt ideology to their wearers.

Our understanding of the religious beliefs of the provinces of the Roman Empire has mostly relied on inscriptions and sculpture supported by metal statuettes and terracotta figurines. The stone dedications may not all have been publically visible as they would have been positioned within a cult center or temple where only the initiated might have had easy access. Even those dedications and figurines kept in domestic shrines would have been largely visible only to family members. Those who could see these obvious declarations of an individual's belief would have shared the same beliefs as the dedicator. A small, brightly colored badge, on the other hand, unless bought for immediate dedication at a cult center, would have been worn in public as a blatant declaration of an individual's personal beliefs in a deity which, due to the paucity of eagles and other attributes of the Capitoline Triad, are likely to have been native to the wearer's homeland.

Webster has suggested that "brooches are a symbol of a bond since they hold together garments or folds of cloth which are pierced by the pin, and thus can be seen as an image of a union";[56] in the case of the zoomorphic brooches the union was between the worshipper and his or her deity. This union would have been important to a believer and regarding the brooches as simply colorful jewelry, introduced randomly as a new fashion, is to miss an important clue to the religious ideology of the time. The Roman invaders brought to Britain the official state gods of Rome but did not attempt to convert the newly conquered to the Roman religions alone. As long as the population paid due reverence to the official deities and the deified emperors on the prescribed days, they were free to worship any deity they wished and as many as they wished. This may suggest a harmonious religious atmosphere throughout the province but there is some evidence that there were clashes of ideology between worshippers of different cults. The altar from Bath, for example, which recorded the restoration of the temple to Virtue and the Deity of the Emperors, which had been "wrecked by insolent hands" (*RIB* 152), indicates friction between the worshippers of different cults, although whether this was on religious or political grounds is not clear in this example. The altar does, however, suggest that wearing a brooch or badge which clearly and firmly declared the wearer's allegiance to a particular and possibly native cult may not have been without its dangers. These people were, in their small way, standing up for their religious ideologies more clearly than the dedicators of altars or the wearers of intaglios and deserve our respect.

Notes

1   Ovid, *Ars Amatoria* III, 149.
2   Ibid., 140.

3   J. P. Wild,"Clothing in the North-west provinces of the Roman Empire,"
     Bonner Jahrbucher, 168 (1968), p. 168; E. Swift and R. Reece, *Regionality in
     Dress Accessories in the Late Roman West*, Montagnac: Éditions Monique Mergoil,
     2000; A. Croom, *Roman Clothing and Fashion*, Stroud: Tempus, 2000.

4   Croom, *Roman Clothing and Fashion*, p. 89.

5   Ibid., pp. 90–101.

6   Ibid., pp. 25–8.

7   L. Allason-Jones, *Women in Roman Britain*, 2nd edn, York: Council for British
     Archaeology, 2005, pp. 104, 110–11.

8   Ibid., p. 109; Wild, "Clothing in the North-West Provinces."

9   Swift and Reece, *Regionality in Dress Accessories in the Late Roman West*;
     Ivleva, T., "Brooches Tell Tales: British-made Brooches in Germania Inferior and
     Superior as Indicators of the Presence of British Emigrants," in K. Huijben, S. J.
     A. G. van de Liefvoort, and T. J. S. M. van der Weyden eds, *SOJA Bundel 2010,
     Radboud Universiteit Nijmegen: Proceedings of Symposium Onderzoek Jonge
     Archeologne* (*Research Symposium for Young Archaeologists*) *held on 19th March,
     Nijmegen*, Nijmegen: 2011, pp. 51–6; T. Ivleva, "British Emigrants in the Roman
     Empire: Complexities and Symbols of Ethnic Identities," in D. Mladenovič and B.
     Russell eds, *TRAC 2010: Proceedings of the 20th Theoretical Roman Archaeology
     Conference, Oxford 2010*, Oxford: 2011, pp. 132–53.

10   Allason-Jones, *Women in Roman Britain*, p. 121; E. Swift, "Personal Ornament,"
     in L. Allason-Jones ed., *Artefacts in Roman Britain: Their Purpose and Use*,
     Cambridge: Cambridge University Press, 2011.

11   Wild, "Clothing in the North-West Provinces," pp. 166–240.

12   C. Johns, "Mounted Men or Sitting Ducks: The Iconography of Roman-British Plate
     Brooches," in B. Raftery ed., *Sites and Sights of the Iron Age: Essays on Fieldwork
     and Museum Research Presented to Ian Mathieson Stead,* Oxbow Monograph 56,
     Oxford: pp. 103–9.

13   Allason-Jones and L. Miket, *Catalogue of Small Finds from South Shields Roman
     Fort*, Newcastle upon Tyne: 1984, no. 3.130.

14   Henig, M., *A Corpus of Roman Engraved Gemstones from British Sites*. BAR Brit.
     Ser. 8 (first published in 1974), Oxford.

15   D. J. Breeze, *Roman Frontiers in Britain*, London: Bristol Classical Press, 2007,
     pp. 23–4.

16   G. L. Irby-Massie, *Military Religion in Roman Britain*, Leiden: Brill, 1999, p. 154.

17   Auchendavy, Scotland: *RIB* 2177 — *RIB* refers to R. G. Collingwood and R. P.
     Wright, *The Roman Inscriptions of Britain*, vol. 1, Oxford: Clarendon Press,
     1965; Carvoran, Northumberland: *RIB* 1777; see also L. Oaks, "The Goddess
     Epona: Concepts of Sovereignty in a Changing Landscape," in M. Henig and
     A. King eds, *Pagan Gods and Shrines of the Roman Empire*, Oxford University
     Committee for Archaeology Monograph 8, Oxford: 1986, pp. 77–84; K. Linduff,
     "Epona: A Celt Among the Romans," *Latomus* 38, 3: 817–37.

18   Irby-Massie, *Military Religion in Roman Britain*, p. 155.

19   L. Allason-Jones, "The women of Roman Maryport," in R. J. A. Wilson ed., *Roman*

Maryport and its Setting: Essays in Memory of Michael G. Jarrett, Maryport: Trustees of the Senhouse Roman Museum, 1997.

20 Ferris, I. M., "Horse and Rider Brooches in Britain: A New Example from Rochester, Staffordshire," *Trans. South Staffordshire Archaeol. and Hist. Soc.* XXVI (1984–5), pp. 1–10.

21 Johns, "Mounted Men or Sitting Ducks," pp. 103–9.

22 R. Hattatt, *Ancient and Romano-British Brooches*, Sherborne: privately published, 1982, p. 162.

23 See, for example, E. Riha, Die 'Römischen Fibeln aus Augst und Kaiseraugst, Forschungen', *Augst* 3, 1979.

24 M. Henig and R. A. Chambers, "Two Roman Bronze Birds from Oxfordshire," *Oxoniensia* 44 (1984): 19–21.

25 J. M. C. Toynbee, *Animals in Roman Life and Art*, London: Thames and Hudson, 1973.

26 Johns, *op. cit.*

27 Ferris, "Horse and Rider Brooches in Britain", p. 2.

28 S. A. Butcher, "Enamels from Roman Britain," in M. R. Apted, R. Gilyard-Beer, and A. D. Saunders eds, *Ancient Monuments and their Interpretation: Essays Presented to A. J. Taylor*, London: 1977, pp. 41–69.

29 R. Leech, "Excavations on a Romano-British Temple and Cemetery on Lamyatt Beacon, Somerset," *Britannia* 17 (1986): 272.

30 M. Henig, "Art and Cult in the temples of Roman Britain," in Rodwell, W., ed. *Temples, Churches and Religion: Recent Research in Roman Britain*, BAR Brit. Ser. 77. Oxford. See also M. V. Taylor, "Statuettes of Horsemen and Horses and Other Votive Objects from Brigstock, Northants," *Antiquaries Journal*, 43 (1963): 264–8.

31 M. Green, *The Religions of Civilian Roman Britain*, BAR Brit. Ser. 24, Oxford: 1976, p. 30.

32 I. M. Stead and V. Rigby, *Baldock: The Excavation of a Roman and pre-Roman Settlement, 1968–72*, Britannia Monograph 7, London: 1986, fig. 49, no. 152.

33 Rutland: Green, *The Religions of Civilian Roman Britain*, p. 167, SK91.

34 M. Green, *The Gods of the Celts*, Gloucester: Alan Sutton, 1986, p. 185.

35 R. E. M. Wheeler and T. V. Wheeler, *Report on the Excavation of the Prehistoric, Roman and Post-Roman Site in Lydney Park, Gloucestershire*, London: Oxford University Press for the Society of Antiquaries, 1932, pl. XXV; see also Toynbee, *Animals in Roman Life and Art*, pp. 122–4.

36 A. Ross, *Pagan Celtic Britain*, 2nd ed., London: Sphere, 1974, p. 423.

37 Toynbee, *Animals in Roman Life and Art*, pp. 197–9.

38 N. Crummy, "Brooches and the Cult of Mercury," *Britannia*, 38 (2007), pp. 225–30; see also Ross, *Pagan Celtic Britain*, p. 417.

39 J. Creighton, *Coins and Power in Late Iron Age Britain*, Cambridge: Cambridge University Press, 2000; J. Foster, *Bronze Boar Figurines in Iron Age and Roman Britain*, BAR Brit. Ser. 39, Oxford: 1977.

40 Ross, *Pagan Celtic Britain*, p. 384.

41 Toynbee, *Animals in Roman Life and Art*, pl. 73.

42 Ibid., p. 65.

43 B. C. Pickard, "Animal Brooches," in Hattatt, *Ancient and Romano-British Brooches*, pp. 158–65.

44 E. Ettlinger, *Die Römischen Fibeln in der Schweiz*, Bern: Francke, 1973, Type 46.

45 Crummy, "Brooches and the Cult of Mercury," p. 224.

46 Ibid., p. 225.

47 Ross, *Pagan Celtic Britain*, p. 302.

48 C. F. Mawer, *Evidence for Christianity in Roman Britain: The Small Finds*, BAR Brit. Ser. 243 (1995).

49 Toynbee, *Animals in Roman Life and Art*, p. 251.

50 Ross, *Pagan Celtic Britain*, p. 437.

51 Johns, "Mounted Men or Sitting Ducks," p. 104.

52 See also S. A. Butcher, "Enamels from Roman Britain," in M. R. Apted, R. Gilyard-Beer, and A. D. Saunders eds, *Ancient Monuments and their Interpretation: Essays Presented to A. J. Taylor*, London: Phillimore, 1977, pp. 41–69.

53 Ferris, "Horse and Rider Brooches in Britain," p. 7.

54 L. Allason-Jones, *Daily Life in Roman Britain*, Oxford and Westport, CT: Greenwood, 2008, pp. 120–31.

55 Henig, *A Corpus of Roman Engraved Gemstones*, pp. 82–5; V. Hutchinson, *Bacchus in Roman Britain: The Evidence for his Cult*, BAR. Brit. Ser. 151, Oxford, 1986, 435–516; Green, *The Gods of the Celts*.

56 G. Webster, "What the Britons Required from the Gods as Seen Through the Pairing of Roman and Celtic Deities and the Character of Votive Offerings," in Henig and King eds, *Pagan Gods and Shrines of the Roman Empire*, p. 60.

Bibliography

Allason-Jones, L., *Daily Life in Roman Britain*, Oxford and Westport, CT: Greenwood, 2008, pp. 105–11.
—*Women in Roman Britain*, 2nd edn, York: Council for British Archaeology, 2005.
—"The Women of Roman Maryport," in R. J. A. Wilson ed., *Roman Maryport and its Setting: Essays in Memory of Michael G. Jarrett*, Maryport: Trustees of the Senhouse Roman Museum, 1997.
Allason-Jones, L. and L. Miket, *Catalogue of Small Finds from South Shields Roman Fort*, Newcastle upon Tyne: Society of Antiquities of Newcastle upon Tyne, 1984.
Breeze, D. J., *Roman Frontiers in Britain*, London: Bristol Classical Press, 2007.
Butcher, S. A., "Enamels from Roman Britain," in M. R. Apted, R. Gilyard-Beer, and A. D. Saunders eds, *Ancient Monuments and their Interpretation: Essays Presented to A. J. Taylor*, London: 1977, pp. 41–69.
Creighton, J., *Coins and Power in Late Iron Age Britain*, Cambridge: Cambridge University Pres, 2000.
Croom, A., *Roman Clothing and Fashion*, Stroud: Tempus, 2000.

Crummy, N., "Brooches and the Cult of Mercury," *Britannia*, 38 (2007), pp. 225–30.

Ettlinger, E., *Die Römischen Fibeln in der Schweiz*, Bern: Francke, 1973.

Ferris, I. M., "Horse and Rider Brooches in Britain: A New Example from Rochester, Staffordshire," *Trans. South Staffordshire Archaeol. and Hist. Soc.* XXVI (1984–5), pp. 1–10.

Foster, J., *Bronze Boar Figurines in Iron Age and Roman Britain*, BAR Brit. Ser. 39, Oxford: 1977.

Green, H. J. M., "Religious Cults at Roman Godmanchester," in M. Henig and A. King eds, *Pagan Gods and Shrines of the Roman Empire*, Oxford: Oxford University Committee for Archaeology Monograph 8 (1986), pp. 29–56.

Green, M., *The Religions of Civilian Roman Britain*, BAR Brit. Ser. 24. Oxford: 1976.

—*The Gods of the Celts*, Gloucester: Alan Sutton, 1986.

Hattatt, R., *Ancient and Romano-British Brooches*, Sherborne: privately printed 1982.

Henig, M., *A Corpus of Roman Engraved Gemstones from British Sites*. BAR Brit. Ser. 8 (first published in 1974) Oxford: 1978.

—"Art and Cult in the Temples of Roman Britain," in W. Rodwell ed., *Temples, Churches and Religion: Recent Research in Roman Britain*, BAR Brit. Ser. 77, Oxford, 1980.

Henig, M. and Chambers, R. A., "Two Roman Bronze Birds from Oxfordshire," *Oxoniensia* 44 (1984), pp. 19–21.

Henig, M. and King, A. eds, *Pagan Gods and Shrines of the Roman Empire*, Oxford University Committee for Archaeology Monograph 8, Oxford: 1986.

Hutchinson, V., *Bacchus in Roman Britain: The Evidence for his Cult*, BAR. Brit. Ser. 151, Oxford: 1986.

Irby-Massie, G. L., *Military Religion in Roman Britain*, Leiden: Brill, 1999.

Ivleva, T., "British Emigrants in the Roman Empire: Complexities and Symbols of Ethnic Identities," in D. Mladenovič and B. Russell eds, *TRAC 2010: Proceedings of the 20th*

—"Brooches Tell Tales: British-made Brooches in Germania Inferior and Superior as Indicators of the Presence of British Emigrants," in K. Huijben, S. J. A. G. van de Liefvoort, and T. J. S. M. van der Weyden eds, *SOJA Bundel 2010, Radboud Universiteit Nijmegen: Proceedings of Symposium Onderzoek Jonge Archeologne (Research Symposium for Young Archaeologists) held on 19th March, Nijmegen*, Nijmegen: 2011, pp. 51–6.

Johns, C., "Mounted Men or Sitting Ducks: The Iconography of Roman-British Plate Brooches," in B. Raftery ed., *Sites and Sights of the Iron Age: Essays on Fieldwork and Museum Research Presented to Ian Mathieson Stead*, Oxbow Monograph 56, Oxford: pp. 103–9.

Leech, R., "Excavations on a Romano-British Temple and Cemetery on Lamyatt Beacon, Somerset," *Britannia* 17 (1986), pp. 259–328.

Linduff, K., "Epona: A Celt Among the Romans," *Latomus* 38,3, pp. 817–37.

Mawer, C. F., *Evidence for Christianity in Roman Britain: The Small Finds*, BAR Brit. Ser. 243 (1995), Oxford.

Maxfield, V., *Excavations at Camelon Roman Forts, 1975–81*, forthcoming.

Oaks, L., "The Goddess Epona: Concepts of Sovereignty in a Changing Landscape," in M. Henig and A. King eds, *Pagan Gods and Shrines of the Roman Empire*, Oxford University Committee for Archaeology Monograph 8, Oxford: 1986, pp. 77–84.

Pickard, B. C., "Animal Brooches," in R. Hattatt, *Ancient and Romano-British Brooches*, Sherborne: 1982.

Riha, E., Die 'Römischen Fibeln aus Augst und Kaiseraugst, Forschungen', *Augst* 3, 1979.

Ross, A., *Pagan Celtic Britain*, 2nd ed., London: Sphere, 1976.

Stead, I. M. and V. Rigby, *Baldock: The Excavation of a Roman and pre-Roman Settlement, 1968–72*, Britannia Monograph 7, London: 1986.

Swift, E., "Personal Ornament," in L. Allason-Jones ed., *Artefacts in Roman Britain: Their Purpose and Use*, Cambridge: Cambridge University Press, 2011, pp. 194–218.

Swift, E. and Reece, R., *Regionality in Dress Accessories in the Late Roman West*, Montagnac: Éditions Monique Mergoil, 2000.

Taylor, M. V., "Statuettes of Horsemen and Horses and Other Votive Objects from Brigstock, Northants," *Antiquaries Journal*, 43 (1963): 264–8.

Toynbee, J. M. C., *Animals in Roman Life and Art*. London: Thames and Hudson, 1973, pp. 264–8.

Webster, G., "What the Britons Required from the Gods as Seen Through the Pairing of Roman and Celtic Deities and the Character of Votive Offerings," in M. Henig and A. King eds, *Pagan Gods and Shrines of the Roman Empire*, Oxford University Committee for Archaeology Monograph 8, Oxford: 1986, pp. 57–64.

Wheeler, R. E. M. and Wheeler, T. V., *Report on the Excavation of the Prehistoric, Roman and Post-Roman Site in Lydney Park, Gloucestershire*, London: Oxford University Press for the Society of the Antiquaries of London, 1932.

Wild, J. P., "Clothing in the North-West provinces of the Roman Empire," *Bonner Jahrbucher*, 168 (1968): 166–240.

5
HOW MUSLIM WOMEN DRESS IN ISRAEL

OZ ALMOG

Introduction—tradition and values

In order to understand fully Muslim female dress in Israel, some basic concepts will be clarified here. Islam, like most other religions, regulates the behavior of its believers.[1] Like other faiths, its legal code lays down rules regarding the related fields of clothing and sexuality.[2] One goal of these strictures is to prevent the exposure and highlighting of certain parts of the body—especially those of women. According to the Prophet Muhammad, God created men and women, but also created, at the same time, clothing to cover those parts of the body that should be covered (7:26, *Surah al-A'raaf*—"The Heights").

Like other religions, Islam is composed of many different sects and schools of religious law. Each of these has its own approach to how women should dress. By and large, however, most Islamic writers and teachers view the female body as a temptation that can cause men's primal urges to overwhelm them. Muhammad himself declared that nothing has a worse effect on men than the temptations of women. He also said: "I looked into hell and saw that most there were women." Mouhamad Abo Rahal, a Muslim cleric in Nazareth and member of the Islamic Movement, adds: "Women are sentenced to damnation for wearing shiny, short, tight, or sheer clothes, tempting men and causing the dissolution of Muslim society."

The *Qur'an* is divided into 114 chapters, each called a *surah*. Each *surah* has a name, in accordance with its content. According to the *Qur'an*, clothing is a divine gift: "And Allah has made for you of what He has created shelters, and He has given you in the mountains places of retreat, and He has given you garments to preserve you from the heat and coats of mail to preserve you in your fighting; even thus does He complete His favor upon you, that happily you may submit" (16:81, *Surah an-Nahl*, "The Bee"). Another verse states: "O children of Adam! We have indeed sent down to you clothing to cover your shame, and (clothing) for beauty and clothing that guards (against evil), that is the best. This is of the communications of Allah that they may be mindful" (7:26, *Surah al-A'raaf*, "The Heights").

Furthermore, *Surat al-Ahzaab* ("The Clans," 33:59), for example, includes a clear injunction to divide men from women: "O Prophet! say to your wives and your daughters and the women of the believers that they let down upon them their over-garments; this will be more proper, that they may be known, and thus they will not be given trouble; and Allah is Forgiving, Merciful." Other verses refer to gold jewelry and silk garments, which are forbidden in this world, but will be the reward of the faithful in paradise.

The seven fundamental rules of women's dress

The Hadith are collections of laws, legends and stories about the Prophet and how he lived, along with precepts learned from his behavior, passed on orally from generation to generation by religious scholars. Most Muslims consider these to be the most authoritative source for interpreting the *Qur'an*. It is important to stress that Islam does not have detailed written dress codes as, for example, ultra-orthodox Judaism does. Rather, there is an oral tradition that mandates that women wear clothes that cover their bodies nearly completely. A Muslim woman must wear a long, loose, opaque garment extending from neck to foot, obscuring all the intimate parts of her body. She is also expected to cover her hair.

All interpreters of the Hadith have been men, and their rulings have been aimed first at protecting male honor, status, and primacy over women. Their patriarchal outlook views women as the property of men. A man is not eager to share his "property" with others; another man's lustful gaze, directed at his wife, is tantamount to trespassing.

Male and female honor are both tied up with the honor of the family, but each is expressed in different ways. Male honor (*sharaf*) is a public matter involving courage, hospitality, and piety. A man may lose his honor, but there are ways for him to regain it. Women's honor (*'ard*) is a private matter with only one component: sexual modesty. Once this is lost (at least in the eyes of others), it cannot be reinstated. If a woman's loss of honor is known only within a closed circle, a reprimand suffices. But if it becomes public knowledge, her male relatives are liable to feel a duty to clean the stain on the family's honor by means that, in extreme cases, may include the murder of the woman.

This concern for female modesty is characteristic of patrilineal societies. Such societies have inbuilt anxiety about the paternity of each child, and about the orderly transfer of inheritance from one male to another.

Throughout history, men in traditional societies have imposed codes on women, as part of enslaving women and treating them as creatures of lower social status than men.[3] Women may not, for example, lead the community or give sermons. Their role, principally, is to obey and serve men. The stricture that a woman may display her sexuality only to her husband also denotes his ownership of her.

There are seven basic rules governing the dress of Muslim women:

1   No part of a woman's body may be seen except her face and her hands;

2   Her garment must be loose, so as not to reveal her figure;

3   The fabric must be thick and opaque, so as not to reveal the color of her skin or the outline of her body;

4   Colors, design, and ornamentation must be muted, so as not to attract attention;

5   A woman may not wear men's clothing;

6   A woman may not wear garments worn by infidels;

7   A woman's clothes must be modest, but not shabby so as to arouse pity.

Girls must begin to dress according to this code as soon as they reach maturity. Islamic texts do not mandate a specific age, but the generally accepted view is that it is the age of the first menses.

Head covering in the Western and Arab worlds

Many modern, non-religious Westerners see Muslim dress as a salient example of the repression of women and denial of their rights.[4] A central finding of a survey conducted in 2006 by the Council on American–Muslim Relations is that nearly half of the Americans surveyed believe that Islam advocates the repression of women. Aysha Hussain, a Muslim woman who works as a journalist in New York, notes that "Many of these people think that if a woman is covered up, it means that she is being oppressed."

Since the covering of the head, and the wearing of a veil in particular, are among the most notable markers of Islamicist affiliation, it is only natural that campaigners against religious coercion have made these their principal targets. This polemic comes not only from the West—it began, in fact, in modernizing Muslim countries during the previous century, such as Atatürk's Turkey during the 1920s. In 1930, the Pahlavi regime in Iran promulgated a law forbidding the wearing of the veil, and Tunisia adopted a similar law in 1986. To this day there are reports about opposition to the veil in relatively liberal Muslim states. In contrast with the veil, which covers the face, attitudes toward the *hijab* (a kerchief that covers the hair but not the face) are positive in most parts of Arab society.

As the Muslim population of Western Europe has grown, the battle over the *hijab* has spread there as well.[5] France recently legislated a prohibition against wearing prominent markers of religious distinction in schools. Similar laws have been passed in about half of Germany's states, on the grounds that the *hijab* has become a symbol of fundamentalism and extremism. The debate has reached the courts of Britain, Belgium, Denmark, and Italy.

The *hijab* and its meaning are central topics in feminist discourse in the Arab world.[6] Those who reject the *hijab* view it as a means of oppression; those who support it offer a variety of defenses: some argue that the *hijab* is an empowering display of identity, women's contribution to Islam's battle against Western culture. One picturesque argument from an Islamic internet site maintains that a woman must be wrapped the way sweets are wrapped, to keep flies and other filthy creatures from landing on her.

Another theory argues that the *hijab* offers women a means of ascending to a higher spiritual and intellectual plane. Thanks to her modest dress, men treat her with respect, and judge her by her personality rather than by outward appearance. The *hijab* liberates women from the pressures that Western society places on them—requiring them to spend time worrying about how they look and exposing as much of their body as possible. Another claim is that the *hijab* protects women from sexual harassment.

Whatever the case, the *hijab* remains an outward expression of a complex reality. After all, the way most Muslim societies treat women has not changed fundamentally. Even women who have shed traditional forms of dress continue to play traditional roles in the family, and are still open to charges of immodesty. The family's honor and her good name still depend on her appearance.

The study of dress in Arab society

To the best of our knowledge, no empirical sociological study of how Arab women dress has yet been conducted in the Arab world, or in Israel. The methodological problems are daunting, given the sensitivity and private nature of the subject. Research on dress is viewed in Arab society as an invasion of privacy. As a result, we have used photography and interviews as our basic information-gathering techniques.

Our data on how Israeli Muslim women dress have been obtained largely through observations in Arab communities and on the campus of the University of Haifa, carried out by Arab students enrolled in the course "An Introduction to Israeli Society." Each student was supplied with a set of basic questions for conducting interviews. They also made observations and took some 500 photographs in Arab communities throughout the country. It should be noted that at the University of Haifa, where about 20 per cent of students are Arab, the full range of dress styles prevalent in Arab society is on display.

The dress code of Muslim Arab women in Israel

Religiosity and secularism in Arab society

Israel's Muslim Arab population lives in about a hundred villages and small cities throughout the country. Surveys show that a decisive majority of Israel's Arab citizens are religious or traditional; only a small minority, most of them of Christian origin, define themselves as non-religious or as not subscribing to any faith at all.

Religious observance among Israel's Arab citizens rose after 1967 and gained momentum in the 1980s as part of broad processes that took place in the Arab and Muslim world at the time.[7] A comparison of photographs of Arabs from 30–60 years ago with contemporary ones shows vast differences, in particular regarding the way women dress.[8] Fundamentalist Islamic dress codes became a notable influence in Israel's Arab sector at the end of the 1990s. But an opposing process appeared at the same time, in the form of daring and less traditional dress. The latter trend is a consequence of the enhanced status of Arab women and their increasing but cautious liberation from the traditional patriarchy.

"Proper" religious garments are imported, largely from Syria, via Jordan, and from Jordan itself. Most mid- to large-sized Israeli Arab communities have shops that specialize in clothing for religious Muslim women. Well-off Muslim women prefer to shop for clothes far from home. Those who live in Haifa used to shop in Jenin, but now go as far as Um al-Fahm, Jerusalem, or even Amman and Cairo. There they feel freer to acquire a double wardrobe: a modern bold one for home, and a conservative, buttoned-up one for the street.

Young and single women tend to be more flexible in how they dress. We surmise that this is a consequence of natural youthful rebellion, and the need young women feel to display their sexual attractiveness in order to obtain a husband.

A Muslim woman is herself the most important force in determining her dress codes, in keeping with her education, her family, the milieu in which she lives, and her personality. According to Muslim Arab society, however, it is generally still accepted that a woman's style of dress must be approved by the men in her family—her father, husband, and in some cases her brothers as well. Mothers and sisters also have considerable influence, but most of the family's authority is invested in its men.

In Israel, the state metes out no punishments against women who violate the religion's dress code, since the judicial system is not subordinate to Islamic law. However, sanctions are taken against a woman who is seen by religious leaders to have violated Islamic dressing codes. According to Khaled Musa Sabah, the imam of the village Abu-Snan (Western Galilee), "We go to her and ask her nicely to mend her ways." Our interviews indicate, however, that the enforcement of these standards can be much less liberal and tolerant. The sanctions against "wayward" girls—that is, those who depart, in the view of those around them, from proper Muslim modesty (hardly a rare occurrence) are imposed by her immediate and extended family and by the community. Her parents are likely to forbid her to leave the house. The community, more often than not, will label her a "bad girl" (an expression used by one of our interviewees). In other words, she is seen as a loose woman, and becomes the subject of evil gossip, scorn, and may even be shunned.

Most women are quite apprehensive about such reactions, which may lead to verbal and physical violence. But even more than violence, they are concerned that such a reputation will make it difficult for them to find husbands, and in particular a "quality" husband—an unbearable punishment for an Arab woman. Neither do they want to stain their families or clans, and they know that a blemish on their reputations will be a blemish on that of their relatives. As a result, even women who are not devout take care to conform to the bare minimum of modesty when they leave home.

Dress in context

The dress code that applies within the home differs significantly from that which applies in public—especially outside a woman's village or neighborhood. The former is considerably more flexible and free. It should be emphasized, however, that standards differ from one community to another. Two male students who aided us in this study said that they were surprised to discover the extent of the differences between the dress code for women they knew from their own villages in the north and the rules that applied in villages they visited in the south.

As a general rule, smaller villages are more religiously observant because of the close social supervision typical of small and isolated communities. A young fashion designer from Tarshiha, a Galilee village, angered Muslim authorities there when, in a local newspaper in June 2006, she said: "In the village there are no few women who go around in the traditional *jelbab* [long traditional dress], and it kills me." The same day a leaflet signed by "women deeply insulted by the insult to their *jelbab*" appeared all over the village, sharply condemning the heretical designer. "We are proud of our *jelbab* and they are an honor and source of pride for us," the signers maintained.

In large cities and settlements that are not exclusively Muslim—Nazareth and Acre, for example—supervision is less strict and women have an easier time flouting convention. Even greater flexibility is available to women in cities of mixed Arab and Jewish population.

It is not easy for a woman to present herself in public in Israel in a long *jelbab* outside Arab communities. The average Israeli views a woman in a traditional Arab dress as something from another world. An Arab woman dressed this way might thus easily find herself the target of invective or even threats. Even worse, she can be suspected as a suicide bomber, both because of her adherence to Islam and because wary Israelis will suspect that her loose clothing is covering an explosive belt.

Dress as a mirror of religious observance

This study is based on the assumption that, for Muslim women, a high level of religious observance correlates with acceptance of strict religious dress codes. These codes forbid baring or highlighting the body, especially those parts of the body considered sexually attractive—breasts, the neck, legs, hair, the waist, the buttocks, and the hips. Throughout the world, in conservative religious societies, sensuality and femininity are also expressed by color—bright colors can call attention to a woman's personal features and attract attention—as well as by clothing, makeup, and jewelry.[9] In other words, the presumption is that the more religious a woman is, the less revealing her clothing will be.

We were unable to prove this assumption categorically in the course of this study, although we found considerable evidence to support it. The difficulty arises from the problem of defining a scale of femininity and eroticism (modesty and eroticism need not be opposites—sometimes they go hand in hand) and because it is also difficult to define a scale of religious observance. In practice, it can be presumed, with all due caution, that the level of a Muslim woman's religious faith is exhibited principally by her religion's standards of modesty, principally its dress code.

It is also reasonable to assume (according to the simplicity principle) that the greater the independence a woman appropriates for herself and the more she allows herself to depart from strict religious standards and dresses as she wishes, the less religion plays an important role in her life. Independent behavior is almost always an expression of liberation from the yoke of religion.

Maneuvering between convention and reality

Israeli Muslims exhibit considerable diversity in their observance of Islamic precepts. This variation derives from the variety of Islamic interpretation, distinctions between local leaders, and the different approaches of groups and individuals within the community regarding their relationship to the Israeli state and other matters. However, while the religious Jewish community includes a number of distinct ideological and theological currents, no such ideological groups exist within Islam. Thus, clothing styles do not necessary reflect different approaches to Islam. To the extent that specific ways of dressing bear meaning, they do so at the individual, *hamula*, or village level, and reflect local customs. In fact, dress constitutes a mirror of the great malleability within Israel's Muslim population and the ever-sharper tension between the strict fundamentalist approach to modesty and the Western–secular approach, which is influenced by prevailing fashion trends in the Jewish population, and especially by the feminist and permissive winds that blow so strongly in the West. These two trends, characteristic of the entire Arab world, are disseminated by the Arabic-language media that Israel's Arabs read, hear, and see.

While Islam is austere, it does not proscribe the cultivation of beauty. It certainly sees beauty as an important marker of status for a woman and her husband. Muslim women thus find themselves walking a tightrope between prudishness and femininity. This maneuvering can be seen in all items of dress, accessories, and makeup. Instead of traditional, all-encompassing *jelbab*, some women wear a skirt of light and supple fabric, a long-sleeved shirt, and perhaps pants. Hair must be hidden under a *hijab*, but sometimes a stray curl may be seen, and not by mistake—this is a compromise between the rules and feminine proclivities.

Muslim women also seek to express their individuality, and use all means at their disposal to do so. Jewelry and accessories (belts, bags, gloves) can provide a personal touch. So can colors and fabrics. The general rule is that the more religious a woman is, the more opaque, dull-colored, and looser her clothing.

Muslim women may seek out detours around religious law, but do so in small increments. Their modes of dress are attractive but not provocative, restrained but not grim. They do not seek confrontation with religious values or provocations; instead they pursue a policy of "creeping femininity." They quietly establish facts, and wait to see how society reacts. If the reactions are sharp, they retreat. In many instances, however, these challenges are met with tacit acceptance, as a result of the gradual erosion of severe approaches to religious law. A Muslim man may not say so explicitly, but he is proud to have a beautiful wife, so he is willing to accept mild violations of the rules of modesty.

The result is a wide variety of fashions. The information we have gathered shows that Muslim women's clothing falls into four principal styles:

1   Classic Muslim religious dress, resembling that of neighboring Arab countries.[10] This consists of a long, loose, dark *jelbab*, complete covering of the hair—usually with two layers—and shoes. It should be stressed that Muslim women in Israel, even the most devout, do not cover their faces—the only exception being a negligible number of Bedouin women.

   The way pious Muslim women dress makes a public declaration: "I am a religious woman who observes all the laws of Islam. My femininity is revealed to my husband alone, and I do not flaunt my eroticism." However, even within the confines of strictly pious clothing, there are fashions, expressed largely in fabrics, colors, and sometimes also in low-key ornamentation. But these are small nuances that take care not to call attention to the garment or to the body.

2   Modest clothing that meets the requirements of Muslim modesty, but at the same time tries to be chic. Women who dress in this way, which we might call "traditional," cover all or nearly all their bodies, including the head and feet, but with a wide variety of different kinds of garments. Some of these are similar or even identical to those commonly worn by Jewish women from the national religious community. For example, instead a *jelbab*, they wear a blouse and skirt (skirts often bring out a woman's figure more than a dress). If they choose to wear a dress, it will be of a more fashionable fabric, such as denim. The clothes are generally more colorful than the classic mode allows. The message they convey is: "I am religious, but I still want to look beautiful and feminine." She signals to those around her: "I take care to cover my body, but the clothes I wear are creative and varied and reflect my personal taste and esthetic sensibility."

   One of our interviewees, a male student at the University of Haifa, interpreted this world-crossing style in functional terms: "A single girl who dresses this way is walking on solid ground. Because conservative and scholarly girls are in the greatest demand in the marriage market, her message is: 'I'm adjustable.'" This style is a way station in both directions—religious and secular. In contrast, completely monochromatic and opaque religious clothing, loose like a robe, is a statement of consistency: it says "I am and will remain religious."

   Note: the traditionalists who constitute a majority in Israel's Arab community believe that Islam can be adjusted to current needs and modernity. Consequently, many women from this group cover their heads but wear colorful clothing and pants. The strictly religious, however, view Islam as an immutable set of laws affecting all areas of life, clothing among them. If a traditional woman marries a religious man, she will change her dress style accordingly.

3   Some women observe the letter of the law when it come to the Islamic dress code, but no more. Such women do not bare their bodies, but instead of a blouse and skirt they wear pants (sometimes pants under a skirt, as in the national religious Jewish sector). The shirt is fashionable and even close-fitting, emphasizing the bust, but not revealing anything of the breasts. Women who choose this style may wear sandals with heels that bare the feet, or high-heeled shoes. Yet they nearly always keep their heads covered. The *hijab* has become the most important marker of the religious Muslim woman. The impression we have received is that Muslim society considers any woman who covers her head in public to be modest. Some of our interviewees explained this phenomenon as a way for young women to send the message that they are good girls who respect their religion, but "I am not too conservative—I am attractive and open-minded."

4   Modern permissive dress, which makes no attempt to comply with the strictures of Muslim modesty. Measuring the prevalence of this style is difficult, because it is characteristic of most Christian Arab women as well. But our impression, from our observations of Arab students at the University of Haifa, is that increasing numbers of Muslim Arab women are dressing in tight pants and shirts, high heels, and colorful fabrics. A minority even allow themselves a bit of décolletage and exposed skin at the waist.

Muslim fashion

Ever more Israeli fashion producers and designers are responding to the special needs of Muslims. In recent years, Arab fashion designers have opened boutiques in Haifa, an Israeli city with a significant Muslim population. Other stores offer clothing produced in Jerusalem, in the West Bank, or in the Israeli Arab city of Um al-Fahm. In advance of an important event such as a wedding, many Muslim women make a shopping trip to Jordan, where they can find a large selection of clothing that accords with Muslim standards. Such stores sell the collections of Lebanese fashion designers, who have gained international recognition in recent years. In the internet age, a huge number of designers, stores, and boutiques sell their wares online, and Israelis are among their customers.

Non-devout Muslim women are gaining interest in permissive Western fashions. Some of them shop in Israeli fashion chains such as *Castro*, *Golf*, and

Renouar, but it is important to note that such stores often do not cater to their special needs. "In the chain stores, the clothes are relatively short and tight. It's less appropriate," said a 20-year-old student at Netanya Academic College. "In Teibe, where I live, there are now nice clothes for my age, not just for 40-year-old women." According to another student, a 27-year-old from Haifa who calls herself a secular, fashion-loving Muslim, "There is an increasing demand for pretty clothes. I see, especially in Haifa, women dressing more nicely, more carefully."

One sign of the Arab community's sector's growing interest in Western fashions is the Israeli website Bukra, which devotes much space to fashion and beauty. Many watch Lebanese and Saudi television shows about women's fashions and read Arabic-language Israeli women's magazines such as *Lilak*. The websites of Lebanese fashion designers who have international careers are also popular.

Clothing items

Jelbab and *abaya*

The garment worn by observant Muslim women in Israel is called the *jelbab* (plural: *jalabeeb*). It is generally made of thick, opaque fabric in a dark color, for example blue or brown. It hangs loosely and does not follow the body's contours.

Only a small minority of Muslim women in Israel—the most strictly pious women, or women who are married to strictly pious men—wear the traditional *jalabiya* familiar among the Bedouin or in the Persian Gulf states. Only a small number, most of them Bedouin, wear a black *jalabiya*. Black is perceived by the great majority of the world's Muslims as the color of mourning, whereas white is seen as denoting purity. Women, however, avoid wearing white because it is liable to be translucent.

Little is known about the process by which the *jelbab* became the mandatory garment for all Muslim women. Conventional wisdom is that the requirement that women cover themselves from head to foot emerged from the Arab encounter with Byzantine culture, when Muhammad's armies moved out of the Arabian Peninsula. What was initially a custom apparently became an obligatory norm at the inception of the Abbasid dynasty, in the mid-eighth century.

The Palestinian *jalabiya* (the *jelbab*) emerged in the 1970s with the rise of the Mujma'al-Islami movement, Hamas's charitable arm. Hamas, founded in 1978 by the Muslim Brotherhood in Gaza, imposed the *jalabiya* and *hijab* or *khimar* (a smaller head covering). The fashion spread from the Gaza Strip to the West Bank, to East Jerusalem, and to Israel as part of the general trend toward increasing Islamic devotion. It is important to note that this set of fashions has become, beyond just a religious command, one of the symbols of the Palestinian national struggle.

The *jelbab* extends from the neck to the ankles. It comes in dark or dull colors—black, brown, dark blue, gray, maroon, or dark green. The hems are machine-embroidered in the same color as the dress or in a contrasting color.

To prevent the dress from unraveling and thus revealing a part of the body, women generally wear a long turtle-necked shirt under the *jelbab*. This is usually in a color similar or identical to that of the dress. Other women wear a sweater closed at the neck. This undershirt is made of opaque fabric and fits loosely, so as to blur the outlines of the body.

Traditional dresses were decorated with hand embroidery (as seen in East Jerusalem after the Six-Day War), but this is now the preserve of older women. Women may wear silk and gold, permitted in accordance with a homily that states that "The Prophet Muhammad ascended to the *manbar* [the place where the prayer leader stands in a mosque], holding gold and silk in his hands, and said that these are permissible for a woman but forbidden to a man."

The *abaya* is an entire set of clothing that includes a long dress (*jelbab*) that covers the entire body and a head covering that covers the hair. Ultra-Orthodox Muslim women also wear a *niqab*, a dark scarf wrapped around the bottom of the face, leaving only the eyes exposed. Very few Muslim women in Israel wear it; most of those who do are Bedouin women from the south of the country. A traditional *abaya* is black, but they can also be seen in an entire range of colors and embroidery patterns. Some women wear only the bottom part of the *abaya*, the dress, without the head covering.

Pants

A believing Muslim woman will not wear pants (*bantalon*) for two reasons. Firstly, pants might reflect the contours of limbs that are supposed to remain hidden. Secondly, items of clothing associated with men are off limits, just as men are forbidden to wear women's clothing. According to the Prophet, Allah curses the woman who dresses in clothing meant for men, and the man who wears clothing meant for women.

Nevertheless, a woman may wear pants within her home. One Muslim woman we interviewed, who had returned to strict religious observance along with her husband seven years previously, walked freely in her home dressed in jeans and a striped knit shirt. The minute she stepped outside, however, she took on a different guise. She donned a long robe over a long, closed dress, and full and proper shoes. Her hair disappeared under a head covering. She maintained that she draws a clear line between her private space, in which her husband and children can see her naturally, and the public space.

Adult women who are not strictly observant and young women wear pants under a dress or long tunic that reaches down below the knees. The pants are dark, generally black, and reach down to the ankles. This "immodest" appearance is balanced by a full head covering, so it is not a blatant violation of the religious dress code. In recent years, more and more Muslim women in Israel's rural regions have begun wearing pants, in particular when they leave their homes to attend big-city schools and colleges. A similar process is underway among older women, as they enroll in enrichment programs, most of which take place in the afternoon. Pants are more comfortable at school, in trips on public transportation and in the city.

Yet, secularization is inexorable. As the years pass, Muslim women become more open, and this is expressed in their adoption of urban fashions—tighter pants, shirts with shorter sleeves and tighter fits, as well as a range of pastel colors rather than the traditional black.

Young and middle-aged women who enjoy financial security and high social status choose items of clothing that mark them as religious, while integrating into them "secular" items. For example, they wear pants despite the religious prohibition, along with gold jewelry that displays their wealth and assertiveness, and need not fear open criticism. Black is the preferred color, so as to avoid an overly impudent look.

Blouses

The *Qur'an* does not explicitly treat individual items of clothing. *Surat al-Hijab* ("The Curtain") includes a general statement that the Prophet commanded the wives and daughters of believers to wear dresses (*jelbab*) that will identify them as believers, and so keep them from harm.

Consequently, at least in formal terms there is no proscription against a woman wearing a blouse (*qamise*, *bluza*) with a skirt or dress, as long as the total ensemble preserves a modest appearance. Given that these matters are open to individual interpretation, many women choose to express themselves and their aspirations through their clothing. A young religious woman will explain that her long-sleeved, somewhat sheer black cotton shirt offers her a way to integrate into the modern society in which she lives. Or she might explain wearing a light-colored shirt because she is looking for a husband, and such a color attracts boys' glances. Here, too, the dressing game runs the gamut from the conservative to the erotic on varying levels of color, opacity, and ornament.

Skirts

The fashion industry produces a rich variety of long, fashionable skirts in different patterns and fabrics. An Islamic woman who seeks to be fashionable but also modest can shop at an Israeli chain store or boutique and find stylish contemporary skirts that meet her religious requirements.

Muslim women, young women in particular, sometimes allow themselves to deviate from strict rules of dress and wear a skirt (*tanura*). This is generally long and made of denim, and is worn with a long-sleeved, long-tailed shirt that breaches the dress code in its color (not dark or black) and fabric (not entirely opaque). This partially religious look is completed with rebellious locks of hair peeking out from under the head covering. The final result expresses a desire to display femininity, rebelliousness, and carefree youth.

Jackets and coats

Jackets and coats are overgarments not meant to cover up the bare body. For this reason, religious rule do not apply to them. Muslim women in Israel choose their jackets and coats in accordance with their budgets, personal taste, and their openness to modernity. Devout women wear simple broad coats, generally in a dark color. Fashionable young women prefer stylish jackets or coats of a quality appropriate to the money they have to spend.

Some Islamic authorities now sanction a jacket worn above a long skirt. A short, trendy skirt is not religious dress because it exposes a woman's legs. Traditional but not strictly religious Muslim women may wear pants suits that are not tight fitting, supplementing them with a head covering, sometimes brightly colored, that in their view meets religious strictures.

Shoes

The *Qur'an*, including the *surah* that addresses clothing (*Kitab al-Libas*) contains no laws about women's footwear. Presumably, women in tribal Arabian societies did not need shoes, since they hardly ever appeared in public.

Shoes hold a place of honor in the wardrobe of Muslim women, whether religious or not. For many Muslims, shoes, and especially high heels, radiate sex appeal. Even when a woman's *jalabiya* reaches down to her ankles, her shoes are still visible and allow the display of a manifestly feminine article of clothing.

Slippers belong to the private wardrobe of the religious Muslim woman. However, when a man who is not her husband visits her home, such a woman prefers closed slippers that conceal her feet.

Cosmetics

Mascara, which has its origin in Iran, is the major form of makeup mentioned in the Hadith. These texts also describe how it is used: a stick is dipped into a vessel containing liquid mascara and is used to apply the color around the eyes. The Prophet himself used mascara, which was believed to sharpen the gaze and encourage the growth of eyelashes.

A devout Muslim woman may decide for herself how often to apply makeup and use cosmetics. Most such women are conscious of their appearance and many (we did not endeavor to find out their precise number) use makeup, perhaps as a kind of compensation for having to cover their bodies from head to foot. But the makeup is almost always minimal and inconspicuous. They do not, for example, use bold red lipstick, which is considered the mark of a prostitute.

In theory, Muslim women are forbidden to use perfume outside their homes. In practice, many do not obey this stricture. In interviews with married religious women, particularly those who had become devout after a non-religious period of life, we often heard them voice an intense desire to sustain their relations with their husbands. The most reliable means available to them are revealing, seductive undergarments, perfume, makeup, and care of their bodies. They were chagrined by their husbands' involvement in manifestly female decisions, such as how they made themselves up or the type of perfume they used. It seems that, in practice, husbands must give their sanction to specific types of cosmetics.

Accessories, jewelry, and body ornaments

Surat al-Haj ("The Pilgrimage") states that "Surely Allah will make those who believe and do good deeds enter gardens beneath which rivers flow; they shall be adorned therein with bracelets of gold and (with) pearls, and their garments therein shall be of silk." Verses such as this one from the *Qur'an* indicate that the Holy Book promises believers a wealth of fine clothing and jewelry in the next world.

Women are permitted to wear gold jewelry in this world as well, despite the general precept of modesty. This may have its source in the male belief that a central part of the female nature is the urge to dress up. As a result, women are permitted to wear silk items over their dresses, as well as gold.

Religious authorities repeatedly remind their followers about the prohibition against *qirqush* (making a jangling or knocking sound), whether with the heels, bracelets, or anklets that jingle when the body is in motion. Jewelry is permitted, but it must not make a sound. The double message leaves a wide area open to personal interpretation. As a result, one finds devout women whose modest garments are overlaid with gold jewelry.

Face tattoos were common among Muslim women in the 1950s. In the Bedouin village Bir al-Maksur, next to Shefar'am in the Lower Galilee, we saw one elderly woman with tattoos around her lips and on her forehead. Facial tattoos may be seen on older Bedouin women of the 'Azazmeh tribe near Maktesh Ramon in Israel's southern Negev desert, and even on some younger women. Such tattoos come out of a tribal culture in which they were seen to have magical, religious, and even class significance.

Tattoos are no longer accepted fashion. Traditional Muslim society now censures young women with tattoos, even though their devout grandmothers had them. Most Islamic authorities oppose tattoos on the grounds that they are an intervention in the plan of creation. They view tattoos as resembling the brands applied to livestock, and do not wish to place women in the same category as beasts. As a general rule, the prohibition against tattoos applies also to men.

Hair and head coverings

Hair in Islam

The Hadith literature views head hair as a sign of divine grace; a Muslim must thus care for it. *Kitab al-Tarajjul* (The Book of Combing the Hair) placed chronologically immediately after *Kitab al-Libas* (The Book of Clothing) stresses the importance of tending the hair. The relevant religious literature reports that the Prophet Muhammad always bore a comb (*mosht*), a mirror, and a vial of hair oil. Nevertheless, in order to restrain the urge to dress ostentatiously, this work states: "The Apostle of Allah (peace be upon him) forbade combing the hair except every second day" (*Sunan Abu Dawud* 33:4147).

It should be noted that the word *tarjjul* (which means combing the hair to remove tangles and debris) has the Arabic root r-j-l, the root of words referring to men and male activity. The work says nothing about women's hair, perhaps because they were, *a priori*, forbidden to bare it in public.

The *Qur'an*'s only reference to tending the hair appears in *Surat al-Fatah* ("The Victory"), which recounts a dream of the Prophet's. In this vision, he saw worshippers entering a mosque in Mecca and, after observing the pilgrimage rite, having their hair cut short. In contrast, many hadith passages address the proper length of the hair and provide guidelines. Three of these are:

1 Women are forbidden to cut their hair short, because of the prohibition against blurring gender differences.

2 Hair is not to be grown below the upper back, because this, apparently, was the length of the Prophet's hair.

3   Haircuts or shaving that results in asymmetry is forbidden. No reason is offered for this prohibition; the commentators on the passage presume that asymmetry is characteristic of a borderline personality, an imitation of pagan hair styles, and an attempt to stand out, in opposition to the principles of simplicity and modesty.

A devout Muslim woman wears a *hijab* that covers her hair. The amount of exposed hair is an unofficial measure of piety. Young single women let their hair show through the *hijab*, with the justification that they seek to attract potential bridegrooms. Some young women who wear long but modern clothing do not cover their hair at all, for the same reason.

The *hijab*

The term *hijab* derives from the word *hajaba*, which means "barrier." The *hijab* is a garment that divides the woman from the outside world; the same word designates a charm worn as protection against the evil eye, the diaphragm used as a contraceptive, and a bodyguard.

The *hijab* is a large kerchief or scarf made of cloth or wool knit that covers the head and is tied under the neck or wrapped around it. Some use a pin to hold the edges of the *hijab* in place. The edges are often ornamented with tassels.

The concealment of women's faces behind a *hijab* was customary even before Muhammad's time among the Arab urban elite. According to tradition, the *hijab* was made mandatory after people who were looking for Muhammad insulted his wives—they claimed that they thought the women were servants. The form of the *hijab* has changed considerably over the intervening centuries. In practice, hundreds of millions of Muslim women over the generations did not wear the *hijab*—it was a luxury that poor families could not allow themselves, since the garment interfered with a woman's ability to work at home and in the fields.

The *hijab* and *purda* (segregation, isolation) are symbols of restrictions whose roots lie in the inequality of the sexes that is built into Muslim society. The Moroccan sociologist Fatema Mernissi has written that Muslim men view women as creatures unable to control their sexuality, and who thus pose a threat to the social order. In other words, their freedom to seduce must be repressed and restrained for society to function in an orderly way.

A devout Muslim woman must cover her head beginning at puberty, immediately after the appearance of her first menses. Traditional Muslim women keep their heads covered even at home. This is the case during visits by members of her extended family, such as cousins and brothers-in-law, whom she may marry, according to Islamic law. A Muslim woman who behaved otherwise would be considered wayward.

Married Bedouin women, older ones in particular, wear a triple-layered head covering. The hair is gathered under a colored, generally blue, *mandil* (kaffiyeh); over this is a kerchief of *shash* (a thin white cotton fabric), which also serves to cover the face, and the margins of which are often crocheted. The two of these are enwrapped in a large black scarf (*quna'*) made of rough cotton of a thickness double that of the *shash*. This long scarf, which sometimes reaches down to the knees, is ornamented with small colored glass beads.

The *hijab* has long since become a fashion accessory and it can be purchased in a variety of designs. The three most popular designs are *hijab ash-shaila*, a thin white knit; *hijab al-amira*, a two-part scarf consisting of a polyester or cotton cap that fits the scalp closely, along with a scarf that is wrapped around the face, holding the *hijab* in place; the third type is *hijab kuwaiti*, a cloth scarf over a knitted layer.

A wide variety of head coverings are available: the *khimar* is a long scarf in white or black that covers the hair, the back of the neck, and the shoulders, but leaves the face bare; the *niqab* is like the *khimar*, but with the addition of a cloth band that covers the face, except for the eyes; the *burqa*, common in Afghanistan, is a cowl that covers the entire head, with a netted slit for the eyes; and the *chador*, a head and body covering in one piece, generally black, is mostly seen in Iran. The last three are not seen among Israeli Muslims.

Conclusion

Israel's Arab citizens live in a secular democratic state. The religious establishment has greater power than is generally the case in other Western democracies. But this power is nevertheless limited, far less than the general rule in Arab and non-Arab Muslim states. Therefore, supervision of how women dress is largely informal, and originates in common practices and negotiation between the individual and the society around her.

Like in the Arab world, Muslim society in Israel has undergone, over the last three decades, an Islamicist religious revival that has produced significantly stricter standards for how Muslim women should dress. Israeli Muslim family photographs from 30 years ago show notable differences between the standards then and now. Then, women did not worry about covering their hair completely, if at all; dresses were not thick and baggy as they are today.

An opposite trend is also evident today—a modern, Western, permissive look.

Both these trends, easily discerned even by the unprofessional eye, are in competition. There is no easy way of knowing which is stronger. Women's ways of dressing, and their fascinating maneuvering between these two poles, is evidence of the struggle. In many cases, it produced an eclectic blending of the demands of religion and of modernism. This cautious maneuvering is, in our view, an intermediate stage prior to the final victory of either conservative religious fundamentalist or modern feminist liberation, as has been argued in many recent studies and books.

We should stress that, as in other areas, clothing culture is not black and white. Religious Muslim women today have a much greater range of personal choice. One of our interviewees, a woman studying at the University of Haifa, put it succinctly: "This special integration of religious and modern dress is the initiative of a particular girl. Today brothers can no longer interfere with how their sisters dress, because they have no right to interfere. They leave it to their parents. Fathers hand the responsibility over to mothers, and the mother is, today, more exposed to the modern world and modern needs of her daughter, and is less concerned about social pressure."

Acknowledgments

The author gratefully acknowledges Ashraf Awawdy's and Dalia Bar-Or's assistance in preparing this chapter.

The author also thanks the interviewees and Ashraf Awawdy, Liza Ayadat, Ameer Mzareeb, Akram Arsheid, Abdalah Abd Alfath, Hiathem Sarhan, Hanan Makazha, Refaat Abdalah, Amani Maray, Wurood Kharanby, Zeinab Abo Leil, Athar Gadeer, Omar Jardie, and Meital Alexander for their help.

Notes

1   Linda B. Arthur ed., "Introduction," *Religion, Dress and the Body*, Oxford and NY: Berg, 1999, p. 1.

2   Steele, Valerie, *Fashion and Eroticism*, *Ideals of Feminine Beauty from the Victorian Era to the Jazz Age*, New York: Oxford University Press, 1985, p. 105.

3   Joanne B. Eicher and Mary Ellen Roach-Higgins, "Definition and Classification of Dress: Implications for Analysis of Gender Roles," in Ruth Barnes and Joanne B. Eicher eds, *Dress and Gender: Making and Meaning*, Oxford and New York: Berg, 1993, pp. 19–21.

4   D. M. Brown, "Multiple Meaning of the Hijab in Contemporary France," in William J. K. Keenan ed., *Dressed to Impress: Looking the Part*, Oxford and New York: Berg, 2001, pp. 105–6.

5   Franco Cardini, *Europe and Islam*, Oxford: Blackwell, 2001.

6   Fatema Mernissi, *Beyond the Veil: Male–Female Dynamics in Modern Muslim Society*, Bloomington: Indiana University Press, 1987, p. xv; Elizabeth W. Fernea and Robert A. Fernea, "Symbolizing Roles: Behind the Veil," in Mary Ellen Roach Higgins ed., *Dress and Identity*, New York: Fairchild, 1995, pp. 290–7; Fadwa El Guindi, *Veil: Modesty, Privacy and Resistance*, Oxford: Berg, 1999, pp. 57–60.

7   B. Lewis, *Islamic History: Ideas, People and Events in the Middle East*, Chicago: Open Court, 1993. Gabriel Almond, Scott R. Appleby, and Emmanuel Sivan, *Strong Religion: The Rise of Fundamentalisms around the World*, Chicago: The University of Chicago Press, 2003, pp. 5–7; S. Gara, *Ideology, Political and Social Activity of the Islamic Movement in Israel*, Ph.D. Thesis, University of Haifa, 2011.

8   Dan Arnon, *Kova'im be-Rosh: al Kisutei Rosh be-Eretz Yisra'el* (in Hebrew), Am Oved, 1995, p. 176.

9   Dick Hebdige, *Subculture: The Meaning of Style*, London: Methuen, 1979, pp. 3–4.

10   H. Hirsh, "Levushan ve-Hitqashtutan Shel Nashim Lefi Meqorot Muslimim Qedumim," M. A. thesis, University of Haifa, 1998.

Bibliography

Almond, Gabriel A., Scott R. Appleby, and Emmanuel Sivan, *Strong Religion: The Rise of Fundamentalisms around the World*, Chicago: The University of Chicago Press, 2003.

Arnon, Dan, *Kova'im ba-Rosh: al Kisuyei Rosh be-Eretz Yisra'el*, (in Hebrew), Am Oved: 1995.

Arthur, Linda. B. ed., "Introduction," *Religion, Dress and the Body*, Oxford and New York: Berg, 1999.

Brown D. M., "Multiple Meaning of the Hijab in Contemporary France," in William J. K. Keenan ed., *Dressed to Impress: Looking the Part*, Oxford and New York: Berg, 2001.

Cardini, Franco, *Europe and Islam*, Oxford: Blackwell, 2001.

Eicher, Joanne B. and Mary Ellen Roach-Higgins, "Definition and Classification of Dress: Implications for Analysis of Gender Roles," in Ruth Barnes and Joanne B. Eicher eds, *Dress and Gender: Making and Meaning*, Oxford and New York: Berg, 1993.

El Guindi, Fadwa, *Veil: Modesty, Privacy and Resistance*, Oxford: Berg, 1999.

Fernea, Elizabeth W. and Robert A. Fernea, "Symbolizing Roles: Behind the Veil," in Mary Ellen Roach Higgins ed., *Dress and Identity*, New York: Fairchild, 1995.

Gara S., *Ideology, Political and Social Activity of the Islamic Movement in Israel*, Ph.D. Thesis, University of Haifa, 2011.

Hebdige, Dick, *Subculture: The Meaning of Style*, London: Methuen, 1979.

Hirsh, H., "Levushan ve-Hitqashtutan Shel Nashim Lefi Meqorot Muslimim Qedumim." M. A. thesis, University of Haifa, 1998.

Lewis, B., *Islamic History: Ideas, People and Events in the Middle East*, Chicago: Open Court, 1993.

Mernissi, Fatema, *Beyond the Veil: Male–Female Dynamics in Modern Muslim Society*, Bloomington: Indiana University Press, 1987.

Steele, Valerie, *Fashion and Eroticism, Ideals of Feminine Beauty from the Victorian Era to the Jazz Age*, New York: Oxford University Press, 1985.

Websites

About.com (2008), "Where to Buy Islamic Clothing Online." Accessed April 7, 2008.

Amir, Dan (2008), "Bein Ha'ala le-Ra'ala: Ha-Paradoqs be-Hofesh be-Levush." Hofesh website. Accessed April 7, 2008.

BBC News (2008), "Muslim Veils in Graphics." Accessed April 7, 2008.

Ezer, Asi (2006), "Nirel Mevi'a Ita Ruah shel Tiqva." NRG, January 26.

Inbari, Itamar (2005), "Derekh ha-Hor be-Khafiyeh." NRG, February 14.

Inbari, Itamar (2006), "So'er be-Tarshiha: Ha-Galabiyya Sofeget Biqoret Ofna." NRG, June 22.

Islam 101 (2008), "The Hijab in the Workplace." Accessed April 7, 2008.

Kristal, Meirav (2007), "Trend Shel Aharei Milhama." Ynet, May 1.

La Perla, Ruth (2007), "Hijab Haute Couture." Ha'aretz online, May 5.

Nana 10 (2006), "Madua' Tzovea' Abu Tir Zeqano be-Tzeva' Katom?" January 26.

Osetzki-Lazar, Sara (2005), "Eizeh Steriotip Mad'ig Yoter." Ha'aretz Online, June 20.

Yakir, Mordecai (2008), "Muslimim ve-Tenu'to Islamiot be-Yisrael bein Haslama be-Hashlama." Department of History website, Tel Aviv University. Accessed April 7, 2008.

Buqra website. Accessed May 11, 2008.

Christian Louboutin, fashion designer (Arabic). Accessed May 11, 2008.

Desertstore. Accessed April 7, 2008.

Elie Saab, fashion designer (Arabic). Accessed May 11, 2008.

Faculty of Education website, University of Haifa. Accessed April 7, 2008.

Gelbab. Accessed April 7, 2008.

Hegab Iran. Accessed April 7, 2008.

Horace Mann's Webpage. Accessed April 7, 2008.

Islam for Today. Accessed April 7, 2008.

Israel Ministry of Education. Accessed April 7, 2008.

Lilak: A Magazine for Women (Arabic). Accessed May 11, 2008.

Ministry of Education, Southern District website. Accessed April 7, 2008.

Modest Clothing Directory. Accessed April 7, 2008.

Sadati website. Accessed May 11, 2008.

Shreiber Magazine. Accessed April 7, 2008.

Zuhair Morad, fashion designer (Arabic). Accessed May 11, 2008.

Wikipedia contributors (2008), "Fulla (Buba)." Wikipedia (Hebrew). Accessed March 25, 2008.

Wikipedia contributors (2008), "Levush Masorti." Wikipedia (Hebrew). Accessed March 25, 2008.

Wikipedia contributors (2008), "Ra'ala." Wikipedia (Hebrew). Accessed March 8, 2008.

Wikipedia contributors (2008), "'Abaya." Wikipedia (Hebrew). Accessed March 8, 2008.

Wikipedia contributors. "Islamic Dress Controversy in Europe." Wikipedia (English). Accessed April 8, 2008.

Wikipedia contributors (2008), "Islamic Dress." Wikipedia (English). Accessed April 7, 2008.

PART THREE
IDENTITY

6

IDEOLOGY, FASHION AND THE DARLYS' "MACARONI" PRINTS[1]

PETER MCNEIL

As John B. Thompson notes, the concept of ideology "first appeared in late eighteenth-century France" via the thinking of the *Philosophe* Destutt de Tracy[2] and has come to mean "'systems of thought', 'systems of belief' or 'symbolic systems' which pertain to social action or political practice.'"[3] Central to the study of ideology is the rise of "mass communication" and its relationship with the state. Writing mainly regarding the influential role of the press in twentieth-century life, Thompson acknowledges its seventeenth- and eighteenth-century precursive forms and remarks that "[t]he reproducibility of symbolic forms is one of the key character-istics that underlies the commercial exploitation of technical media by institutions of mass communication, and the commodification of symbolic forms which these institutions pursue and promote."[4] If ideology is promulgated by and within mass communication and viewing positions, how then are we to interpret the matter of looking at an eighteenth-century caricature? How might an ideological effect work within what was considered a "low" art form and what was caricature's relationship with "high art"? What intensity of viewing is necessary—how many people need to be able to "see"—for there to be an "ideological" impact? Is there a concrete difference between the reception of a political caricature, and one concerning manners, such as arose in very large numbers in the last third of the eighteenth century in England? How can we determine the ideological function of eighteenth-century printed satires of the subject of fashion? What was the ideological role of the "witty expressions and humorous sallies" that were popular consumer items, as d'Archenholz observed of the many such broadsheets being sold in the streets of London in 1786? What is known about the people who might have perused them?

In this chapter I focus upon one genre of the printed satirical material of the eighteenth century and indicate some of the problems of interpreting the corpus. The macaronies form the largest subset within the English graphical social satires produced in abundance from the early 1770s. "Macaroni" was a topical term connoting ultra-fashionable dressing in England *c.* 1760–80.[5] Although used occasionally to refer to women, the term generally referred to the styling of men. The commonly held explanation for the title "macaroni," that it was derived from a fondness for that Italian dish, may be supplemented in that "macaronic" refers also to a type of Latin poetry which revolved around wit, a hallmark of the macaroni stereotype. The macaroni association was closely associated with Continental travel, which was not considered at the time to result necessarily in the corruption of young English men. There was also a long history of discourses reaching back to the sixteenth century concerning the value of travel in generating cosmopolitan values and urbanity (including husbandry, politics, artistic knowledge, manners, and fashion).[6] "Macaroni" identity was a lively topic linking fashion, taste, aesthetics, and consumption within metropolitan life.

The development of the caricature as a specific form of humourous print in eighteenth-century England can be viewed not simply as social commentary on politics and manners, but also by considering its opposite, the respectful portrait, and contemporary understandings of idealized aesthetics. Connected to ideas about fashion, it also rested upon a metropolitan notion of the *beau monde*, in which the elites could recognize references to each other, as Hannah Greig has recently persuasively argued.[7] This chapter will take as its focus a close reading of the relationship between the ultra-fashionable English "macaroni" (c. 1760–85), and the caricatures re-presenting this figure. The public understanding of the macaroni was also negotiated through a range of media and sites including paintings, painted copies of caricatures, the theatre, the masquerade, the written press, popular songs and jokes, and newly designed products, including mass-produced ceramics and textiles.

Men as socially disparate as Sir Joseph Banks, Dr Daniel Solander, the politician Charles James Fox, the preacher William Dodd, and the painter Richard Cosway were caricatured as macaroni in their day. Ideologically, the figure functioned as a sign of effete, urbane, un-English, and suspect masculine consumption. The recurrence of the macaroni reveals much about so-called cultural "anxieties" surrounding the redefinition of middling-sort gender and sexuality in this period, which also entailed the sexing of commodities within the rapidly evolving consumer markets of Enlightenment England. However, all periods of history are "anxious" about many matters—particularly gender relationships—and this generalized statement requires further contextualization. Caricatures are by their nature frequently scurrilous and scathing, although others invite identification with the seductive allure of those caricatured. Some do both at the same time. The chapter argues that the "reflection model" that dominated analysis of such material until the 1970s is particularly inappropriate for satires of fashion, as fashion is sometimes an image before it is actuality. The double-mirror nature of fashion/image accounts for both its fascination and frustration as subjects try to reach for its ideal and effects.

The Macaroni craze

Painted caricatures began on the "Grand Tour" as private jokes shared between young men and their tutors. Private Italian painters working in Florence inspired the English development of this field. Etchings were made by Pier Leone Ghezzi (1674–1755) and Pietro Longhi (1702–85), and painted in Rome by English artists including Sir Joshua Reynolds and Thomas Patch (1725–82). Horace Walpole wrote in his journal thus: "Patch was excellent in Caricatura, and was in much favour with the young English nobility who visited Florence; many of whom allowed him to represent them and their governors ludicrously."[8] The expression used in a letter of 1765 to capture Patch's process of making a caricature was that of being "encanvassed," in which the suggestion was that subjects might cut their own throats:

> Patch has by this time encanvass'd you, and I dare say made us as ridic-ulous, as his Genius will admit of. After all 'tis absurd enough for a Man to sit seriously down to be laugh'd at, in the Copy of his figure, who at the same time wou'd cut one's throat for grinning at the original. I soon expect a letter, which, amongst other good intelligence, will bring me that of the fate of our Caricatura … Pray give [my compliments] to Stuart and the rest of my ken at Charle's [sic] …[9]

The long eighteenth century created its own histories and historiographies regarding the "invention" of caricatures. There was a wide general awareness amongst the well educated that the caricature tradition drew upon and extended that of the Renaissance physiognomic studies or "caprices" by Leonardo da Vinci, Giuseppe Arcimboldo and Albrecht Dürer, and the Baroque caricatures of Annibale and Agostoni Carracci (Heads, c. 1590) and Gianlorenzo Bernini. Such images were in fact illustrated, along with ancient Greek masks, in one of the frontispieces of J. P. Malcolm's An Historical Sketch of the Art of Caricaturing with Graphic Illustrations (1813). Non-Western art was also advanced within Malcolm's antiquarian study as an explanation for what was considered the "universality" of caricature, a "universality" that he felt had been brought to fruition in England. South Pacific tribal art, freshly topical following the voyages and collecting activities of Captain Cook, Sir Joseph Banks, and others to that region, was claimed by Malcolm to be one of the most original and ancient origins of caricature. Completely misunderstanding the aesthetic belief systems

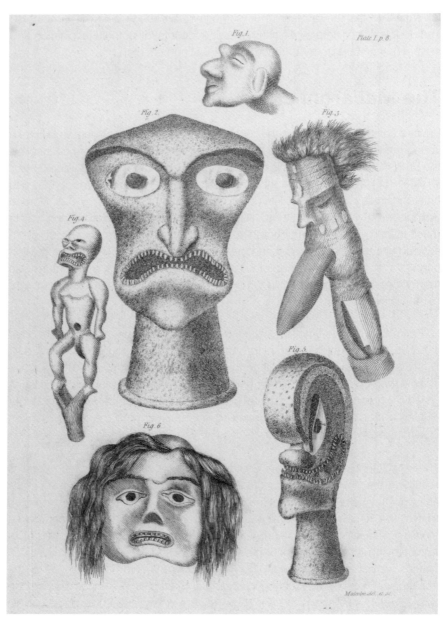

Figure 6.1   "Fig. 1 is a head in stone; Fig. 3 a weapon, Fig. 4 a non-descript
carving; and Fig. 5 a mask in wood with real hair; all are from the South-sea Islands."
Frontispiece, J. P. Malcolm, *An Historical Sketch of the Art of Caricaturing with Graphic
Illustrations. J. P. Malcolm. FSA. Author of London Redivivum, Manners and Customs of
London &* c., London: Longman, Hurst, Rees, Orme & Brown. 1813, described at p. 8.
Photograph courtesy Lewis Walpole Library, Yale University.

of South Pacific peoples, Malcolm noted that "Nature has permitted caricaturing from the earliest stages of creation" (p. v) and that:

> The specimens we have of their idols are busts more ingeniously composed of red feathers … all are from the South-sea Islands … Mothers and nurses often implant an expression of alarm and terror on the features of infants … Such are the sources whence artists in all ages have derived their ideas of Caricature … This is also the case with certain ingenious natives of countries still in a state of uncultivated nature; and it must be acknowledged they excel all competitors antient [sic] or modern in the art I am treating of, and have done so from time immemorial.[10]

Such a comment of highly ambivalent cultural ranking is equally important in terms of fashion, as many of the new extreme fashions of the second half of the eighteenth century were described and joked about in terms of non-Western peoples. Thus the "Hottentot" was an expression that was often used to refer to the large posterior padding of late eighteenth-century women's dresses (Isabelle Paresys, communication with the author). French women's hair, Tobias Smollett argued, was also copied from that of the "Hottentots," and was surely "the vilest piece of sophistication that art ever produced."[11] Note here the important suggestion that people are certainly not natural, and almost no longer human, as a result of contemporary fashions and the propensity of travel. Thus the deviation from Western ideals of beauty—of face, body, but also of clothing—came together in order to reinforce notions of ideals and conceptions of ugliness, or the artificial, at the very least.

An expanding field

Malcolm's account of caricature repeated the widely held belief that "[t]he History of Caricaturing … would naturally narrow into that of English Caricatures; for the obvious reason that in no other country has the art met with equal encouragement, because no other portion of the globe enjoys equal freedom."[12] The period from the 1760s witnessed a great expansion of satirical printmaking in England. About 10,000 different caricatures survive in the British Museum from the reign of George III, and there are several thousand more in the Library of Congress, acquired from the Royal collection. About 3,000 examples not included in the British Museum collection are to be found in the Lewis Walpole Library, Farmington, Connecticut, where they were collected by the great Horace Walpole devotee Mr W. S. Lewis.[13] In the 1760s, 1,033 social and political prints were published; in the 1770s, 964; in the 1780s, 2,027; in 1784, 410 alone.[14] Caricature in late eighteenth-century England enjoyed a golden age unparalleled anywhere in Europe, except the Dutch Republic. English Case Law established in 1699 demanded that libel had to be against an identifiable person. Certain political satires and libels were particularly good earners, as affronted individuals had to buy up the whole set in order to censor the image; this guaranteed profits for the print shops that were gathered around St James's and the West End. Cruikshank's receipt for a £100 bribe he took not to caricature George IV "in any immoral situation" is in the Royal Archive.[15] Researchers have not found one example of a legal prosecution of a political caricature or loose graphic satire in England. Printed books with offensive images were occasionally prose-cuted, such as the infamous trial of William Hone, who was acquitted, at any rate. Social caricature is often thought of as the quintessential English form,[16] although the French and the Germans produced a number of engravings which are very similar in their crude style and subject matter to English examples.

In the second half of the century, numerous English print makers who were also print sellers switched their output from political caricatures to social ones, in which fashion formed the principal subject. Print sellers exhibited their wares publicly in shop windows and printed single-sheet caricatures, which were sold in folio sets, reproducing the designs of others such as John Collett, Robert Dighton, Henry W. Bunbury, and Thomas Rowlandson (1756–1827).

Who could see?

Often hand-colored or sold in suites, English prints were relatively expensive, sought out by the aristocracy, the gentry, and collected even by the king. In England, satirical prints were kept in folios, or in the 1790s, visited in exhibi-tions. D'Archenholz claimed in 1789: "The print-shops are actually so many galleries of painting. To the number of privileges enjoyed by these islanders may be added that of publishing *caricatures*, which ridicule the occurrences of the times."[17] There has been some dissent within print scholarship as to the extent of exposure to the better quality prints. Eirwen E. C. Nicolson has disputed the primacy of the quite common image of the "print shop window" as proving that there was extensive popular viewing of the more expensive large and hand-colored caricatures: "Although the print shop window is cited as the main source of plebian exposure to prints of the quality of [Gillray], there is little reason to believe that prints of this kind would have been viewed in this fashion other than by a limited number of Londoners."[18]

George III had the latest Gillray print sent to him when he was out of town.[19] Countryside gentlemen ordered prints from London dealers too.[20] The practice of collecting prints was not a passive activity; a famous example is the print room at Calke Abbey, Derbyshire, in which images were pasted on the walls. Aristocrats themselves engraved prints in England as a hobby. Folios were also "lent out for the evening," for example, by the printmaker Isaac Cruikshank in 1795, which might have been a practice more common late in the century than earlier, although there is no reason to presume this practice might not have started earlier.[21] Social caricatures were also pasted into folios with comments and suggestions as to their true identity, as is the case with the well-known album of Horace Walpole.[22] Expatriates were fervent collectors of prints, and this is probably what Sir Horace Mann refers to when writing to Horace Walpole in 1780:

> I received three packets from England with your letter … That of the former date and many others anterior to it confirm me in the opinion that in all stations of life our country produces more extravagant characters and more madmen than any other we know or have heard of. I am unwilling to attribute this to our liberty, though I fear that it is the effect of it.[23]

Ladies' fans frequently featured satirical prints, and many that survive were expressly printed for that purpose rather than adapted, which seems to have been the suggestion of Herbert M. Atherton regarding English examples. A French fan now in a Danish collection, for example, crafts an integrated composition in which a *trompe-l'oeil* print of a funerary urn suggestive of the destruction of the *ancien régime* is surrounded by untidy promissory notes and *assignats*, the paper currency or mortgage bonds issued between 1789 and

Figure 6.2   Fan, French, 1790–6, printed paper, Den Gamle by, Denmark, 27L, 224:39. With permission from Tove Engelhardt Mathiassen.

1796 that resulted in inflation and the fear of depreciation.[24] The exact role of such a fan in a fashion scenario—social connection, souvenir, ironic comment, barbed point, being topical, contemporary fashionable attribute?—is yet to be clarified. From humble Staffordshire tea caddies to the more expensive tea and coffee wares attributed to Vienna, people viewed but also carried, poured, and drank from wares that sometimes also carried copies of illustrated fashion innovations.[25] Some of these sources were respectful Paris fashion images, but others were caricatures of fashion. Such images become "frozen" on objects that had a much longer life than either fashion itself or the more ephemeral category of cheaper prints. Might this be a transient commodity fetishism, to get the thing sold while it was new?

The matter of cost clearly has a relationship to the ability "to see." Most of the caricatures owned by Sir Joseph Banks had cost between 1 and 3 shillings; in the 1770s labourers and journeymen made between 12 and 15 shillings per week; though some trades like printers were better paid—in 1777 printers earned 24 shillings for a week of six 12-hour days.[26] Hogarth's *Industry and Idleness* sold for 12 shillings complete. Woodcut versions of the last two *Stages of Cruelty* were 1 shilling each and, according to Nicolson, "beyond the means of those at whom they were directed," although Hogarth would likely have been well aware of that.[27] Roy Porter notes that at around sixpence a sheet, or two shillings for colored examples, the political print was never cheap and three times the cost of a newspaper.[28] The cost of commissioning a political print was high: in 1789 Gillray charged two guineas for working up an ordinary design, which was an artisan's monthly wage. The Cruikshanks charged three guineas for a broadsheet caricature, including copper, design etching, and colored template.[29] The average run of a political print was 500 to 1,500 impressions, a fraction of the run of a newspaper.[30]

Considerable detail is known regarding the print holdings of one well-to-do and famous London household. Sarah Sophia Banks (1744–1818) was a virtuoso collector, like her brother Sir Joseph, the explorer, though in her case it was a collection of printed and other ephemera rather than natural history; she owned a large annotated collection of prints, amongst them macaroni images, including one of her brother.[31] Sophia made notes on many of her prints including the suggested date. She owned many caricatures of fashion, which she described in an inventory. The prints were kept in the house in Soho Square in appropriate folios; prints of members of the Royal Family were kept in the "Room, Wardrobe where Court Hoop is" [sic] – that is, a hoop or paniers to wear to the court. In a folio in Joseph Banks's room were "The French Man in London" (shaving); "Citizen going to his Country House"; "The Maccaroni on Horseback or the Contrast"; "O The Roast Beef of Old England," Hogarth; "The Bath Beauties"; "French Maccarony." He also owned "Bunbury's Prints" and "Sayer's Prints," probably folio sets. "French caricatures" are listed but not itemized; these are probably about the French, not by the French. Prices paid for the caricatures were listed; most were 1s.; the dearer ones 3s. 6d; *Hyde Park* cost 12s.

Joseph Banks owned many more prints relating to kings and queens of the past, judges, lord mayors, aristocrats, and the Pretender than satirical material, which suggests that in some housholds the social caricatures might have appealed more to women. Banks's library included the periodicals *Town and Country* 1769–78, *Universal Magazine* 1757, 1784, 1792, *Universal Museum* 1762–70, and *Westminster Magazine* 1775. In the 1780s either Sophia or Joseph Banks, but probably Sophia, took the new French fashion periodicals *Cabinet des Modes*, *Journal de la Mode*, *Costumes Parisiens à Paris*, and *Gallery of Fashion*. Sarah bequeathed her own material to her sister-in-law Lady Dorothea Banks, who presented it to the British Museum in 1819; it numbered 19,000 items.

Mirror to an age?

Art historian Diana Donald observed 20 years ago that there are few major works that examine English caricature "as complex artefacts" compared with the work undertaken on French political prints.[32] What to make of these copies, impressions, and reflections? As print expert Maidment notes, many studies which use prints as evidence are not much concerned with the problems of visual sources:[33]

> Instead of using Dorothy George's [author of the British Museum catalogue of English political and personal satires] model of analysis and explication, where a direct correlation is sought between verifiable social events and their representation in contemporary prints, it may be more productive to look at the intersection between represented event and mode of representation, especially when those modes of representation are themselves undergoing profound change.[34]

Dorothy George's magisterial analysis of the British Museum collection was "reductive," in that it argued generally for one meaning for any one image and posited caricatures as reflections or one-way representations of pre-existing events. The reflection model used by George is particularly inappropriate for satires of fashion, as fashion was sometimes likely to be an image before it was actuality. That is, it might be worn by very few members of society before it was more widely known and experienced. Recent research published by Hannah Greig on the fashions of the super-rich metropolitan *beau monde* would tend to support this view.

Caricaturists played on the image of affronted individuals, including macaronies, viewing caricatures which resemble them exactly.[35] Who reflects whom in this scenario? Without George's catalogue, any study of this printed material would be daunting. However, to her essentially empirical work can be brought post-structural theories of representation, and new data concerning the distribution and reception of prints and their role in crafting social identities. Rather than viewing the corpus as stable, a study of the prints indicates that a wide range of meanings was possible within the genre. As Morton comments: "Satire, whether in literature or fine arts, seems to have a double audience; the person or persons attacked and the spectators to the exuberant assault."[36] The satirist need not be "the conserving moralist holding revolution at bay ... If no longer the presiding arbiter of enlightened society, the satirist may well be seen as the most sophisticated manipulator of the century's art forms."[37] While Ernst Gombrich argued that the aim of the printmaker and dealer was to sell the product, and that the cartoonist "did not in fact want to disturb his audience,"[38] Paulson wrote that within graphic satire a range of explanations are true and not mutually exclusive.[39] In this chapter I am arguing for a matching of the functions of both macaronies and caricatures. Their mutual dependence as entities is evinced in their proliferation within the history of one another; witness the large number of caricatures of macaronies, and the macaroni consumption of caricatures that takes place in the "print shop window" type. This would surely go a long way towards explaining the proliferation of these images in the 1760s and 1770s.[40]

The macaronies are best known through caricature but the public understanding of this type was also negotiated through the theatre, the masquerade, the press, popular songs and jokes, and the decorative arts. David Garrick, for instance, owned a huge collection of prints, including 106 plates by Hogarth, and a parcel by his good friend Charles Bunbury.[41] Noted for a new naturalism in acting style, Garrick was remarkable for the flexibility of his face and the enormous variety of facial expressions he could hold. The imagery of the macaroni type would inevitably have informed the way in which he performed such roles on stage, performances which in turn would have inflected both the reading and production of prints. Garrick and his wife were extremely interested in fashion, and were retained by the Duke of Devonshire in the countryside as a "proxy shopper" to advise on the purchase of his metropolitan court dress.[42] In an interesting indication of how such prints might have appeared within a contemporary interior, some of the engravings and mezzotints of Garrick's collection were "glazed, framed and hung throughout ... [his] two mansions."[43] Matthew Darly dedicated his 1772 suite of *Macaronies, Characters, Caricatures* to the actor. Stone and Kahrl state this dedication was "In recognition of Garrick's patronage of engravers and print sellers."[44]

Addressing your friends

Caricature was a popular hobby amongst some of the nobility and men "of family and estate," such as H. W. Bunbury and the 4th Viscount, 1st Marquis Townshend; they produced sketches that were engraved by professionals.[45] Lady Diana Beauclerc sketched "Doctor la Cour's Wife and her Sister, and a Jew Beau, Drawn at Bath," 1776.[46] Horace Walpole wrote of her in his journal: "Lady Diana Beauclerc, eldest daughter of Charles Spencer, 2nd Duke of Marlborough … had an amazing genius from [sic] drawing, music, and all the arts, and the most exquisite taste. She drew caricaturas admirably and cut them out in paper like Monsr. Hubert of Geneva." This comment indicates the transnational flows of *genres* and artistic traditons across Europe.

"Lady Di's" actions tell us something about the function of the caricature amongst the aristocracy; many of them simply seem to laugh at the pretensions of the lower orders who emulate the manners and dress previously reserved for their social betters. Nicolson should be considered here, when she reflects on the significance of the emblematic in "graphic satire" (her preferred word to "caricature"):

> Indeed, it can be argued that so far from representing a more "popular" and accessible idiom, caricature, as it emerged in the political prints between 1750 and 1800, was potentially more exclusive and elitist than the established graphic mode of graphic comment and satire … The success of a caricature depends to a considerable degree on the spectator's familiarity with the original; such familiarity is essential if the distortion effected by the caricaturist is to be appreciated … Later eighteenth-century political caricature, in particular, was characterised by what might be described as an "intimate topicality"; it was an idiom for insiders.[47]

Nicolson goes so far as to argue that:

> caricature as it was adopted in England was an idiom that amused and flattered as much as it abused and subverted … [the joke was] in most cases, tempered by the shared social values of the caricaturist, subject and audience … To be the subject of such mild ridicule was, after all, to receive confirmation that one had achieved an elevated position and could be "brought down" wittily without any … permanent loss of authority. Such an "attack" was therefore actually capable of reinforcing the sitter's sense of invulnerability and confirming his status within an elite group whose members exclusively enjoyed the right to mock one another … Why else were such satires collected and preserved by their victims?[48]

I have argued elsewhere this relationship was dependent on the social standing and prestige of the individual satirized; therefore Sophia Banks might proudly pen next to the macaroni image of Sir Joseph Banks, that this was her brother. This is not the only meaning, however, of fashion satires. As Maidment notes of the early nineteenth-century "literary dustman" type, "in form and technique, this print asserts the energy and vitality of its labouring class subjects even as it satirises their aspirations and pretensions."[49] Patten agrees: "Caricatures helped people see their lives in relation to national and abstract issues and to conceive of their own existence not as meaningless, obscure or archetypal, but as narrative, consequential and individual."[50] Different readings emerged when the lower orders viewed the numerous satires of the gentry and nobility. Of the graphic satire *Taking Physick—or—the news of Shooting the King of Sweden* (BM 8080) [1792], in which the king is shitting next to the queen on a close stool, Nicolson makes the very significant point that far from dehumanizing its victims, "the use of facial caricature can render them [such as monarchs] more human, and is therefore not without limitations as a 'weapon'."[51] Many of the social caricatures of the eighteenth century are printed with letters missing. As Nicolson astutely observes, this encourages empathy and interaction between the viewer and the artefact: "In the case of blanks, one sees the complicity between the satirist and reader which is one of the accepted features of satires; the spectator can be relied upon to supply the deficit."

Harry Bunbury, the famous caricaturist who savaged Bath residents, was also well born, like "Lady Di"—he was the brother to Sir Charles Bunbury, whose wife Sarah was the aunt of the Whig politician Charles James Fox. H. W. Bunbury was also well placed to draw macaroni caricatures, of which *The St. James's Macaroni*, 1772, *The Fish Street Macaroni*, *The Full Blown Macaroni*, and *The Houndsditch Macaroni*, December 20, 1772 are his, etched and published by J. Bretherton in 1772. The nineteenth-century cataloguer of the British Museum collection, Frederic Stephens, called these "lower-sort" types "imitation macaronies."

39, Strand

The print sellers and printmakers Matthew and Mary Darly were the first to capitalize extensively on the macaroni phenomenon. Indeed, they helped to invent it; Darly issued six sets of twenty-four caricatures, which he re-issued in six volumes, each with a title page, between 1771–3. Simultaneously, he issued at least two other similar sets of larger prints. Many were re-issued in January 1776, and as late as 1779, thus enjoying a long circulation.[52] Matthew Darly began his career as a designer and printer of wallpapers, a paper stainer, and an engraver; he was selling prints as early as 1749.[53] During the Seven Years'

War he began to etch the political caricatures of George Townshend, which attacked Henry Fox, amongst others.[54] Dorothy George notes that: "After 1770, Darly, who had been the chief publisher of political prints during the fifties and sixties, devoted himself almost entirely to personal and social satires, in which, especially during 1771–2, macaronies took a leading part."[55]

Mary Darly, also an etcher, published a book on caricature drawing, *The Principles of Caricatura*, around 1762.[56] The Darlys' shop moved to the well-known premises at 39 Strand from 1765.[57] Darly advertised that at his premises:

> Gentlemen and Ladies may have Copper plates prepared and Varnished for etching. Ladies to whom the fumes of the Aqua Fortis are Noxious may have their Plates carefully Bit, and proved, and may be attended at their own Houses, and have ev'ry [*sic*] necessary instruction in any part of Engraving, Etching, Dry Needle, Metzotinto [*sic*] &c … Ladies & Gentlemen sending their Designs may have them neatly etch'd [*sic*] and printed for their own private Amusement at the most reasonable rates, or if for Publication, shall have evry [*sic*] grateful return and acknowledgement for any Comic Design …[58]

As print sellers and entrepreneurs, Matthew and Mary Darly traded on this association with aristocratic amateur sketchers when they produced their macaroni suites from 1771. By 1773 the Darlys held caricature exhibitions of up to 300 images, which Donald argues were a gentle parody of those of the Royal Academy and the Society of Artists.[59] Caricature was thus always challenging the boundaries of itself and art.

Matthew Darly's macaroni images tend to be crude.[60] Style in itself carries meaning: Nicolson points out that the speech scrolls can be clear and attractive or spikey and crude, and this too means something.[61] Darly's work became so closely associated with the genre that in July 1772 he published a piece which pointed up the circularity of art and life, *The Macaroni Print Shop*, his own store, no. 39 Strand, outside which various ridiculous figures peer at the ridiculous types engraved within. In another layer of circularity, they peer at identifiable images which had been published by Darly. The viewers include a wide range of ages, and several sport either a sword, a cane, striped stockings, large bag-wig, or pig tails, which were the mark of the macaroni. The macaroni at right peers at his twin with a cane pictured in the window. As contrast, a John Bull figure is included in a rustic frock coat and boots. The size of the prints has been exaggerated for effect; Stephens noted that they are all much smaller than a pane of glass.[62] They do not simply look, but react, to each other and to the images therein.

Darly's first suite was entitled *Caricatures by Several Ladies, Gentlemen [sic], Artists &c. Pubd. by M. Darly. Strand* and some of this set were after the well-known caricaturists H. Bunbury and E. Topham. It included many French references, such as *Monr. Le Frizuer* [*sic*]; *French Peasant*; *The Paris Shoe Cleaner*. *My Lord Tip-Toe. Just Arrived from Monkey Land* manages to attack the French and fashion simultaneously. This group played on the stock theme of the poor Frenchman or peasant in patched finery. Darly also included notables in the set, who were recognizable to parts of the public from the start. *The Turf-Macaron* is The Duke of Grafton, *The Lilly Macaroni* The Earl of Ancrum, according to Stephens. These identifications have been made by cataloguers of the collection on the basis of puns, annotations in old hands, and recognizable similarities to portraits. The most consistent aspect of macaroni dress that recurs in this imagery is the wig. Macaronies wear a powdered wig, caricatured as towering, with the options of either a large wig-bag, *queue* or clump of hair depending at the rear, or pig-tail.[63] Baldness was only acceptable as a topos for certain types of portrait busts.[64] Other elements include high-heeled shoes, often small slippers, a tightly cut silk suit, pastel or patterned, nosegay, silk stockings, sometimes spotted or striped, snuff box, cane, and dress sword or hanger adorned with a large tassel.

Darly's second suite of caricatures, published in 1772, was entitled *Vol. II of Caricatures. Macaronies & Characters, By Sundry Ladies, Gentlen* [*sic*] *Artists &c*. The title page announces parodic intention: the elaborate swags of laurel leaves and pompous architectural fragment refer to the contemporary craze for the archaeologically informed neo-classicism of Robert Adam and James "Athenian" Stuart. It both announces the contents as topical, and pokes fun at yet another fashion, an architectural style by no means universally acclaimed. The set included a wide range of types, and styles of varying technical sophistication. In a gesture which was typical of Darly's output, the more low-born the person depicted, the more crude the illustrative style. The images have been described by Dorothy George, who emphasizes their reference to topical events and individuals. In *The Tiger Macaroni, or Twenty More, Kill'em*, macaroni status is used to deride Lieutenant Alexander Murray, the officer in charge of the Guards at the Massacre of St. George's Fields, May 10, 1768, which George notes was still a pressing issue.[65] An *excessive* number of killings is the macaroni-related joke. *Billy Button, Master of the Ceremonies to an Eighteen Penny Rout & Assembly* refers to a character in Samuel Foote's play *The Maid of Bath*, as well as to the Master of Ceremonies at venues such as Bath's Assembly Rooms. The play had premiered on June 26, 1771, indicating the topicality of this imagery.[66] *The Oxford Macaroni*, with large club of hair and balletic posture, and *A Law Macaroni*, are refined in manner and appearance and drawn accordingly in a more refined manner, appropriate in fact to the fashion plate that had emerged in France in the late 1760s. These differences perpetuate the belief that the orders are inherently either vulgar or superior depending on rank, as well as highlighting the joke contained in the overstepping of sartorial boundaries from group to group. Social hierarchy accentuates deviation in other respects. The

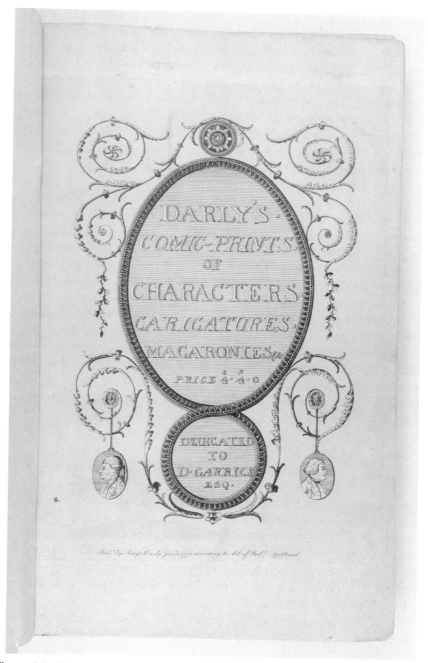

Figure 6.3 Title page, *Darly's Comic-Prints of Characters, Caricatures. Macaronies. Dedicated to D. Garrick. Esq.* Published by Mary Darly, January 1, 1776, 39 Strand. Courtesy Lewis Walpole Library, Yale University.

most ridiculous macaroni, *The Unfortunate Macaroni*, is sub-human in his ugly mask-like features and inelegant posture, and is also given the most ridiculous outfit, with a patched face and sprigged stockings with clocks (embroidery on the lower leg). George suggests that he is an unlucky gambler. Dress swords jut out level with the crotch and in varying states of erection or deflation, which highlights the hilarity and the barbed attack; *Captn Cut-lass* is an example. What Darly emphasizes in this suite is the "universality" of the macaronic infection, which affects everyone from *The Clerical Macaroni*, who is burlesqued in garments with no resemblance to clerical dress, to *A Temple Macaroni*, whom George argues resembles Richard Grenville-Temple, 1st Earl Temple (1711–79), and who is treated less savagely.

Darly's third suite, whose title page read, *1772, Vol. III of Macaronies, Characters, Caricatures &c. Designed by the Greatest Personages, Artists &c. Graved & Pubd. by M. Darly, 39 Strand*, this time in a frame encircled with roses, featured the accessories of fashionable dress wielded by the macaroni. Artisans and court-followers were mocked in this suite. We view the tasselled cane and enormous shirt-lace of *The Porter Macaroni*, with his disproportionate head and beak-like nose; the lorgnette and dress-sword of *The Ridicule*; long phallic *queue* of *A Dancing Master Macaroni*, engraved in a self-consciously French manner to underline his distance from English traditions; and the lace stock and cane with built-in bejewelled snuffbox, carried by *The Macaroni Provider*, probably a procurer. Other figures such as *The Macaroni Haberdasher* and *The Catgut Macaroni*, a violinist, suggest the theatre of the street.

Volume IV was also concerned with the ludicrous spread of macaronic fashions. *The Farmer-Macaroni* carried the verse:

E'en Farmers dress & mount their Ponies,
And all alike, are Macaronies.

Other caricaturists took the theme of the city boy or girl returned to the country to shock their horrified parents (*What is this my Son Tom*, published by Sayer and Bennett, 1774).[67] This is, in part, an internalization of Grand Tour degeneracy. Images in Darly's set included *The Southwark Macaroni*, *A Curtesan [sic] and Frizeur*, *The St James's Macaroni*, who was in turn followed by *The Newmarket Macaroni* and *The Picadilly Macaroni*, the latter stout and plain. Rank recurred again in *The Margate Macaroni*, which George notes already had plebian overtones. The group included the macaroni of colour, *A Mungo Macaroni*, probably Julius Soubise. Darly's funniest coup was in calling Richard Cosway *The Miniature Macaroni*. Darly made the image half the size of the rest and also depicted the painter of miniatures as very tiny, overshadowed by his sword.

In preparing his works, Darly had several older traditions to draw upon, which would have resonated with the more educated parts of the viewing public as an immediate context for the macaroni caricatures. Thomas Patch (1725–82) had produced a large repertoire of painted and engraved images of fops; his paintings of nobles and gentry on the Grand Tour exposed the fine line between luxury and the ludicrous. Like Sir Joshua Reynolds' satirical painting of aristocrats in Rome, *Lord Ailesbury, Mr Ward, Lord Milltown and Mr Henry of Straffan* (1751), these paintings mocked the props of the Grand Tour. The works depict the dress and demeanor of the aristocrat abroad when the mask of civility has slipped under the influence of alcohol; undone stockings, falling wigs, the suggestion of an uncivilized body always ready to burst forth once the polite veneer of clothing is lost. The artificial performance of genteel or aristocratic "superiority" is exposed, and the class distinction undermined. These paintings in turn refer to Hogarth's satires on male behavior and debauchery in his engravings of the 1730s (Hogarth died in 1764).

Brewer notes that the conventions of the printmaker insisted that the common people be depicted either as comic and grotesque, or as "worthy, deserving and industrious."[68] The former applied when "commons" stepped out of their place in the social hierarchy by adopting the manners of their betters. More often than not, the plebian was "depicted with ungracious, ill-formed features."[69] Certain types had particular resonance. The macaroni tradesman type is drawn from the stock images that represented nationality, social standing, and trades by the use of physiognomy, body types, costume, and tools. The butcher, who is often paired with the macaroni, was depicted as amorous, thus virile; stout, thus well-fed, and nationalistic, for he prepared the roast beef of England. By contrast, the French cook preparing frogs was skinny and miserable. Barbers were depicted with a comb in their hair or a wig-box, a convention which was taken over into the macaroni typology. A French or German hairdresser was indicated with similar tools, but an especially monstrous visage and scrawny body. The macaroni hairdresser, with excessive hair and equally absurd clients, was translated into a variety of inter-related media including theatrical performances, caricature prints, and Ludwigsburg porcelain figurines. The public thus could recognize both trades and nationalities in an instant. Forerunners and variants of "John Bull" were positioned against the effeminate Frenchman but also against the "emaciated and scabrous Scot," who was almost as unpopular as a Frenchman.[70] Thus there were intra- and international symmetries at work.

Darly was joined by competitors producing macaroni imagery from 1773. Carington Bowles, map and print seller at no. 69 St Paul's Church Yard, London, catered for the country trade. He produced hand-colored mezzotint caricatures of macaronies in 1773. Donald notes that Bowles used mezzotint for long print runs. He did not produce political themes.[71] His macaroni images include *Docking the Macaroni* and *How d'ye like me* [*sic* – the lack of a question mark is pertinent here; it becomes statement and assertion], probably the most reproduced macaroni image today. Bowles was well known for the captivating series peopled by Miss Prattle, Miss Rattle, and Lady Betty Bustle; their names come from the theatre and also from the jokes contained in the periodical press.

Another competitor, John Bowles, whose shop was at no. 13 in Cornhill, entered the fray with *Miss Macaroni and her Gallant at a Print-Shop*, a fine mezzotint by J. R. Smith, and the devestatingly mordant *The Macaroni: A Real Character at the Late Masquerade*, by Philip Dawe. In the former, a fashionably dressed macaroni indicates out a "portrait" to his female partner, whilst a dog fouls the shoe of the more sober man viewing the images in surprise, a topos taken from seventeenth- and eighteenth-century Dutch art. The text makes the point of this self-reflexive print doubly clear:

> While Macaroni and his Mistress here,
> At other Characters, in Picture, sneer,
> To the vain Couple is but little known,
> How much deserving Ridicule their own.

Real caricatures included in the window include *How d'ye like me*; *The Macaroni Painter* and *The Paintress of Macaroni's* [*sic*], which refer in turn to Richard Cosway and probably Angelica Kauffman, and *Lady Betty Bustle Dressing for the Pantheon*.

In the late 1770s Mary Darly resumed production of her husband's specialty. Her next major set was produced from January 4, 1776, with a significant dedication to David Garrick. *Darly's Comic Prints of Characters, Caricatures, Macaronies & c.* was priced a £4 4s, a substantial sum. It is as if the price of art is taken in with the conspicuous expenditure it illustrates. The title page is particularly interesting. It is not just a matter of fashion. The drawing is laboured, creaking, naïve and deliberately distorted. The text sitting on the elegant framed lines (resembling the engraving or engine-turning on say a snuff box, as well as the form, resembling a fashionable mirror), is crude and misjudged in form. The two pendants that hang from the elegant crestings (which in themselves are slightly absurd), make the point; rather than elegance, we see a pinched face on the left and a very banal visage of a late-middle-aged man on the right. This series includes some of the satires upon fashion best known today, which by this date had extended to comment as strongly on women as on men. They include *The Preposterous Head Dress, or the Featherd* [*sic*] *Lady*, *Oh Heigh Oh or a view of the back settlements*, and *The Vis A Vis Bisected or the Ladies Coop*, in which two women crouch on the floor of the carriage in order to fit their hair and head-dresses.

What historical figures such as Cosway, but also Sir Joseph Banks (South Sea explorer and scientist), Charles James Fox (the prominent Whig politician), the Reverend William Dodd (chaplain to the king), Soubise (a man of color and freed slave of the Duchess of Queensbury), Humphrey Repton (famed garden

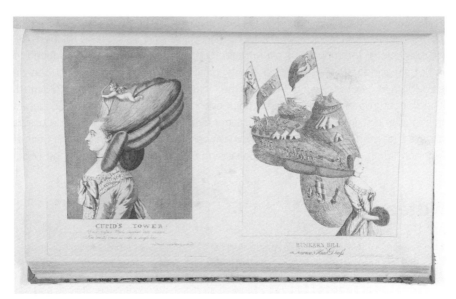

Figure 6.4   "Cupid's Tower" (March 1776) and "Bunker's Hill or America's Head Dress." *Darly's Comic Prints*, 1776. Courtesy of the Lewis Walpole Library, Yale University.

designer), and John Cobb (luxury upholsterer) have in common is a recognition and exploitation of the power of dress. All of these figures were popular subjects of the field of caricature. Underlying this insight is a more or less self-conscious understanding of the performance of identity. Dress is constructed as a costume that creates a reality, rather than as a straightforward expression of some inherent character. The power this construction afforded was put to diverse ends by different personages, and was practiced with varying degrees of self-consciousness. Charles James Fox made an explicit statement of cultural alignment with French culture in order to annex an authority of taste in opposition to the Tories. All the other macaronis might be said to have exploited different versions of this cosmopolitan authority to their own ends: Banks, for example, to assert the dilettantism of the aristocracy; Cosway to celebrate and perpetuate his new socially esteemed self. As Amelia Rauser argues somewhat differently but in accordance with this chapter "The paradox is that the macaroni, icon of inauthenticity, became through the unmasking effect of portrait caricature a real individual—known, individuated, perhaps eccentric but also thereby authentic—a modern manly Englishman."[72] Over the course of the nineteenth century, these types become romanticized within a generalized "Georgian past." Yet the dress of such figures was not simply a matter of folly or "fun for the young."

The essay has examined the dyad of "macaroni" and "caricature" as genres or types. This is not to say that there is the possibility of further mixed genres, as in the caricature crossed with the portrait or the "conversation piece" (a type of portrait genre in an indoors or outdoors setting), as well as low and high art, as, for example, in the macaronis either depicted on or made of ceramic. Caricature is not simply a reflection of social reality, distorted for comic effect, but can be said to have created the site in which the "macaroni" identity was consolidated. The caricatures of the caricatured figures consuming visual caricatures depict this occurring. In this sense, the macaroni's representation in caricature is always that medium's portrait of its own power. The macaroni, indeed, is neither fact nor fiction, but represents the collapsing of a distinction between the two.

Notes

1   Versions of this chapter were presented as "Macaroni Caricature: Portrait of itself as a Genre" within the session Portraiture: A Complex Web at the AAANZ (Art Association of Australia and New Zealand) Conference, Canberra, November 2009 and at Fashioning the Early Modern, penultimate conference, Victoria and Albert Museum, September 2012. The more recent research has been supported by Lewis Walpole Library/Yale University Fellowship and the Humanities in the European Research Area/Fashioning the Early Modern Project. I have benefitted from recent discussions with Giorgio Riello, John Styles, Matthew Martin, and Patrik Steorn. Richard Read was particularly helpful and read the draft.

2   John B. Thompson, *Ideology and Modern Culture: Critical Social Theory in the Era of Mass Communication*, Stanford: Stanford University Press, 1990, p. 2.

3   Thompson adds: "For social life is, to some extent, a field of contestation, in which struggle takes place through words and symbols as well as through the use of physical force." Ibid., p. 10.

4   Ibid., p. 166.

5   Valerie Steele, "The social and political significance of Macaroni Fashion," *Costume*, 19 (1985): 94–109; Aileen Ribeiro, "The Macaronis," *History Today*, 28, 7 (1978): 463–8; Peter McNeil, "Macaroni Masculinities," *Fashion Theory*, 4, 4 (2000): 373–404; Peter McNeil, "'That doubtful gender': Macaroni dress and male sexualities," *Fashion Theory*, 3, 4 (1999): 411–47; Amelia F. Rauser, "Hair, authenticity, and the self-made Macaroni," *Eighteenth-Century Studies*, 38, 1 (2004): 101–17.

6   Daniel Carey, *Continental Travel and Journeys Beyond Europe in the Early Modern Period: An Overlooked Connection*, The Hakluyt Society, Annual Lecture, 2009.

7   Hannah Greig, *The Beau Monde: Fashionable Society in Georgian London*, Oxford: Oxford University Press, 2013.

8   Horace Walpole, "Book of Materials" (LWL Walpole, 49 2615 II, 1771).

9   Written by Clarke, a Derbyshire man, then on his way to Florence from Milan. Frederick A. Pottle ed. *Boswell's London Journal 1762–1763*, Melbourne, London, and Toronto: William Heinemann, 1950.

10   J. P. Malcolm, *An Historical Sketch of the Art of Caricaturing with Graphic*

Illustrations. FSA. Author of London Redivivum, Manners and Customs of London, London: Longman, Hurst, Rees, Orme and Brown, 1813.

11   Tobias Smollett, Travels Through France and Italy, 1766, p. 105.

12   Malcolm, An Historical Sketch, p. v.

13   Diana Donald, The Age of Caricature: Satirical Prints in the Reign of George III, New Haven and London: Yale University Press, 1996, p. 1.

14   As listed in the B. M. cat., quoted in John Brewer, The Common People and Politics, 1750–1790s: The English Satirical Print 1600–1832, Cambridge: Chadwyck-Healey, 1986, p. 30.

15   Eirwen E. C. Nicholson, "English Political Prints and Pictorial Argument c.1640–c.1832: A Study in Historiography and Methodology," Ph.D. thesis, University of Edinburgh, 1994, p. 351.

16   Donald, The Age of Caricature, p. 1.

17   M[onsieur] D'Archenholz (Formerly a Captain in the Service of the King of Prussia), A Picture of England; Containing a Description of the Laws, Customs, and Manners of England … Vol. I, London: Edward Jeffery, 1789, p. 152.

18   Nicholson, "English Political Prints," Plates to Part I, ch. VIII, plate 2.

19   Lorna Rempel, "Carnal satire and the constitutional king: George III in James Gillray's monstrous craws at a new coalition feast," Art History, 18, 1 (March 1995): 11.

20   Cited in Nicholson, "English Political Prints," pp. 277, 132.

21   Isaac Cruikshank, "Deputy Pendulum's motion for an address," published by S. W. Fores, London, November 29, 1795, publisher's advertisement follows the imprint "Folios of caractures [sic] lent out for the evening" (Lewis Walpole Library, 795.11.29.01), Impression 2.

22   Walpole also acquired the original sketch by "Miss Hoare of Bath" (1776) for the caricature. See Donald, The Age of Caricature, p. 91.

23   March 11, 1780 in S. Lewis Wilmarth ed., The Yale Edition of Horace Walpole's Correspondence, New Haven and London: Yale University Press, 1937–83, vol. 25, p. 23.

24   Herbert M. Atherton, Political Prints in the Age of Hogarth: A Study of the Ideographic Representation of Politics, Oxford: Clarendon Press, 1979, p. 17. Another printed and painted fan depicting assignats is in the Museum of Fine Arts Boston [1976.237]. The Museum also holds an English fan printed in 1795 with a row of caricature portrait faces along the fan edge [1976.310]. See Anna Gray Bennett, Unfolding Beauty: The Art of the Fan. The Collection of Esther Oldham and the Museum of Fine Arts, Boston, New York: Thames & Hudson, 1988. For a superb reading of the printed and painted representations of the assignat as post-Revolutionary 'traumatic mimesis' see Richard Taws, 'Trompe-l'Oeil and Trauma: Money and Memory after the Terror', Oxford Art Journal, 30:3 (October 2007): 353–76.

25   This is the subject of a forthcoming work by McNeil.

26   M. Dorothy George, London Life in the Eighteenth Century, Harmondsworth: Penguin, 1966, pp. 166–7. For Banks's collection see Arlene Leis, "Displaying art and fashion: ladies' pocket-book imagery in the paper collections of Sarah Sophia Banks," Konsthistorisk tidskrift/Journal of Art History, 82, 3 (2013): 252–71.

27 Nicholson, "English Political Prints," p. 233.

28 Ibid., p. 268.

29 Ibid.

30 Ibid., p. 337.

31 John Gascoigne, *Joseph Banks and the English Enlightenment: Useful Knowledge and Polite Culture*, Cambridge: Cambridge University Press, 2003, p. 67.

32 Donald, *The Age of Caricature*, p. vii.

33 B. E. Maidment, *Reading Popular Prints, 1790–1870*, Manchester & New York: Manchester University Press, 1996, p. 12.

34 Ibid., p. 56.

35 See *The Caricaturist's Apology*, S. Howitt (pub.), 1802, in Donald, *The Age of Caricature*, p. 17.

36 Richard Morton, "Introduction: Satire and Reform," in J. D. Browning ed., *Satire in the 18th Century*, New York and London: Garland, 1983, p. 2.

37 Ibid., p. 5.

38 Freud lecture, Yale University, 1979, on which see Ronald Paulson, "Gillray: The Ambivalence of the Political Cartoonist," in Browning, *Satire in the 18th Century*, p. 150.

39 Ibid., pp. 150–1.

40 This idea was advanced in my Ph.D. thesis, "Fashion Victims: Class, Gender, Sexuality and the English Macaroni, circa 1765–1780," 2 vols, University of Sydney, 1999.

41 George Winchester Stone and George Morrow Kahrl, *David Garrick: A Critical Biography*, Carbondale: Southern Illinois University Press, 1979, p. 456.

42 Greig, *The Beau Monde*, p. 118.

43 Winchester Stone and Kahrl, *David Garrick*, p. 457.

44 Ibid., pp. 456–7.

45 Frederic George Stephens and Edward Hawkins, *Catalogue of Prints and Drawings in the British Museum: Division I. Political and Personal Satires*, vol. IV, A.D. 1761–c. A.D. 1770, London: Trustees of the British Museum, 1883, p. xxxviii.

46 Illus. Donald, *The Age of Caricature*, pl. 18.

47 Nicholson, "English Political Prints," p. 254.

48 Ibid., pp. 322, 323.

49 Maidment, *Reading Popular Prints*, p. 90.

50 Cited by Nicholson, "English Political Prints," p. 297. Patten is probably the author of *George Cruikshank: Life and Times and Art*, London: Rutgers University Press 1992.

51 Eirwen E., C. Nicholson, "English Political Prints and Pictorial Argument c. 1640–c. 1832: A Study in Historiography and Methodology," PhD Thesis, University of Edinburgh, 1994.

52 Mary Dorothy George, *Catalogue of Political and Personal Satires Preserved in the Department of Prints and Drawings in the British Museum*, vol. V, 1771–1783, London: Trustees of the British Museum, 1935, p. 236.

53   Atherton, *Political Prints in the Age of Hogarth*, pp. 18–19.

54   Donald, *The Age of Caricature*, p. 3.

55   George, *Catalogue*, vol. V, p. xxxiv.

56   Atherton, *Political Prints in the Age of Hogarth,* p. 21.

57   Ibid.

58   From the engraved page placed after the title-page of Darly's macaroni prints, quoted in George, *Catalogue*, p. xxxiv.

59   Donald, *Age of Caricature*, p. 3.

60   At the time of going to press, I read Joseph Monteyne's *From Still Life to the Screen. Print Culture, Display, and the Materiality of the Image in Eighteenth-Century London*, New Haven and London: Yale University Press, 2013. Monteyne writes therein an innovative chapter entitled '"Modern Enigmas by a High Headed Sphynx": Matthew and Mary Darly's Abstract Architecture of the Body'. He explores the 'experimental fusion of fashion and ornament' in a print by Benedetto Pastorini and extends this to the practice of Matthew and Mary Darly [p. 88]. He argues for the term 'macaronic' to be extended to works that create a 'hybrid and mixed composition, a jumble of two or more representational languages' [90]. Parts of the argument regarding the inter-relationship of printed ornamental designs and printed caricatures find a counterpoint in a work that was prepared around the same time, Peter McNeil and Patrik Steorn, 'The Medium of Print and the Rise of Fashion in the West," *Konsthistorisk tidskrift: Journal of Art History*, 82, 3 (2013), 135–56. Monteyne argues his point much further in an interesting way, claiming that in the work of the Darlys, 'The caricature of the body has been displaced by the caricature of things' [107].

61   Nicholson, "English Political Prints," page not known.

62   Stephens and Hawkins, *Catalogue*, p. 786.

63   Peter McNeil, "'Beyond the Horizon of Hair": Masculinity, Nationhood and Fashion in the Anglo-French Eighteenth Century," in D. Freist and F. Schmekel eds, *Hinter dem Horizont Band 2: Projektion und Distinktion ländlicher Oberschichten im europäischen Vergleich*, 17.19. Jahrhundert, Aschendorff, Münster, 2013, pp. 79–90.

64   Ibid.

65   George, *Catalogue*, p. 71.

66   Ibid., p. 72.

67   Illus. Donald, *The Age of Caricature*, pl. 90.

68   Brewer, *The Common People and Politics,* p. 18.

69   Ibid., p. 21.

70   Ibid., p. 29.

71   Donald, *The Age of Caricature*, p. 3.

72   Amelia Rauser, *Caricature Unmasked: Irony, Authenticity, and Individualism in Eighteenth-Century English Prints*, Newark: University of Delaware Press, 2008, p. 76.

Bibliography

Atherton, Herbert M., *Political Prints in the Age of Hogarth: A Study of the Ideographic Representation of Politics*, Oxford: Clarendon Press, 1979.

Bennett, Anna Gray, *Unfolding Beauty: The Art of the Fan. The Collection of Esther Oldham and the Museum of Fine Arts, Boston*, New York: Thames and Hudson, 1988.

Brewer, John, *The Common People and Politics, 1750–1790s: The English Satirical Print 1600–1832*, Cambridge: Chadwyck-Healey, 1986.

Burke, Peter, *Popular Culture in Early Modern Europe*, London: Temple Smith, 1978.

Carey, Daniel, *Continental Travel and Journeys Beyond Europe in the Early Modern Period: An Overlooked Connection*, London: The Hakluyt Society, Annual Lecture, 2009.

Carretta, Vincent, *George III and the Satirists from Hogarth to Byron*, Athens and London: University of Georgia Press, 1990.

Carter, Harold B., *Sir Joseph Banks (1743–1820): A Guide to Biographical and Bibliographical Sources*, St Paul's Bibliographies and the British Museum (Natural History, 1987).

Donald, Diana, *The Age of Caricature: Satirical Prints in the Reign of George III*, New Haven and London: Yale University Press, 1996.

—*Followers of Fashion: Graphic Satires from the Georgian Era*, London: Hayward Gallery, 2002.

Gascoigne, John, *Joseph Banks and the English Enlightenment: Useful Knowledge and Polite Culture*, Cambridge: Cambridge University Press, 2003.

George, Mary Dorothy, *Catalogue of Political and Personal Satires Preserved in the Department of Prints and Drawings in the British Museum*, vol. V, 1771–83, London: Trustees of the British Museum, 1935.

—*London Life in the Eighteenth Century*, Harmondsworth: Penguin, 1966.

Greig, Hannnah, *The* Beau Monde: *Fashionable Society in Georgian London*, Oxford: Oxford University Press, 2013.

Harris, Eileen, *The Townshend Album*, National Portrait Gallery, London, Her Majesty's Stationery Office, 1974.

Leis, Arlene, "Displaying art and fashion: ladies' pocket-book imagery in the paper collections of Sarah Sophia Banks," *Konsthistorisk tidskrift/Journal of Art History*, 82, 3 (2013): 252–71.

Maidment, B. E., *Reading Popular Prints, 1790–1870*, Manchester & New York: Manchester University Press, 1996.

Malcolm, J. P., *An Historical Sketch of the Art of Caricaturing with Graphic Illustrations. FSA. Author of London Redivivum, Manners and Customs of London*, London: Longman, Hurst, Rees, Orme & Brown, 1813.

McNeil, Peter and Patrik Steorn, "The medium of print and the rise of fashion in the west," *Konsthistorisk tidskrift/Journal of Art History*, 82, 3 (2013): 135–56.

McNeil, Peter, "'Beyond the Horizon of Hair': Masculinity, Nationhood and Fashion in the Anglo-French Eighteenth Century," in D. Freist and F. Schmekel eds, *Hinter dem Horizont Band 2: Projektion und Distinktion ländlicher Oberschichten im europäischen Vergleich, 17.19. Jahrhundert*, Aschendorff, Münster, 2013.

—"Fashion Victims: Class, Gender, Sexuality and the English Macaroni, circa 1765–1780," 2 vols, Ph.D. thesis, University of Sydney, 1999.

—"Macaroni masculinities," *Fashion Theory*, 4, 4 (2000): 373–404.

—"'That doubtful gender': macaroni dress and male sexualities," *Fashion Theory*, 3, 4, 1999, pp. 411–17. McWilliam, Neil, "The Age of Caricature ... by Diana Donald" [review], *Art History* 20, 1, (March 1997).

Morton, Richard, "Introduction: Satire and Reform," in J. D. Browning ed., *Satire in the 18th Century*, New York and London: Garland, 1983.

Nicholson, Eirwen E. C., "English Political Prints and Pictorial Argument c.1640–c.1832: A Study in Historiography and Methodology," Ph.D. Thesis, University of Edinburgh, 1994.

—"English Political Prints: 'Emblem v. Caricature—a Tenacious Conceptual Framework'," in Alison Adams, Laurence Grove, and Amy Wygant, *Glasgow Emblem Studies, Vol. 1. Emblems and Art History: Nine Essays*, Department of French, University of Glasgow, 1996, pp. 141–67.

Pottle, Frederick A. ed., *Boswell's London Journal 1762–1763*, Melbourne, London, and Toronto: William Heinemann, 1950.

Prevost, M., and Roman d'Amat eds, *Dictionnaire de Biographie Française*, vol. 7, Paris, Librairie Letouzey et ané [*sic*], 1956.

Rauser, Amelia, *Caricature Unmasked: Irony, Authenticity, and Individualism in Eighteenth-Century English Prints*, Newark: University of Delaware Press, 2008.

Rauser, Amelia F., "Hair, authenticity, and the self-made Macaroni," *Eighteenth-Century Studies*, 38, 1, 2004: 101–17.

Rempal, Lora, "Carnal Satire and the constitutional king: George III in James Gillray's *monstrous craws at a new coalition feast*," *Art History*, 18, 1 (March 1995): 4–23.

Ribeiro, Aileen, "The Macaronis," *History Today*, 28, 7 (1978): 463–8.

Saumarez Smith, Charles, *Eighteenth-Century Decoration: Design and the Domestic Interior in England*, London: Weidenfeld and Nicolson, 1993.

Smollett, Tobias, *Travels through France and Italy. Containing Observations on Character, Customs, Religion, Government, Police, Commerce, Arts, and Antiquities, with a particular description of the Town, Territory, and Climate of Nice: to which is added, a Register of the Weather, kept during a residence of Eighteen Months in that City,* 2 vols, London: R. Baldwin 1766, reprinted as *Travels Through France and Italy,* ed. Frank Felksenstein, Oxford: Oxford University Press, 1979.

Steele, Valerie, "The social and political significance of macaroni fashion," *Costume*, 19, 1985: 94–105.

Stephens, Frederic George and Edward Hawkins, *Catalogue of Prints and Drawings in the British Museum: Division I. Political and Personal Satires*, vol. IV, A.D. 1761–c. A.D. 1770, London: Trustees of the British Museum, 1883.

Thompson, John B., *Ideology and Modern Culture: Critical Social Theory in the Era of Mass Communication*, Stanford: Stanford University Press, 1990.

Vickery, Amanda, "Mutton dressed as lamb? fashioning age in Georgian England," *Journal of British Studies*, 52, 4 (2013): 858–86.

Walpole, Horace, "Book of Materials" (LWL Walpole, 49 2615 II, 1771).

Waterhouse, Ellis, *Painting in Britain 1530 to 1790*, London: Penguin, 1953.

Waterhouse, Ellis et al., *British Painting in the Eighteenth Century*, exh. cat., Montreal: Montreal Museum of Fine Arts et al., 1957–1958.

Welch, E., "Objects of Fashion in the Renaissance," in Giorgio Riello and Peter McNeil eds, *The Fashion History Reader: Global Perspectives*, Oxon and New York: Routledge, 2010.

Wilmarth, S. Lewis ed., *The Yale Edition of Horace Walpole's Correspondence*, New Haven and London: Yale University Press, 1937–83, vol. 25.

Winchester Stone, George and George Morrow Kahrl, *David Garrick: A Critical Biography*, Carbondale: Southern Illinois University Press, 1979.

7

FEMINIST IDEOLOGIES IN POSTMODERN JAPANESE FASHION: REI KAWAKUBO MEETS MARIE ANTOINETTE IN DOWNTOWN TOKYO

ORY BARTAL

In November 1970 Yukio Mishima, a three-time Nobel Prize-nominated writer, stepped on to the balcony of the headquarters of Japan's Self-Defense Forces. His purpose was to inspire the soldiers to launch a *coup d'état* and restore the powers to the emperor. Mishima, whose literature expressed yearning for beauty, masculinity, eroticism, and death, believed in the traditional *bushido* values[1] and declared his wish to become a *samurai*. In 1967 he formed a private unarmed army called *takenokai* (shield society) and swore to protect the emperor. Like any other fascist movement, *takenokai* was also connected to aesthetic fetishism. Mishima was highly committed to aesthetics, and when choosing the uniform for *takenokai*, he made an unusual choice. Instead of opting for a traditional Japanese military style, he asked the successful French fashion designer of the time, Pierre Cardin, to design the uniform. The wrapping of his *samurai* vision in Pierre Cardin's uniform is firmly engraved in the collective memory of the Japanese people mainly because after he failed in his mission, Mishima returned to the commandant's office and committed *seppuku*, being beheaded by one of the members of *takenokai*.

The horrifying suicide in traditional manner by one of Japan's most well-known personae of the time created a national trauma. After years of asceticism and frugality, the youthful post-war generation was yearning for a new and modern lifestyle. These transitional years led to the birth of the late consumer culture of the 1980s that challenged the power of bureaucratic establishment and cultural structures, creating new cultural possibilities based on new values. This chapter will analyze Japanese contemporary fashion via its expression in the late consumer culture that merged economics and aesthetics, creating a contemporary social ideology in Japan.

Socio-historical context

In the 1970s, the modernistic social paradigm collapsed in many post-industrial countries. In Japan, it resulted in the falling apart of the homogeneous culture that hailed collectivism. Various groups began to form. In 1970s Tokyo, the *Karasu-Zoku* (raven tribe) emerged as a parallel to the British Punk movement. Alongside the *karasu-zoku* was the *an-non-zoku*, a young and fashionable "tribe" consisting of women who enjoyed reading the magazines *an-an* and *non-no*. The idea of tribes forming around style and fashion became even stronger in the 1980s in Yoyogi Park, situated in the heart of Harajuku neighborhood, when the bamboo tribe (*take-no-ko-zoku*) appeared, rebelling against the establishment by smoking cigarettes, using grease in their hair, and dancing in the streets. They vacated their place in the mid-1980s to the "Bands" tribe (*bando-zoku*), who played and danced in the streets on Sundays. Later, these were followed by the *visual-kei-zoku* and the Gothic Lolita Tribe, who together were known as *harajuku-zoku*. Additional tribes formed among the young women of Tokyo, including the *ganguro-zoku* (Ganguro tribe) that developed in the Shibuya and Ikebukuro neighborhoods, the *otaku-zoku* (Otaku tribe) in Akihabara, and the *kurisutaru-zoku* (Crystal tribe) in Aoyama neighborhood.[2]

The 1970s collapse of the modernistic social paradigm led to a process of departure from homogenic culture with people seeking new frames of reference. Like Mishima, the Lolita-tribe of Harajuku expressed itself in a French style, but this time it was an appropriation of late Baroque and Rococo style of a different "drama-queen"—Marie Antoinette. Oddly enough, Mishima and the French queen—who were both passionate about style—shared the same fate: they were both beheaded.

The emergence of these sub-cultures, each uniting around unique aesthetics that differentiates them from one another, is a type of Totemism, which according to Claude Levi-Strauss is the unavoidable structure of human society. Totemism is the human attempt to unite around an object that becomes the sign of the group. The sign gives identity, inspiration, and strength to its followers and protects them from the constant threat of scattering.[3] In the late consumer culture, the Totem gives an almost spiritual or magical meaning and identity to each group. Via style and preferences, which are expressed in the brand's sign, the individual declares affiliation to a group or a sub-culture. In other words, the style of a product is not naïve and meaningless, but rather an element that creates identity, association, and social meaning. The sociologist Pierre Bourdieu broadens this saying, claiming that style creates both separation and power struggle between different social groups. Furthermore, he says that preference and style, which are usually considered personal issues that are based on intuition or subconscious decisions, are an acquired social cultural construction, just like a language.[4] The customers choose a style in order to form a personal identity, and acquire a social status by declaring their affiliation to a specific group or sub-culture, while they differentiate and separate themselves from other groups. This is how "style" transformed from what seemed to be a meaningless decoration into the "doorman" guarding the borders separating between various statuses and groups.

Jean Baudrillard explains how this mechanism triggers the late consumer culture. He argues that products in the post-modern economics no longer were meant to provide materialistic needs alone, but social needs as well: the market follows psychological patterns as opposed to economic logic. Baudrillard presents the postmodern economic system as a social system.[5] According to Baudrillard, the new consumer society is driven by two forces, Need and Desire, both of which are social and not economic: the need for difference and the desire for social meaning. Consequently, it is the desire which comes into question in a rich consumer society.[6] In other words, when consumers buy fashion brands, the actual "product" they buy is their identity. Researcher Stuart Ewen presented the blurring of borders between products identity and personal identity, naming this phenomena "The Commodity Self."[7]

The formation of this new socio-economic ideology occurred throughout the post-industrial world. But, in 1980s Japan, the new consumer culture reached new peaks that turned its economy into a speculative bubble. Marilyn Ivy, who researched the economic bubble era in Japan, refers to it as an "accelerated symbolic consumerism" era.[8] Some of the signs being purchased were clothes: total spending on clothing in Japan grew from 376.6 billion Yen in 1988 to 826.5 billion Yen in 1990.[9] Fashion took the role of an identity marker, since other products such as cars, house, furniture, or interior design are not flauntingly displayed in typical Tokyo lifestyle. According to Patricia Mears, the importance of fashion in Japan goes beyond trendiness or consumer products: Japanese believe that design of objects or clothes can lead to intellectual and spiritual places.[10] In the 1980s, consumers used various styles and brands as tools to form identity, becoming "fashion victims." Suzuki Kyoichi photographed fashion collectors who dedicate entire apartments for their collections, similar to art collectors in other countries. He named his book *Happy Victims: You Are What You Buy*.[11]

From the wide style spectrum seen on Tokyo's streets, I will focus on two specific styles in this chapter: firstly, the *avant-garde* style of Rei Kawakubo, which developed in Aoyama neighborhood, and secondly, the cute and obsequious baroque style that developed as Lolitas, flourishing in the Harajuku neighborhood and corresponding with the femininity of Marie Antoinette. At their core, these styles present different ideological concepts of femininity in Japan. But at the meta-level they present the values of the late consumer culture that dictates consumer identity in form of signs and style.

Rei Kawakubo and the anti-fashion movement

Kawakubo broke into the fashion world in 1981 in Paris. Her clothes countered the strict rules and codes of the European fashion of that time. European designers used patterns that presented the "ideal" woman's body and high-quality materials that emphasized glamour and wealth. In contrast, Rei Kawakubo's clothes were characterized by the breaking of codes. First and foremost, they re-wrapped the body in a way that does not consider the shape of the body but rather the space surrounding it. The clothes presented asymmetry and random sewing patterns, resulting in sculptural objects dressed on the body. She brought to the world an aesthetics of poverty not at all desired in Europe and thus received ice-cold reviews, such as "Les Japonais jouent *Les Misérables*" ("The Japanese play *Les Misérables*").[12]

Some researchers saw Kawakubo's clothes as an aesthetic link to *muromachi* period traditions, when the ideology of Zen Buddhism was developed and expressed via monochromatic coloring, the beauty of the incomplete and the aesthetics of *wabi-sabi*.[13] But I will argue here that the work of Rei Kawakubo was much more influenced by foreign ideas and global trends than by the traditional Japanese aesthetics.[14]

Aesthetic sources

The earliest source to influence Rei Kawakubo was the cultural revolution (followed by visual revolution) that took place in the 1960s worldwide, including Japan. The *avant-garde* movements at that time—*gutai, neo-dada, butoh* and *mono-ha*—created subversive, experimental art that protested against values of established institutions of government, industry, and culture, against accepted beauty values, and struck out against the rigid hierarchy of Japanese pre-modern art. An example of this anti-art can be seen in Tanaka Atsuko's Electric Dress from 1957 that presented the new discourse of body politics.

At the same time foreign art and design trends found their way to Japan. The 1960s Italian anti-design trend was created by groups like Studio de Pas, D'Urbino Lomazzi,[15] and studio Gatti, Paolini, Teodoro, as well as by individual designers like Gaetano Pesce and Ettore Sottsass. These designers, who were influenced by Arte Povera and other subversive paths in Italian art, broke all that was expected of modern design furniture and undermined the "Good Design" of modernism, which believed in functionality, perfect ergonomics, and timeless design solutions. These objects raised questions about the purposes of design in general. The radical designers wanted to create a design that blurs the social class issue and sought new visual strategies that redefine the role of design, the status of the designer, and the relationship between design and society. They called their works anti-class, anti-consumer, anti-marketing and thus also anti-design. The resulting design had social and political messages that successfully excluded it from the capitalistic system. One example that shows this influence is the Sacco "Beanbag" Chair, designed in 1969 by the Italian studio Gatti, Paolini and Teodoro. This was a legless chair, which looks like a punching bag, giving no indication regarding the proper place and direction for sitting. This anti-design chair has an unusual volume compared to a modernist chair, looking more like a sculptural element. These characteristics, as well as its black color, remind us of the elements in Kawakubo's clothes and show the influence of such design on her work.[16] The radical Italian design, which blurred the boundaries between art and design and tried to cancel socio-economic elements within design, arrived in Japan via designers such as Umeda Masanori and Shiro Kuramata, influencing Kawakubo.

Conceptual sources

Kawakubo studied philosophy and literature in Keio University and never received any formal fashion training. According to Patricia Mears, her skills are not in her hands or her patterns, but rather in her ability to engage in theoretical discourse.[17] During her studies, deconstruction and feminist ideas were highly influential on the spirit of the era. Deconstruction, which was largely the heritage of France's philosophy departments and American literature departments, spread to art, architecture, and design. When it reached the fashion arena, deconstruction broke the dominance of the modernist fashion that produced cuts that fit the body and were polished and finely finished.

Deconstructive fashion presented clothing with an unfinished look, including loose frayed hems and edges. The clothes appeared to be falling apart or made of a combination of different parts. Deconstructed patterns tended to hide the body rather than show it. These clothes were quite the opposite of glamour and presented a poor look of devastation and degradation. Patricia Mears writes that the deconstruction theory was the driving force behind Rei Kawakubo's work. Rei Kawakubo was the first to formalize and appropriate it completely with the monochromatic coloring, asymmetric baggy look that destroyed modernist patterns. French journals, in reference to her new draping, called Rei Kawakubo "Le Destroy."

Rei Kawakubo's ragged edges, irregular hemlines, crinkled fabrics, and loose-fitting layers that fell aimlessly over the body eventually came to be known as "World War Three survival look." Via these protest clothes, Kawakubo fought against the rigid social and cultural codes of Japan, just like the Italian designers who fought against social class concepts using design.

It is possible that her protest was like that of some of the Japanese *avant-garde* movements that sought to perpetuate the memory of the Second World War destruction and the atomic bomb, a memory that was repressed under the economic miracle of the 1970s that brought along both European bourgeois taste and a nostalgic return to the traditional Japanese aesthetics of the Edo era.[18]

With the development of her style, Kawakubo seemed also to be influenced by the postmodern freedom with the use of irony and paradox. As such, she started to quote from neo-punk or Walt Disney. In addition, Kawakubo was also influenced by social ideologies. Although Kawakubo never referred to herself as a feminist, it seems to me that she joined the radical feminism ideology that was just reaching Japan at the time, influenced by Japanese creative women such as art director Eiko Ishioka. Ishioka created a revolutionary advertising campaign in the 1970s for the Parco department store, folding feminist messages into advertisements. One of Ishioka's advertisements showed Indian women in the Rajasthan desert carrying heavy water containers on their heads, bearing the slogan "Are they career women?" The power of women in her advertisements was not presented via glamorous models but rather by highlighting the female roles that had been previously unacknowledged. Ishioka dared to present male nudity, for the first time referring to the female point of view. The male pop star Sawada Kenji (known as Julie) was shown in the nude with the slogan "It's time to gossip about men."

Other feminist *avant-garde* artists included Yoko Ono of Fluxus. In 1964 Yoko Ono presented a famous installation titled "Cut Piece." In this installation, she sat on stage wearing a black dress, and invited the audience to cut her clothes. Via the medium of the black dress that refers to "la petite robe noire," Ono raised a difficult issue, namely the mutuality between the attacker and the victim.

Another artist active in the 1970s was Kusama Yayoi, who had just returned from a stint with Andy Warhol in New York. Kusama's work is conceptual in nature, but is often described as feminist art that presents "otherness."

Comparing Ono's black cut dress or Ishioka's statements, it seems to me that these creative women undoubtedly had a major influence on Kawakubo's work. In 1972, Kawakubo called her company Comme des Garçons, a name that not only insinuates her gender concept of equality between men and women, but also tries to change the basic concept that fashion creates power relationships in which the woman is dressed in order to seduce a man, with a sexy appearance. Kawakubo claimed at the time that she wished for women who wear her clothes to be financially independent with strength and self-esteem. In an interview, she reiterated "We must break away from conventional forms of dress for the new woman of today. We need a new strong image, not a revisit to the past."[19]

This concept differed from the feminist concept of Coco Chanel, who freed women from exhibitionistic Belle Époque clothes and dressed them in comfortable, modern, and modular wardrobes, and Yves Saint Laurent, who dressed women in trousers and men's clothes to demonstrate equality. Rei Kawakubo's feminist concepts were expressed concretely in her stepping out against standard patterns typical of the designers who gave women perfect patterns and a sexy appearance. The designers of the 1970s and the 1980s in Europe not only presented fine material and faultless finish, but also patterns that relate to a body with the "correct" and "perfect" proportions, which were drafted mathematically. Yael Taragan defines this imaginary body as a timeless body that prohibits any other body type—distorted, short, bent, tattered, or disproportional—from the fashion world. The approach of the fashion world at the time saw such bodies as bodies whose faults should be fixed, blurred, or concealed by clothing.[20]

Rei Kawakubo fought against this concept, wishing to present the entire spectrum of the human body, especially the woman's body, which in most cases does not match the proportions dictated by fashion designers. At times she designed her clothes as one size, to wrap up the body rather than show it off. This one-size look flew in the face of the highly sexualized silhouettes that are normally associated with the taste of the 1980s. Thus it can be said that Kawakubo embraced feminist ideals within the fashion world. Her perception inverts our notions of the highly sexualized body.[21] Her clothes challenged the conventions and ideas regarding the ideal woman's body and the ideals of beauty that were established in our conscience for many years by the fashion world.

Later, the idea developed into the presentation of "other" bodies—the distorted and the different. In the 1997 collection "Dress Meets Body, Body Meets Dress", which was also called "Quasimodo", Kawakubo designed a hunchbacked dress. This dress, made out of stretchy, synthetic fabrics printed in pink or blue gingham, had pockets into which she placed down-filled pillows. But rather than pad the breasts to enhance the feminine form, she put the pockets and pillows on the necks, upper backs, hips and rear ends.

This dress, with its unusual bulk, was part of a highly controversial collection that explicitly expressed what Kawakubo tried to demonstrate throughout the years: not to hide the different body, but rather to expose it. The construction of a different space around the body represented an alternative to the Western beauty ideals. The dress was made of a material with a grid pattern, a core concept in modernist aesthetics creation that was based on machine aesthetics and the idea of "form follows function." The dress distorted the shape of the body and broke the traditional grid in order to challenge our idea of the "ideal" woman's body. The clothes protest against the harsh determinations of "correct" body proportions for a woman.[22]

This feminine and deconstructive platform, in combination with the *avant-garde* aesthetic visual expression of Japanese art and Italian anti-design in the 1960s, found a voice in Kawakubo's work. As Dorinne Kondo explains, her style did not come from kimono design, as was commonly thought.[23] In fact, Kawakubo resisted any connection and actively challenged Japanese fashion traditions, just as the art movements of the 1960s challenged Japanese traditional aesthetics. The clothes blur boundaries between art and design, high and low, global and local, and paradoxically between *avant-garde* and luxury. Her work represents the complexity of the new avant-garde visual culture that developed in Japan, based on a new conceptual platform that goes against both Japanese and European traditional aesthetic values and most of all against the aesthetics of the fashion world in which she serves as a cultural hero.

Rei Kawakubo raises questions about modernist patterns, the mask created by fashion, the masculine perspective on the feminine body as well as more general questions such as "What is beauty? What is our perception of the human body?" These questions served as a foundation for an alternative ideological line for women who refused to consider the masculine perspective. Her work presents an *avant-garde* style based on new and defiant conceptual platform. The breaking down of modernist patterns and reconstruction of the body are not aesthetic acts, but ideological ones that present the complexity of creation in the new visual and *avant-garde* culture that developed in Japan in the 1980s.

Marie Antoinette reincarnated in downtown Tokyo

Geographically close to Rei Kawakubo's flagship boutique, but on the opposite side of the scale conceptually, a fringe-style culture known as *Kawaii* developed in the 1970s. This style would eventually make its way to the mainstream in the 1980s, in parallel to consumer culture.

This style was influenced by, among others, a Manga series called "Rose of Versailles," written by Ikeda Ryoko in 1973. The story, set in Versailles, initially focused on Marie Antoinette and was illustrated as *shoujo* (girls' Manga) heroine, but very soon the secondary character, Oskar, became the main character in the story. Oskar was born as a woman but was raised as a man in order to gain a position as a guard in Marie Antoinette's royal court. The story was published serially in *Margaret Magazine* during the 1970s and was bound in 10 volumes in 1982. It presented Oskar's love affairs and all the women with whom he interacted, assuming he is a man. The story raised issues of gender, thus transforming Cinderella–Prince Charming relations into a new type of man–woman relationship. It became one of the most influential Manga ever written, with 12 million books sold. The books were adapted as an Anime movie,[24] a cinematic movie,[25] a ballet, an opera, and a French–Japanese movie,[26] in addition to numberless plays in the popular Takarazuka Theater.

The popularity of the Manga created a boom in the study of the French language and travels to France, particularly Versailles, a popular tourist destination for Japanese. Versailles became, as Susan Napier states, "a particularly good example of idealized Western Otherness."[27] Its decorative style presenting fantasy, luxury, and exoticism became an unrealized myth, real and unreal simultaneously, just like the Manga narrative. As such, it became an object of fantasy and desire. This Rococo style, which began with Manga, found its place in the fashion world under the auspices of the *Kawaii* style. The *Kawaii* style positioned itself as a central ideology of the popular culture.

Style and ideology—the Kawaii

During the 1970s, Japanese youth began to rebel against their country's rigid social codes. The word "*Kawaii*," which originally meant "cute," adopted a wider connotation of childishness that included naivety, purity, simplicity, and vulnerability. These youth wished to free themselves from the burden of the gloomy and full-of-compromises adult life. Their protest was embodied by childlike behavior, speech, and writing, and by choosing cute products designed in childish style.[28] This style was characterized by a saccharine look or fairy-tale style, devoid of any maturity power or sexual attributes.

Kinsella revealed in 1990 that most youngsters were not sure of their political affiliation or to which social class they belonged. However, they knew with certainty that they belong to the *Kawaii* culture, which defined their identity.[29] Unlike a typical teenage revolution, in which youngsters seek to achieve adult rights and independence, this childishness movement was a type of revolt in which young Japanese women presented a way of life in which they do not accept responsibility or independence as an alternative for maturity. Cultural anthropologist Eiji Otsuka explained that as opposed to the worldwide post-war protest movements (punk, rap), the *Kawaii* ideology was led by women. These young women preferred fantasy over reality since it protected them from the difficult role of women according to Japanese traditional social codes.[30] It differed from the feministic ways of Rei Kawakubo, Yoko Ono, or Eiko Ishioka, but it was still a form of feminist protest.

Even though the *Kawaii* style was supposedly created in an air of lacking awareness (since this is an important part in the childishness), part of the young women's protest presented a life that revolves around their own personal pleasure, with an overconsumption of products. The young Japanese women of the 1970s who had recently joined the workforce remained by and large at home living with their parents. This left them with disposable income, turning them into the richest sector in Japan and a powerful consumer group.[31] Their exaggerated consumption was perceived as anti-social, immoral, and irresponsible (thus childish).

Kawaii has to be analyzed in the context of the ideology created through the late consumer culture. The *Kawaii* style was created in the margins, but businesses quickly recognized its market potential, and created products that fitted the needs of the target audience. The new consumer culture and the attempt to express a new femininity via cuteness and sweetness brought prosperity to the fashion houses such as Milk, Pink House Ltd., and Angelic Pretty, who created fantasy and fairy-tale like clothes in the Harajuku neighborhood. They created a trend of young women dressed in Lolita clothing.

These fashion houses produced clothes that were meant to give the wearer a feeling of cuteness. They were designed with white and pink colors, with ribbons and fringes that hinted at the French Rococo style. Milk was the premiere fashion house of the trend. Established in 1970, it quickly became synonymous with gothic Lolita fashion. Pink House Ltd. also flourished in the 1980s and created a movement of young women wearing pink, named the Pink House Movement. The designs from Pink House imitated children's clothes, but used stretch materials that enabled expansion to three or four sizes larger. This way, teens and young adults could purchase "kids'" clothes and have a closet resembling that of a young girl.

At the same time, a new fashion magazine named *Cuties* was launched. This magazine changed the childish look to one of humorous chic, as androgenic and eccentric as that of children's fairy tales. The magazine changed the direction of this fashion, as it showed these youngsters to be simultaneously cute and bad, projecting a sense that they were doing something individualistic, rebelling against the responsible adult culture. Part of the new direction was the music industry *visual-kei* Band trend. A major element of these music bands was the visual. They dressed in a style that was often inspired by the Manga look. One of the most famous bands, the Malice Mizer, performed in a style influenced at first by the French classic style, and later the Gothic Victorian. The band's leader, Mana, would dress in women's clothes, and later created his own fashion brand called Moi-même-Moitié, which included both the dark and the sweet styles.

Angelic Pretty, established in 1979 and specializing in Pink Lolita clothing, that most strongly established the trend. The Lolita style that developed in the fashion houses in Japan extolled not only the Marie Antoinette Rococo style as illustrated in Manga for young women (*Shoujo* Manga), but also the clothing of Marie Antoinette, as designed by Marie Jeanne Rose Bertin. This style reached maturity in the 2000s in the designs of Hiroko Naoto, the designer of the successful "h. Naoto" line, which specialized in sub-culture styles deriving from the gothic and punk Lolita style.[32] The Rococo style supplied the *Kawaii* culture believers with a children's fairy tale fantasy, an escape route with a Western touch.

From street to art and back again

The new popular sub-culture, together with the consumer culture, was the primary and leading stream of the entire 1980s and 1990s Japanese culture. Art and design responded in part to the aesthetics and new styles that emerged from the Japanese street. The *Kawaii* style influenced Japanese contemporary artists, and the influence of their art objects eventually bounced back into the design scene as well.

Murakami Takashi, the most influential pop-artist of the time, creates works of art that present the consumer culture and its products as a reflection of thinking patterns and cultural structures. His works present the seduction motif and narcissistic structure of the *Kawaii* culture. Murakami exposed the narcissistic structure of *Kawaii* and presents it as a dangerous social phenomenon, as it makes its users dependent. One of Murakami's exhibitions was held in Versailles. This exhibition expressed Murakami's view on the culture and the contemporary Japanese visual language, which was closer to the Rococo-ornamented style of the palace than to the Orientalist image of Japanese visual culture as minimalist and monochromatic. Murakami states that the first time he heard of Versailles was in the "Rose of Versailles" Manga. He claims that approximately 20 percent of Japanese people associate the palace directly with the Manga and the Takarazuka Theater: "In this way, you could say that for us, the Palace is both a symbol of Western history and a dream world with its own aesthetics."[33] This point of view on Versailles is also counter-Orientalist and was very influential on the visual culture, art, and psychology of the Japanese consumer.

From pop art to elite fashion

Pop art and street culture influenced the elite fashion designers, who started to co-operate with artists. Murakami Takashi created artworks as consumer products, thus checking the new boundaries between art and consumer culture.[34] He redesigned Louis Vuitton items with Multi-color monogram, the Cherry Blossom bag, and the Eye Love monogram, all inspired by the *Kawaii* style.

The legitimization that the popular cute style received via contemporary pop art even influenced back on the works of *avant-garde* designers such as Rei Kawakubo, who, at first, avoided the sweet or sexy look.[35] In 1995, Kawakubo launched the "Sweeter than Sweet" collection, which was pink, with fringes and small aprons. In winter 2002 she designed an entire line of fashion inspired by lingerie with a look of an *avant-garde* hooker. In spring–summer 2005, she put on a show that related between the beauty and the power of a ballerina/bike-rider, blurring between the delicate and the aggressive. She returned to the color pink in 2007 with pink clothes in kids' sizes.

In 2009, Rei Kawakubo cooperated with Murakami Takashi: she opened Magazine Alive, a concept shop in association with Japanese *Vogue* magazine. The first show in this new forum was titled Takashi Murakami Magical Princess, with Murakami's works shown alongside Kawakubo's clothes. Another influence on Murakami was a limited-edition Louis Vuitton series by Rei Kawakubo. Rei Kawakubo also supports Tao Kurihara and Fumito Ganryu, who are influenced by street culture and work under the Comme Des Garçons line. Similarly, Naoki Takizawa, who designed clothes for Issey Miyake, co-operated with artist Aya Takano, a member of Murakami Takashi's Kaikai Kiki studio. In addition, there are many independent fashion designers, including Akira Onozuke for the brand Zucca and Kunihiko Morinaga for the brand Anrealage, who are influenced by the "Cool Japan" style.

Vogue magazine in Japan acknowledged the connection between Japan's elite fashion and street fashion and published an issue called "Manga Takes the Catwalk," which focused on the connection between Manga and clothing. This issue presented different Manga-style categories (My Manga Sweetheart, Power Play, Sexy Planet, and School-Girl Chic) and showed how to match different clothes to your preferred Manga style, not as a cosplay but as a look that delivers different feminine message of each Manga. One of the categories was dedicated to the romantic style of the characters from Rose of Versailles, as interpreted through Chanel and Lanvin clothes.

Another side of Japanese design that was influenced by art combined the cute with scary and beautiful with ugly. Designer Jun Takahashi's fashion company *Undercover* adopts this style, with clothes that have a strange-but-beautiful aura. He described his first collection, which launched in 2002 entitled Scab, as cute but scary, beautiful but ugly.

Conclusion

This chapter has presented Japanese fashion as an expression of various ideologies that flourished in Japan, as well as the changes that transpired within the multi-hued postmodern-era society. This unique fashion was regarded as a "Japanese fashion." However, despite the fact that the designers worked in Japan and designed for a Japanese target market, they were individual creators. In interviews, they repeatedly say that they view themselves as international, claiming that viewing their work as deriving from Japanese tradition is actually a foreign viewpoint that limits the understanding of their work.[36]

The examples presented in this chapter—the dialog of Mishima with Pierre Cardin, the Comme des Garçons brand influenced by French deconstructionist philosophy, the nationwide obsession with the Rococo and the *Kawaii*—show that the French influence was much more noticeable than the influence of traditional Japanese fashion. Any attempt to force Japanese fashion into a national framework and to present it as an expression of Japanese ideology is a Western Orientalist perspective. These urban styles were closer to the styles of other large cities throughout the industrial world than it was to that of other areas in Japan. Fredric Jameson claims that the configurational characteristics of postmodernism express a more profound logic of the late capitalist social system. These styles are not connected to aesthetic traditions or traditional Japanese ideology, but rather respond to social, economic, and technological changes, giving expression to globalization and establishing a new discourse regarding the bubble economic era. Nevertheless, even if these styles were influenced by global trends, they developed in Japan and differed from anything seen elsewhere at the time. We should see them as an interpretation of the international values to the Japanese language and culture. In other words, the fashion definitely has Japanese flavors, but not such that are connected to the Orientalist image of the "Japanese Culture,"—rather to the new socio-economic paradigm that expresses the triumph of the consumer culture as a central ideology of the postmodern *zeitgeist* in Japan. Japanese fashion is not just a final product—it is also part of a social process. This fashion created and aroused social, economic, and aesthetic forces that together dictated new values, initiated a new social paradigm, and raised various concepts femininity. In other words, it created a new social ideology, generating a new visual culture that helped to establish Japan's new identity between "cool" and "*avant-garde*" in the postmodern era.

Notes

1   Bushido values originated from the Samurai moral code and stressed frugality, loyalty, martial arts mastery, and honor until death.

2   *Kurisutaru zoku* were branded a social group after the success of the novel *Nantonaku Kurisutaru* (Somewhat Crystal). This group name was referring to Japanese yuppies who were swept up in the economic boom of the 1980s in Japan and became conscious of their image and brand names.

3   Judith Williamson, *Decoding Advertisements*, New York: Marion Boyars, 1978, pp. 45–50.

4   Marita Sturken and Lisa Cartwright, *Practices of Looking: An Introduction to Visual Culture*, Oxford: Oxford University Press, 2001, pp. 227–8.

5   Jean Baudrillard, *For a Critique of the Political Economy of the Sign*, St Louis: Telos Press, 1981, p. 78; Jean Baudrillard, *The System of Objects*, London and New York: Verso, 1996; Jean Baudrillard, *Consumer Society: Myths and Structures*, London: Sage, 2004.

6   Hiroshi Kashiwagi, "Post War History in Advertising Design," in *Advertising History 1950–1990* (exhibition catalogue), Tokyo: East Japan Railway Culture Foundation (Pub.), 1993, pp. 14–15.

7   Sturken and Cartwright, *Practices of Looking*, pp. 198–203.

8   Marilyn Ivy, "Critical Texts, Mass Artifacts: The Consumption of Knowledge in Postmodern Japan," in H. D. Harootunian and Masao Miyoshi eds, *Postmodernism and Japan*, Durham and London: Duke University Press, 1989, pp. 40–2.

9   Makoto Akabane and Saito Maki, "Du Materiel au Spirituel: Changement de Société au Japon et son Reflect dans la Publicité après L'effondrement de la Bulle Speculative," in Tching Kanehisa, *Société et Publicité Nipponnes*, Paris: Editions You-Feng, 2002, p. 3.

10 Patricia Mears, "Formalism and Revolution," in Valerie Steele, *Japan Fashion Now*, New Haven: Yale University Press, 2010, pp. 152–5.

11 Kyōich Tsuzuki, *Kidaore Hōjōki: Happy Victims*, Kyoto: Seigensha, 2008.

12 Mears, "Formalism and Revolution," p. 158.

13 Kondo, *About Face: Performing Race in Fashion and Theater*, London: Routledge, 1997, p. 57.

14 On Rei Kawakubo: Fukai Akiki, Barbara Vinken, Susannah Frankel, and Hirofumi Kurino, *Future Beauty: 30 Years of Japanese Fashion*, London: Barbican Centre, 2010, pp. 161–81; Kawamura Yuiya, *The Japanese Revolution in Paris Fashion*, Oxford: Berg Press, 2004, pp. 125–51; Bonnie English, "Fashion as Art Postmodernist Japanese Fashion," in Louise Mitchell ed., *The Cutting Edge: Fashion from Japan*, Sydney: Museum of Applied Arts and Sciences, 2006, pp. 29–40; Mears, "Formalism and Revolution," pp. 141–208.

15 David Raizman, *History of Modern Design*, London: Laurence King Publishing, 2003, pp. 345–6.

16 Mears, "Formalism and Revolution," p. 171.

17 Ibid., p. 162.

18 Ibid. p. 181.

19 Ibid., p. 183.

20 Yael Taragan, "Altering the 'Basics': Basic Patterns and Basic Assumptions in Fashion," "Altering the 'Basics': Basic Patterns and Basic Assumptions in Fashion," *Protocolim*, online magazine of the department of history and theory, Bezalel, 16— Modes of Creation: Jewelry and Fashion (April 2010).

21 Mears, "Formalism and Revolution," p. 161.

22   Ibid., p. 163.

23   Kondo, *About Face*, p. 67.

24   The Anime *The Rose of Versailles* had 40 episodes. It ran on Japanese TV from October 1979 to September 1980.

25   *Inochi arukagiri aishite* was released in 1987.

26   *Lady Oscar* is a French–Japanese co-production film, written and directed by Jacques Demy in 1979, and shot in France.

27   Susan J. Napier, "Vampires, Psychic Girls, Flying Women and Sailor Scouts," in Dolores Martinez ed., *The Worlds of Japanese Popular Culture: Gender, Shifting Boundaries and Global Culture*, Cambridge: Cambridge University Press, 1998, p. 107.

28   Sharon Kinsella, "Cuties in Japan," in Brian Moeran and Lise Scov eds., *Women, Media and Consumption in Japan,* Honolulu: Curzon and Hawaii University Press, 1995, pp. 220–1.

29   Ibid.

30   Midori Matsui Midori, "Beyond the Pleasure Room to a Chaotic Street," in Murakami Takashi ed., *Little Boy: The Arts of Japan's Exploding Subculture*, New Haven: Japan Society at Yale University Publishing, 2005, pp. 208–12.

31   Karen Kelsky, *Women on the Verge: Japanese Women*, *Western Dreams*, Durham: Duke University Press, 2001, p. 85; Brian Moeran, "Homo Harmonicus and the Yenjoy Girls: Production and Consumption of Japanese Myths," in *Encounter*, London, 72, 5 (1989), pp. 19–24.

32   Valerie Steele, "Is Japan Still the Future?" in Valerie Steele, *Japan Fashion Now*, New Haven: Yale University Press, 2010, pp. 96–7.

33   Thierry Taittinger, *Murakami Versaille*, Ivry-sur-Seine: Beaux Arts Editions + TTM editions, 2010, p. 7.

34   Scott Rothkopf, "Takashi Murakami: Company Man," in Paul Schimmel ed., *Murakami*, New York: Rizzoli International, 2007, pp. 146–53.

35   Steele, "Is Japan Still the Future?" p. 81.

36   Mears, Patricia, "Formalism and Revolution," p. 144; Kondo, Dorinne, *About Face*, pp. 68–9; Lise Skov, "Fashion trends, Japonisme and postmodernism, or 'What is so Japanese about *Comme des Garçons*?'," *Theory, Culture and Society*, 13 (1996): 129–51.

Bibliography

Akabane, Makoto and Maki, Saito, "Du Matériel au spirituel: changement de société au Japon et son reflet dans la publicité après l'effondrement de la bulle spéculative," in Tching Kanehisa, *Société et Publicité Nipponnes*, Paris: Editions You-Feng, 2002.

Baudrillard, Jean, *Consumer Society: Myths and Structures*, London: Sage, 2004 (1970).

—*For a Critique of the Political Economy of the Sign* (trans. with introduction by Charles Levin), St. Louis: Telos Press, 1981.

—*The System of Objects*, J. Benedict (trans.), London and New York: Verso, 1996 (1968).

English, Bonnie, "Fashion as Art Postmodernist Japanese Fashion," in Louise Mitchell ed., *The Cutting Edge: Fashion from Japan*, Sydney: Museum of Applied Arts and Sciences, 2006.

Fukai Akiki, Barbara Vinken, Susannah Frankel, and Hirofumi Kurino, *Future Beauty: 30 Years of Japanese Fashion*, London: Barbican Centre, 2010.

Ivy, Marilyn, "Critical Texts, Mass Artifacts: The Consumption of Knowledge in Postmodern Japan," in H. D. Harootunian and Masao Miyoshi eds, *Postmodernism and Japan*, Durham and London: Duke University Press, 1989.

Kashiwagi, Hiroshi, "Post War History in Advertising Design," in *Advertising History 1950–1990* (exhibition catalogue), Tokyo: East Japan Railway Culture Foundation (Pub.), 1993.

Kawamura Yuiya, *The Japanese Revolution in Paris Fashion*, Oxford: Berg Press, 2004.

Kelsky, Karen, *Women on the Verge: Japanese Women*, *Western Dreams*, Durham: Duke University Press, 2001.

Kinsella, Sharon, "Cuties in Japan," in Brian Moeran and Lise Scov eds., *Women, Media and Consumption in Japan*, Honolulu: Curzon and Hawaii University Press, 1995.

Kondo, Dorinne, *About Face: Performing Race in Fashion and Theater*, London: Routledge, 1997.

Kunimoto, Namiko, "Tanaka Atsuko's Electric Dress and the Circuits of Subjectivity," *The Art Bulletin*, XCV, 3 (September 2013), pp. 465–83.

Mears, Patricia, "Formalism and Revolution," in Valerie Steele, *Japan Fashion Now*, New Haven: Yale University Press, 2010.

Midori, Matsui, "Beyond the Pleasure Room to a Chaotic Street," in Murakami Takashi ed., *Little Boy: The Arts of Japan's Exploding Subculture*, New Haven: Japan Society at Yale University Publishing, 2005.

Moeran, Brian, "Homo harmonicus and the Yenjoy girls: production and consumption of Japanese myths," *Encounter*, 72, 5 (1989).

Napier, Susan J., "Vampires, Psychic Girls, Flying Women and Sailor Scouts," in Dolores Martinez ed., *The Worlds of Japanese Popular Culture: Gender, Shifting Boundaries and Global Culture*, Cambridge: Cambridge University Press, 1998.

Raizman, David, *History of Modern Design*, London: Laurence King, 2003.

Rothkopf, Scott, "Takashi Murakami: Company Man," in Paul Schimmel ed., *Murakami*, New York: Rizzoli, 2007.

Shamoon, Deborah, "Revolutionary Romance: The Rose of Versailles and the Transformation of Shōjo Manga," in Frenchy Lunning, *Mechademia 2: Networks of Desire*, Minneapolis: University of Minnesota Press, 2007.

Skov, Lise, "Fashion Trends, Japonisme and Postmodernism, or 'What is so Japanese about *Comme des Garçons*?'," *Theory, Culture and Society*, 13, 3 (1996).

Steele, Valerie, "Is Japan Still the Future?" in Valerie Steele, *Japan Fashion Now*, New Haven: Yale University Press, 2010.

Sturken, Marita and Lisa Cartwright, *Practices of Looking: An Introduction to Visual Culture*, Oxford: Oxford University Press, 2001.

Taittinger, Thierry, *Murakami Versaille*, Ivry-sur-Seine: Beaux Arts Editions, TTM editions, 2010.

Taragan, Yael, "Altering the 'Basics': Basic Patterns and Basic Assumptions in Fashion," *Protocolim*, online magazine of the department of history and theory, Bezalel, 16— Modes of Creation: Jewelry and Fashion (April 2010).

Tsuzuki, Kyōich, *Kidaore Hōjōki: Happy Victims*, Kyoto: Seigensha, 2008.

Williamson, Judith, *Decoding Advertisements*, New York: Marion Boyars, 1978.

8

MILITARY DRESS AS AN IDEOLOGICAL MARKER IN ROMAN PALESTINE

GUY D. STIEBEL

In recent decades military dress has become a significant source of information in the study of the identity of institutionalized martial bodies such as the Roman army and the opposing local militias within the boundaries of the Empire. It has proven to be a valuable medium that reflects social aspects of soldiership and not least of the societies in which the military bodies operated.[1]

Military dress, in its wider sense, comprises of martial attire and equipment. Undeniably, the design of military equipment is first and foremost functional, offensive weapons were firstly designed to inflict damage whereas the design of defensive equipment was a "struggle" between two ends: the requirement to provide maximum protection whilst still allowing an efficient functioning. Yet, from a very early age it was given ornamental attention, which followed personal tastes and stylistic trends as well as status-related and symbolic meanings.[2] The present chapter wishes to dwell upon the use of military dress as an ideological messenger and marker.

In the entry for the word "ideology" in the *Oxford English Dictionary* one reads: "a system of ideas and ideals, especially one which forms the basis of economic or political theory and policy" and thereafter "the set of beliefs characteristic of a social group or individual." Turning to military dress, the attire and most notably the equipment clearly defined soldiers. In the words of the Mishnah: weapons were ornaments to men (Shabbat 6.4). Defining the soldier as an individual and as a member of a community, the symbolic functions of weapons appear to emphasize further the important place military life had among the peoples in which these military societies existed and operated. Following the presentation of the military dress of both rivalling sides—Roman and Judean—we will unveil and discuss a wide spectrum of ideological expressions and practices that took place during the early Roman period (63BCE–CE135) in Palestine.

What did they look like?

Only a few instances from the Roman Empire actually provide scholars with near-complete assemblages of panoplies, and most rare of all are the remains that derived directly from conflict lands. In addition to the celebrated navy soldier from CE79 Herculaneum,[3] one may mention the soldier from the well in Velsen (NL).[4] In the East one such very informative example is reported from Tower 19 countermine, Dura-Europos.[5] To these very few examples I add the remains of L. Magus from Gamala.[6] In light of this circumstance, the diverse images of the warriors have to be constructed from the patchy archaeological evidence. One of the challenges of artefactual studies is to draw beyond the endless technical lists of types in an attempt to reconstruct the actual image of the fighting parties. The recent decade has witnessed the abandonment of the quest for a globalized Roman military appearance in favor of what Hingley has called the *fragmentation of identities*.[7] The following paragraphs present narrated reconstructed images of the varied foot soldier warriors that served in Roman Palestine. Given the limited scope of the chapter, I have chosen to focus upon the Roman legionaries and the Jewish militia soldiers alone, most notably due to considerations of coherence and common basis for discussion, despite the well-established fact that a large variety of Roman soldiers, units, and forces was evidently present in Judea.[8]

The Roman Legionaries in Palestine

Many scholars have discussed the question of whether there was "legionary" equipment.[9] In the Roman East we have had only dependable data regarding legionary equipment from Dura-Europos, so far.[10] As far as early Roman Judea is concerned, Josephus provides a first-hand testimony in which he describes the equipment of the legionaries as follows:

> the infantry are armed with cuirass and helmet and carry a sword on either side; that on the left is far the longer of the two, the dagger on the right being no longer than a span ... the regiments of the line have a javelin and oblong buckler (*BJ* 3.94–5).

The dramatic discovery of Roman panoply at Gamala enables us to reconstruct the image of one legionary in CE67 almost to its full extent. Wearing a tinned

Haguenau (Coolus) type helmet, L. Magus was clad in *"lorica segmentata"* armour, the plates of which were laced to each other through riveted tie-loops, and which featured a sliding rivet mechanism upon its backplate. His right hand was seemingly protected by a tinned *manica*. The soldier's *gladius* was sheathed in a copper-alloy scabbard that was decorated by an eagle emblem, executed in a somewhat provincial way, with palmette designs, and this terminated in a silver-plated tip. In addition he carried a *pugio* and his belt had mounts with a central rosette decoration. The soldier was further furnished with a *pilum* and a *scutum* that was reinforced by flat iron bars and framed by U-binding. Two *tabulae ansatae* that flanked the *umbo* bore his name and that of his officers. He wore typical nailed *caligae*. The data from Masada provides further details. The legionaries wore *tunicae albae*, as well as red tunics and snuggled in kilted *sagi*. The sword was set in a red tooled leather scabbard that hung from copper-alloy frogs. The frogs were suspended from a leather belt that was decorated by silver-plated mounts. The dagger was suspended from elaborate D-shaped loops. The *scutum* that had integral leather facings was red in color; the facing was stretched upon a glue-soaked layer of textile. Others may have used wickerwork shields, although these more commonly furnished native warriors.[11]

The imaginary legionary of the second century CE, or the Second Revolt period, wore a Weisenau-type helmet and dressed in stiffer scale armor, with each of its scales fastened to three others. The armor had a collar or a shoulder-piece that protected his upper torso. Shin-guards of iron greaves protected the legs of the soldier. His sword was set in a u-guttering scabbard and he held either a tanged or a socketed *pila*.

We possess little data that may be linked with an officer or high ranking position. The earlier figure would have carried a *vitis* or a cane/reed, while the clothes or belt of the latter would have been decorated by a "benefiziarierlanzen" badge. Josephus further describes the picked infantry that formed the general's guards, noting them to "carry a lance (*hasta*) and round shield (*parma*)" (*BJ* 3.9). The depiction of these elite troops may be gleaned from the Flavian relief of Plazzo della Cancelleria and the Great Trajanic Frieze.[12] The use of muscle armor by high-ranking officers is further attested.[13]

Jewish militia

The poorly equipped David and the fundamental distinction between his wooden staff and stones compared to the much more advanced panoply of his opponent Goliath appear to serve us well in the attempt to describe the condition that prevailed in Palestine on the eve of the outbreak of the First Revolt. The rebels, who were organized in militias, were not expected to exhibit any standardization in their equipment, a picture that is clearly reflected from the archaeological repertoire, although varied trends and typical designs are identifiable. Their panoplies may be described as combinations of peasants' equipment, looted and old weapons, as well as locally manufactured and ethnic weapons. According to Philo, the Essenes manifested a marked anti-war attitude, one of the expressions of which was the absence of weapon manufacturers. This indicates that craftsmen were expected to be found elsewhere in Palestine: "as no one, in short, attending to any employment whatever connected with war, or even to any of those occupations even in peace which are easily perverted to wicked purposes" (Philo, *Every Good Man is Free*, 12.78).

The Jewish warrior would commonly fall under the category of κούφους (light-armed) (*BJ* 2.543). Despite Roman pressure, it appears that Jewish men used to carry swords, or at least possessed edged weapons even under Roman rule (Mt. 26.47, 55; Mk 14.43, 48; Lk. 22.35–8, 52), possibly as gender and status indicators. The most celebrated edged arm in Judea was the *sica*, a local carved dagger [Fig. 1], which gave a rebel group its name—*Sicarii*. The latter had a linen head-band (unpublished examples are known from Masada), and he dressed

Figure 8.1   Sica and sheath, En Gedi (Courtesy of Gideon Hadas; Photo by Guy Stiebel; after Stiebel 2007, Vol. 3, Pl. I.8:2).

in a short-sleeved tunic, across which he wore a leather belt, from which was suspended the sheathed *sica*. The rebels of the Second Revolt carried clasp knives, set in decorated leather scabbards, the popularity of which may hint that they served as a status symbol, indicating them as men or warriors, similarly to the ornate curved knives that are carried by Near Eastern men, most notably in Yemen (*jambiyas*). Our imaginary rebel of the First Revolt carried a solid iron-shafted weapon, with a flat leaf head.[14] Some of his comrades carried old weapons (*BJ* 2.576), like *gladii Hispaniensis*.

Unlike Roman soldiers, most rebels were not regularly armored. In addition, there is no evidence for Jewish rebel use of helmets during the two revolts. Nonetheless, one should not rule out the possibility of the use of looted Roman headgear. An additional explanation may have to do with the dangers of the typical heat.[15]

The finds from the Second Revolt allow me to illustrate the images of two types of Jewish rebels: a heavy warrior and a light warrior. The first is depicted after the incised warrior from Kh. as Salantah.[16] He held with both his hands a long, heavy spear and protected himself using a round shield. In addition, the rabbinical literature mentions the employment of wickerwork bucklers, which appear to have been common in the East. The light warrior was equipped by a backed dagger and the above noted clasp knives that were set in tooled leather sheaths. He held light throwing javelins with a typical collared head, which were seemingly butt-less. In addition, the rebels held improvised shafted weapons like the "field modification" from the Figs Caves that was composed from a re-used Roman catapult head.[17]

The status factor

Carrying weapons clothed in military dress defined soldiers from the civil population.[18] Weapons have clearly been a key defining feature of individual rebels and militia groups; as aforesaid, one Jewish rebel party in Judea was named after its characteristic weapon—the *Sicarii* [Fig. 1]. The very act of carrying arms identified the bearers as warriors not only in the eyes of the local civilian population, but in the eyes of the Roman authorities and as such bore hazardous implications. The fate of Jewish captives at Jerusalem was very much related to their status: "since the soldiers were now growing weary of slaughter, though numerous survivors still came to light, Caesar issued orders to kill only those who were found in arms and offered resistance, and to make prisoners of the rest" (*BJ* 6.414). Primarily, weapons reflected the status of their bearer, hence the pride of the individual Roman soldier in his arms that is expressed by his fondness for gleaming appearance.[19] In addition to being a manifestation of personal taste and a reinforcement of the identity felt by the individual soldier, the shiny appearance of equipment was further intended to intimidate the enemy, a lavish example being the Roman exercise of the *hippika gymnasia*.

It appears that Roman military equipment distinguished units (most notably the nations), and at times identified ranks. A prominent example is the *vitis*, which was carried by centurions and served as disciplinary tool as well as a status symbol. This was true also in the eyes of the local Jewish population, which associated the rank *ba'al zmorah* (lit. the owner of the *vitis*), with harsh and vicious behavior. Some of the fittings were clear badges of office, like the *beneficarius* badge from Jerusalem.[20] In the absence of a means of fastening it seems that these spear-models were pinned on to the soldier's belt or to his garment. These badges were meant to be a visual indicator of the position and authority of the bearer. It should be noted that the growing number of Eastern examples appears to undermine the suggestions that these badges were typical of Upper Germany alone and that each province had its own distinguishing markers,[21] pointing rather at a more homogenous symbolic grammar that has been used on widespread scale at least for this specific official.

The sovereignty factor

Weapons commonly appeared in official propaganda, being a symbol that represented the sovereignty of the ruler and the state. The shield, for example, had an important place in the coinage of late Hellenistic and early Roman Palestine. What has solely been identified as a star and tiara, the attribute on the coins of Alexander Jannaeus,[22] is in fact an emblem of the Macedonian shield.[23] The helmets on Herod's and his heirs' coins are similarly interpreted as a symbol of sovereignty.[24] Motifs that reflect Roman governmental propaganda often appeared on weapons.[25] The promotion of the "cult of personality" as part of the Roman imperial propaganda was very much on the agenda of Augustus. His initiation brought about the manifestation of politico-religious symbols, like the Capricorn, on the equipment of Western legions.[26] This, however, was not the case in early Roman Judea. Only during the First Revolt does one find these motifs in the decorative repertoire. It seems that geopolitical circumstances dictated a different grammar of motifs. This trend presumably skipped Judea in the days of Augustus, owing to the fact that during most of his reign the client kingdom was not part of the Empire, in addition to the dominance of Herod that seemingly prevented its introduction. Furthermore, the expression of this propaganda was more common among citizen forces, which were not present in Judea until the First Revolt.

One of the expressions of triumph by victorious rulers that did diffuse into Judea, despite religious reservations, was the presentation of spoils of arms in the temples—a well-rooted tradition in the Classical world. Weapons taken as booty were presented on the walls of the Temple and theatre in Jerusalem (*AJ* 15.402, 272, 276).

The spiritual factor

The Romans regarded themselves as the most spiritual nation in the ancient world, a fact that in their eyes granted them the assistance and protection of the divine. Interestingly, the notion that Roman rule was partly the result of divine intervention or decree was similarly prevalent among the occupied nations (*BJ* 1.390, 2.390, 3.293). The Roman pantheon of gods and in particular the military pantheon were much enriched from the multinational origin of its soldiers. Soldiers addressed the gods to receive their goodness, hospitality, to ensure good health, help, protection, and preservation from harm in the hostile environment of the battlefield.[27] It is not surprising to find that religion has been, and still is, interwoven in all the aspects involved in the act of war, being manifest in many different spheres. The ways war is experienced by the state, the army as a community, the individual commander or, no less important, by the individual low-ranked soldier, differ dramatically. Therefore, the way weapons were perceived and used, in the spiritual sense, appears to shed light upon the nations, communities and individuals concerned and their ideologies.

Weapons were often symbolically used in state ceremonies, which played an important part in the formation and maintenance of the identity of these societies.[28] The ceremonial manifestations that occurred previous to, during and following the fighting made an intensive use of weapons, aspects of which are hereby discussed. While at the state level, weapons functioned as symbols of sovereignty and formed an important part in imperial propaganda that was designed to strengthen its coherence, among the comrades in the military community *militaria* appears to define the identity of soldiers and manifest the hierarchy of this closed society. Moreover, as part of their *Kriegethik* (military ethic), the Romans regarded weapons as an entity with virtues that could be violated by improper behavior. The individual soldiers used their equipment as a platform for the manifestation of symbols; the decoration and the shaping of varied fittings in the image of sacred motifs was aimed at ensuring protection and successful operation in battle. In not a few instances the stylistic choice reflects the religious affiliations of the soldiers and manifested imperial propaganda. Inscribed leaden slingshots were often accompanied by religious symbols, such as the *fulmen* or trident, and contemptuous icons, like the phallus. Painted Roman shields similarly manifested values of unity, and the symbols adorning them were commonly drawn from religious themes, like winged *fulmen*.[29] In addition, weapons were often used as actual "messengers" in psychological warfare. The celebrated example is the inscribed leaden slingshots that bore both supportive and blasphemous slogans (Stiebel 1997).[30]

The ritual factor

Weapons provide power. Yet, in the mental atmosphere of the ancient world, it was not harmful to recruit the assistance of the gods through weapons. The design of some fittings as well as elements that decorated *militaria* seems to have been carefully chosen in order to ensure the alliance of the gods with the right side. These motifs coupled with the far better studied epigraphic evidence hint at the social and religious background of part of the Roman forces operating in Palestine.

As in the West, harness fittings are found to exhibit a strong affinity with viticulture, while the combination of the solar and lunar motifs in lunate pendants (*lunulae*) was also favored by Roman cavalrymen. Both symbols were intended to protect the horseman and his mount.[31] The same protective function was assigned to phallic elements. Phallic pendants were used to decorate equine harnesses, while a complete wooden phallus is reported from siege-camp F at Masada [Fig. 8.2]. It is interesting to note the marked differentiation in the nature of the populations that used these pendants between the civil and military communities. Whereas among civilians the *lunula* and the phallus were nearly confined to women and children, among the Roman army these motifs were very popular as harness ornamentations during the early principate and later.

The Roman pantheon is further represented by Isis and Harpocrates that appear on two amulets from Masada.[32] These rare objects testify to the popularity of the Eastern and particularly the Egyptian goddess among soldiers. Young Eros appears on the chalcedony *phalerae* that seemingly served as harness fittings.[33] The popularity of Jupiter is attested by the *fulmen* known on slingshots and shields. One the chief symbols of the legion and Rome has been the eagle. Its image is seen on several first-century *gladii* scabbard chapes from Gamala.[34]

On the other hand, Jewish religion regarded weapons as tools of destruction. It was thus forbidden to enter the Temple in Jerusalem, as well as religious schools, armed (*Babylonian Talmud*, *Sanhedrin* 82$_{a-b}$). This *raison d'être* stood behind the ban over the use of iron for the shaping of the large stone altar in the Temple and fighting during the Sabbath, a thoroughly discussed theme. As a society that at least during the early Roman period still perceived itself as being under occupation, it was necessary to provide an explanation for the continuous Roman success and the repeated Jewish failures (*BJ* 5.399). Josephus justified this state of affairs by divine intervention (ibid., 1.390, 2.390, 3.293).

Conclusions

The study of the military dress and fittings from Palestine can be seen as a chronicle of a struggle, which reflects a bitter ideological conflict between the

Figure 8.2   Wooden phallus pendant, Camp F at Masada (Courtesy of Benjamin Arubas and Haim Goldfus, Photo by Guy Stiebel; after Stiebel 2007, Vol. 3, Pl. III.20E:1).

societies involved. The period under discussion included turbulent political upheavals, which apparently formed some of the most dramatic events that shaped the futures of this region and the Jewish nation to this day. In just under 200 years, the political status of Judea gradually shifted from an independent kingdom to a client monarchy, which was later annexed into the Roman Empire. Following several decades of unrest it experienced two major revolts, finally deteriorating to the unprecedented status of identity elimination, when the name of the province was changed, to *Syria Palestina*. During this period, the country experienced the destruction of its traditional capital while its religious and civil ruling classes lost their power and authority. The destruction of the Temple had tremendous consequences, undermining national links both to land and place (as well as to the heavens). This shift, which was at the same time a shift of state of mind, necessitated the formation of a new ideology and social organization in order to ensure continuity of national existence. This succeeded, as seven decades after the suppression of the First Revolt, the fire of nationalistic aspirations was still burning. Indeed, it seems to me that the gradual nature of these processes and the time these changes lasted, rather than a single swift conquest, allowed the endurance and development of anti-Roman tendencies.

In the social landscape of the Roman Empire, the Jewish people formed a society with unique, even exotic, national characteristics. Jews were prohibited to carry weapons on the day of Sabbath (Mishnah, Shabbat 6.4, 11.8); hence in early periods they were known not to fight during that day even in the face of grave danger. This prohibition lies in the more fundamental debate that took place between Jewish Sages, concerning the significance of weapons. Most of the Sages regarded them as nothing but tools of destruction,[35] echoing an apparent moral and educational position. When entering a religious study-house it was customary for the warrior to remove the head of a shafted weapon and to put it in one's legging (*fascia*) (Palestinian Talmud, Sanhedrin 10 28d). Others, like Rabbi Eliezer, considered weapons as a man's jewelry (Mishnah, Shabbat 6.4). The latter notion stems from a more practical perception of daily life, clearly indicating the ordinariness of carrying weapons in Roman Palestine. Being monotheistic and holding strict idiosyncratic views Jews might have appeared in bystander's eyes as arrogantly secluded, regarding the world as "us and them."[36] They practiced dietary taboos, circumcision, and did not fight during the Sabbath. In practice, this social seclusion reduced many aspects of interaction between Jews and Romans.

By stating this, I am not suggesting that no cultural negotiations and interfaces were in existence. Adoptions of "Roman" designs and symbols are apparent in all fields of material culture and life by Jews in Roman Judea, like dress, leisure time, architecture, and, of course, military equipment. Nonetheless, the picture was far more complex, and none of this new consumer-like attitude, being blinded by the dazzling wealth of designs and possible new relations and opportunities provided by the contact with the Empire, represents a wish of the Jewish population to adopt Roman identity.[37] From a Roman perspective, it is clear that the exploitation and enslavement of marginal societies were very much on the Imperial agenda. Still, one must take into account that this was not an entirely asymmetrical relationship and that Roman conduct passed with no reaction from the native peoples. There are clear indications for the existence of an opposition, both active and passive. In the East, the political opposition that was manifested in internal unrest is exemplified by the frequency of banditry.[38] Of special interest are the subsurface manifestations, most of which are drawn from literary evidence. It is evident that in Judea there were inherent social restrictions on relations with the Romans. One of the clearest examples is the Jewish ban over selling not only weapons but any item that could have been used against them, like mounts. Although this act may well be interpreted as an ideological expression of opposition, the clear literary context of safety considerations indicates that the chief rationale had more to do with self-preservation of the native people than with resistance to contemporary Roman cultural domination.

The "unfriendly interface"[39] nonetheless took place between the *military* societies of these two peoples. The social environments in which Jewish warriors and the contemporary Roman soldiers operated were utterly different, functioning in totally different cognitive spheres. Despite the very diverse ethnic composition of the Roman army, its soldiers managed to form and maintain a surprisingly unified soldierly identity—a community of "fellow soldiers" (*commilitones*),[40] or "collective mentalities."[41] Military equipment and dress were elements that both distinguished and united soldiers, creating individual as well as unit identity-senses within the army and in the eyes of non-military people. In addition to the panoply *per se*, one may further mention soldierly dress items, badges, harness equipment, and the use of religious objects that manifested and materialized this communal sense. This standpoint appears to accord well with the conceptualization of the Roman soldier who invested much in a shiny and jingly appearance and regarded them as status symbols. This social bonding that formed an important factor in the consolidation of the Empire in peace time, also contributed much to the *esprit de corps* in war.[42]

Thus, in Roman Palestine, Roman military dress and fittings, as well as those of the Jewish warrior, were both identity markers. Moreover, they concretized their antithetic origins: the Roman military apparel was the perfect materialization of an imperialist ideology, while the look of the Judean warrior represented an exotic, nationalist ideology.

Notes

1   M. C. Bishop and J. C. N. Coulston, *Roman Military Equipment: From the Punic Wars to the Fall of Rome*, 2nd edn., Oxford: Oxbow, 2006, pp. 253–78.

2   Ibid., pp. 266–7.

3   R. Gore, "2000 Years of Silence: The Dead Do Tell Tales at Vesuvius," *National Geographic*, 165 (1984), pp. 557–613; S. Ortisi "Pompeji und Herculaneum—Soldaten in den Vesuvsdäten," *Archäologie der Schlachtfelder—Militaria aus Zerstörungshorizonten, Tagungsakten der 14*, ROMEC Konferenz Wien 2003, Carnuntum Jahrbuch, 2005, pp. 143–51.

4   J.-M. A. W. Morel and A. V. A. J. Bosman, "An Early Roman Burial in Velsen I," in C. van Driel-Murray ed., *Roman Military Equipment: The Sources of Evidence, Proceedings of the Fifth Roman Military Equipment Conference*, Oxford: British Archaeological Reports, International Series 476, 1989, pp. 167–91.

5   S. James, "The Deposition of Military Equipment During the Final Siege at

Dura-Europos, with Particular Regard to the Tower 19 Countermine," *Archäologie der Schlachtfelder—Militaria aus Zerstörungshorizonten, Tagungsakten der 14. ROMEC Konferenz Wien 2003, Carnuntum Jahrbuch*, 2005, pp. 189–206.

6   G. D. Stiebel, "'Dust to Dust, Ashes to Ashes': Military Equipment from Destruction Layers in Palestine," *Archäologie der Schlachtfelder: Militaria aus Zerstörungshorizonten, Tagungsakten der 14.* ROMEC Konferenz Wien 2003, Carnuntum Jahrbuch, 2005, pp. 99–108.

7   R. Hingley, *Globalizing Roman Culture, Unity, Diversity and Empire*, London and New York: Routledge, 2005, p. 91ff.

8   G. D. Stiebel, *"Armis et litteris*: The Military Equipment of Early Roman Palestine in Light of the Archaeological and Historical Sources," Ph.D. dissertation submitted and approved at University College London, University of London, 2007, pp. 211–23.

9   Bishop and Coulston, *Roman Military Equipment*, pp. 253–9, with references.

10 S. James, *The Arms and Armour and other Military Equipment, The Excavations at Dura-Europos Conducted by Yale University and the French Academy of Inscriptions and Letters 1928 to 1937, Final Report VII*, London: 2004, pp. 168–9.

11 Stiebel, *Armis et litteris*, pp. 77–9.

12 F. Magi, *I relievi flavi del Palazzo della Cancelleria*, Rome: 1945; A.-M. Leander Touati, *The Great Trajanic Frieze: The Study of a Monument and of the Mechanisms of Message Transmission in Roman Art*, Stockholm: Svenska Institute i Rom, 1987.

13 Stiebel, *Armis et litteris*, pp. 51–2.

14 Ibid., III.12/H.1.

15 James, *The Arms and Armour and other Military Equipment*, p. 102.

16 Stiebel, *Armis et litteris*, PL. V.32A: 2.

17 Ibid., V.21/H.1.

18 J. C. N. Coulston, "How to Arm a Roman Soldier," in M. Austin, J. Harries and C. Smith eds., *Modus Operandi: Essays in Honor of Geoffrey Rickman*, London: BICS supplementary, vol. 71, 1998, p. 184; James, *The Arms and Armour and other Military Equipment*, pp. 57ff., 246ff.).

19 Coulston, "How to Arm a Roman Soldier," p. 184.

20 Stiebel, *Armis et litteris*, Pls. VI.3: 3–4.

21 Oldenstein, J., "Zur Ausrüstung römischer Auxiliareinheiten: Studien zu Beschlägen und Zierat an der Ausrüstung der römischen Auxiliareinheiten des obergermanisch-raetischen Limesgebietes aus dem zweiten und dritten Jahrhundert n. Chr.," *BRGK* 57 (1976), pp. 49–284, Taf. 9–90.

22 Y. Meshorer, *A Treasury of Jewish Coins From the Persian Period to Bar-Kochba*, Jerusalem: Yad Ben-Zvi Press (2001) (in Hebrew).

23 G. G. D. Stiebel, "Power and Rule: Jerusalem Coins of Alexander Jannaeus," in D. Amit, G. D. Stiebel, and O. Peleg-Barakat eds, *New Studies in the Archaeology of Jerusalem and its Region, Vol. V*, Jerusalem: 2011 (in Hebrew), pp. 179–84 (in Hebrew).

24 Meshorer, *A Treasury of Jewish Coins*, pp. 61, 73–5.

25 M. Feugère, *Les armes des Romains, de la République à l'Antiquité tardive*, Paris: Errance Editions, 1993, pp. 260–26.

26 E. Künzl, "Politische Propoganda auf römischen Waffen der frühen Kaiserzeit," in M. Hofter, V. Lewandovski, and H. G. Martin eds, *Kaiser Augustus und die verlorene Republik, Ausstellungskat. Berlin 1988*, Mainz: 1988, pp. 541–5.

27 Le Bohec, Y., *The Imperial Roman Army*, London: Batsford, 1994, pp. 237–8.

28 R. Laurence, "The Destruction of Place in the Roman Imagination," in J. B. Wilkins ed., *Approaches to the Study of Ritual, Italy and the Ancient Mediterranean*, London: Accordia Research Centre, 1996, pp. 112–21; Y. Yadin, *The Scroll of the War of the Sons of Light Against the Sons of Darkness*, Oxford: Clarendon, 1962.

29 G. Stiebel, "Notes on M. Hershkovitz's Article in *Qadmoniot* 124 'A Carved Bone Plaque from Tel Dan'," *Qadmoniot*, 125 (2003): 56–7 (in Hebrew).

30 G. Stiebel, '"… You were the word of war" – A sling shot testimony from Israel', *Journal of Roman Military Equipment Studies* 8 (1997): 301–7.

31 M. C. Bishop, "Cavalry Equipment of the Roman Army in the First Century AD," in J. C. N. Coulston ed., *Military Equipment and the Identity of Roman Soldiers. Proceeding of the Fourth Roman Military Equipment Conference*, Oxford: British Archaeological Reports, International Series 394, 1988, pp. 107–8.

32 Stiebel, *Armis et litteris*, PL. III.19Z: 3–4.

33 Ibid.; G. D. Stiebel, "Chalcedony *phalera* from En-Gedi," in E. Stern ed., *En Gedi Excavations I, Final Report (1961–1965)*, Jerusalem: 2007, pp. 294–6.

34 Stiebel, *Armis et litteris*, PL. III.3AB: 1–2.

35 M. D. Herr, "The Problem of War on the Sabbath in the Second Temple and the Talmudic Periods," *Tarbiz*, 30 (1961), p. 356 and note 5.

36 J. P. V. D. Balsdon, *Romans & Aliens*, London: Duckworth, 1979, pp. 235–6; T. Rajak, "The Jewish Community and its Boundaries," in J. Lieu, J. North, and T. Rajak eds, *The Jews Among Pagans and Christians in the Roman Empire*, London and New York: Methuen, 1992, pp. 9–28.

37 P. Freeman, "'Romanisation' and Roman Material Culture," *JRA*, 6 (1993), pp. 438–45; for culture's consumption, R. Hingley, *Globalizing Roman Culture, Unity, Diversity and Empire*, London and New York: Routledge, 2005, p. 105 ff.

38 B. Isaac, *The Limits of Empire: The Roman Army in the East*, Oxford: Oxford University Press, 1992, ch. 2.

39 Adopted from David Nicolle's article title: "Medieval warfare: the unfriendly interface," *The Journal of Military History*, 63 (1999): 579–600.

40 S. James, "The Community of the Soldiers: A Major Identity and Centre of Power in the Roman Empire," in P. Baker, C. Forcey, S. Jundi, and R. Witcher eds, *TRAC 1998: Proceedings of the Eighth Annual Theoretical Roman Archaeology Conference, Leicester 1998*, Oxford: Oxbow, 1999, pp. 14–25.

41 Y. Le Bohec, *The Imperial Roman Army*, London: Batsford, 1994, pp. 235–6; R. MacMullen, "The Legion as society," *Historia*, 33 (1984), pp. 440–59.

42 A. K. Goldsworthy, *The Roman Army at War 100BC–AD200*, Oxford: Clarendon Press 1996, p. 252ff.

Abbreviations

AJ: Flavius Josephus, *Antiquitates Judaicae*, trans. R. Marcus and A. Wikgren, Cambridge: Loeb, 1933, 1963.
BJ: Flavius Josephus, *Bellum Judaicum*, trans. H. St. J. Thackeray, Cambridge: Loeb, 1927.

Bibliography

Balsdon, J. P. V. D., *Romans and Aliens*, London: Duckworth, 1979.
Bishop M. C., "Cavalry Equipment of the Roman Army in the First Century AD," in J. C. N. Coulston ed., *Military Equipment and the Identity of Roman Soldiers. Proceeding of the Fourth Roman Military Equipment Conference*, Oxford: British Archaeological Reports, International Series 394, 1988.
Bishop, M. C. and J. C. N. Coulston, *Roman Military Equipment: From the Punic Wars to the Fall of Rome*, 2nd edn., Oxford: Oxbow, 2006.
Coulston, J. C. N., "How to Arm a Roman Soldier," in M. Austin, J. Harries and C. Smith eds., *Modus Operandi: Essays in Honor of Geoffrey Rickman*, London: BICS supplementary, vol. 71, 1998.
Feugère, M., *Les armes des Romains, de la République à l'Antiquité tardive*, Paris: Errance Editions, 1993.
Freeman, P., "'Romanisation' and Roman material Culture," *JRA*, 6 (1993): 438–45.
Goldsworthy, A. K., *The Roman Army at War 100BC–AD200*, Oxford: Clarendon Press 1996.
Gore, R., "2000 years of silence: the dead do tell tales at Vesuvius," *National Geographic*, 165 (1984): 557–613.
Herr, M. D., "The problem of war on the Sabbath in the second temple and the Talmudic periods," *Tarbiz*, 30 (1961): pp. 242–56, 336–41 (in Hebrew).
Hingley, R., *Globalizing Roman Culture, Unity, Diversity and Empire*, London and New York: Routledge, 2005.
Isaac, B., *The Limits of Empire: The Roman Army in the East*, Oxford: Oxford University Press, 1992.
James, S., "The Community of the Soldiers: A Major Identity and Centre of Power in the Roman Empire," in P. Baker, C. Forcey, S. Jundi, and R. Witcher eds, *TRAC 1998: Proceedings of the Eighth Annual Theoretical Roman Archaeology Conference, Leicester 1998*, Oxford: Oxbow, 1999.
James, S., "The Deposition of Military Equipment During the Final Siege at Dura-Europos, with Particular Regard to the Tower 19 Countermine," *Archäologie der Schlachtfelder—Militaria aus Zerstörungshorizonten, Tagungsakten der 14. ROMEC Konferenz Wien 2003, Carnuntum Jahrbuch*, 2005.
—*The Arms and Armour and other Military Equipment, The Excavations at Dura-Europos Conducted by Yale University and the French Academy of Inscriptions and Letters 1928 to 1937, Final Report VII*, London: 2004.
Künzl, E., "Politische Propaganda auf römischen Waffen der frühen Kaiserzeit," in M. Hofter, V. Lewandovski, and H. G. Martin eds, *Kaiser Augustus und die verlorene Republik, Ausstellungskat. Berlin 1988*, Mainz: 1988, pp. 541–5.
Laurence, R., "The Destruction of Place in the Roman Imagination," in J. B. Wilkins ed.,

Approaches to the Study of Ritual, Italy and the Ancient Mediterranean, London: Accordia Research Centre, 1996.

Le Bohec, Y., *The Imperial Roman Army*, London: Batsford, 1994.

Leander Touati, A.-M., *The Great Trajanic Frieze: The Study of a Monument and of the Mechanisms of Message Transmission in Roman Art*, Stockholm: Svenska Institute i Rom, 1987.

MacMullen, R., "The Legion as society," *Historia*, 33 (1984), pp. 440–59.

Magi, F., *I rilievi flavi del Palazzo della Cancelleria*, Rome: Bardi Editore, 1945.

Meshorer, Y., *A Treasury of Jewish Coins From the Persian Period to Bar-Kochba*, Jerusalem: Yad Ben-Zvi Press (2001) (in Hebrew).

Morel, J.-M. A. W. and A. V. A. J. Bosman, "An Early Roman Burial in Velsen I," in C. van Driel-Murray ed., *Roman Military Equipment: The Sources of Evidence, Proceedings of the Fifth Roman Military Equipment Conference*, Oxford: British Archaeological Reports, International Series 476, 1989.

Nicolle, David, "Medieval warfare: the unfriendly interface," *The Journal of Military History*, 63 (1999): 579–600.

Oldenstein, J., "Zur Ausrüstung römischer Auxiliareinheiten: Studien zu Beschlägen und Zierat an der Ausrüstung der römischen Auxiliareinheiten des obergermanisch-raetischen Limesgebietes aus dem zweiten und dritten Jahrhundert n. Chr.," *BRGK* 57 (1976), pp. 49–284, Taf. 9–90.

Ortisi, S., "Pompeji und Herculaneum—Soldaten in den Vesuvsdäten," *Archäologie der Schlachtfelder—Militaria aus Zerstörungshorizonten, Tagungsakten der 14*, ROMEC Konferenz Wien 2003, Carnuntum Jahrbuch, 2005.

Rajak, T., "The Jewish Community and its Boundaries," in J. Lieu, J. North, and T. Rajak eds, *The Jews Among Pagans and Christians in the Roman Empire*, London and New York: Methuen, 1992.

Stiebel, G. D., "'... You were the word of war' – A sling shot testimony from Israel," in M. Feugère ed. L'Équipment Militaire et L'Armement de la République (Ive-Ier s. avant J.-C.), *Journal of Roman Military Equipment Studies*, 8 (1997), pp. 301–7.

—"Notes on M. Hershkovitz's Article in *Qadmoniot* 124 'A Carved Bone Plaque from Tel Dan'," *Qadmoniot*, 125 (2003): 56–7 (in Hebrew).

—"'Dust to Dust, Ashes to Ashes': Military Equipment from Destruction Layers in Palestine," *Archäologie der Schlachtfelder: Militaria aus Zerstörungshorizonten, Tagungsakten der 14. ROMEC Konferenz Wien 2003*, Carnuntum Jahrbuch, 2005.

—"*Armis et litteris*: The Military Equipment of Early Roman Palestine in Light of the Archaeological and Historical Sources," Ph.D. dissertation submitted and approved at University College London, University of London, 2007.

—"Chalcedony *phalera* from En-Gedi," in E. Stern ed., *En Gedi Excavations I, Final Report (1961–1965)*, Jerusalem: 2007.

—"Power and Rule: Jerusalem Coins of Alexander Jannaeus," in D. Amit, G. D. Stiebel, and and O. Peleg-Barakat eds, *New Studies in the Archaeology of Jerusalem and its Region, Vol. V*, Jerusalem: 2011 (in Hebrew).

Yadin, Y., *The Scroll of the War of the Sons of Light Against the Sons of Darkness*, Oxford: Clarendon, 1962.

PART FOUR
POLITICS

9
FASHION AND FEMINISM

SHOSHANA-ROSE MARZEL AND HENRIETTE DAHAN-KALEV

Fashion has often been associated with women's obedience to codes of dressing that aimed at their objectification and rendering them sexual objects for men. Therefore, feminist and gender critiques study fashion and dress as oppressing patriarchal tools. However, clothing has also been part of feminist combat for more than 200 years. In this chapter we wish to shed light on the ways in which feminist movements have used clothing in order to promote their agendas over the last two centuries.

Our working hypothesis is that the issue of dress in the feminist movement has been instrumental, as it has in other ideological movements. However, within feminist movements, contrary to others, dress forms changed over time. They began with the female demand to wear pants during the French Revolution and continue today with the contemporary struggle over the feminine Islamic dress in Europe. Thus, in the feminist perspective, freedom and civil rights equal the right to wear whatever a woman wants. Moreover, clothes in the feminist struggle frequently contain an important symbolic dimension, often taken as a subversive act against gender oppression.

The thread linking the French Revolution to present time's "burka scandal" shows that great political events propel cultural changes, and clothing is one of the most important. Proper attention can provide us with significant knowledge about the effect of clothing as a political factor during these events. The same can be said concerning gender research: not a lot has been written on clothing, although there is much on the body (Bordo, Irigaray, and Kristeva are only a few among the many dealing with this topic).[1]

Dress and the struggle for female civil rights during the French Revolution

During the French Revolution, dress became an important issue: one of the ways in which revolutionaries' values were to be obtained and symbolized was through the adoption of class-less styles of clothing, which expressed the ideals of Fraternity, Liberty, and Equality.

Several decrees concerning clothing and gender issues were also passed. For instance, as it became easier for women than for men to get food, some men disguised themselves as women in order to do so. To prevent this, a new decree was voted and approved on August 7, 1793, stating that "a man wearing woman's clothes, will be punished by death."[2]

Moreover, on October 29, 1793, a new revolutionary edict stated that:

> No person of either sex may constrain any female or male citizen to dress in a particular manner. Everyone is free to wear whatever clothing or adornment of his sex seems right to him, on pain of being considered and treated as a suspect and prosecuted as a disturber of public peace.[34]

As much as this decree sounds neutral, it is not: although every French person has the right to wear whatever clothing or adornment he or she wishes, no one has the right to wear clothes outside of her or his gender.

Moreover, the history of this decree's promulgation reveals women's conflicts during the French Revolution: it was promulgated after a group of women appeared at the National Convention complaining that another group of women had tried to force them to wear the red cap of liberty as a sign of their adherence to the Revolution. The National Convention immediately passed a decree reaffirming liberty of dress (above), at the same time rethinking the old code of dressing. On the following day, October 30, 1793, Jean-Baptiste Amar (1755–1816) spoke for the Committee of Public Security as follows:

> In the morning at the market and charnel-house [mortuary] of the Innocents, several women, so-called women Jacobins, from a club that is supposedly revolutionary, walked about wearing trousers and red caps; they sought to force the other citizenesses to adopt the same dress. Several have testified that they were insulted by these women. [...]
>
> Your committee [the women's committee] believed it must go further in its inquiry. It has posed the following questions: (1) Is it permitted to citizens or to a particular club to force other citizens to do what the law does not command? (2) Should the gatherings of women convened in popular clubs

in Paris be allowed? Do not the troubles that these clubs have already occasioned prohibit us from tolerating any longer their existence?

Thus, after having answered negatively to these questions, Amar proposed a decree suppressing all women's political clubs, which passed with virtually no discussion.[5] Hence, in a very cynical way, male leaders of the Revolution exploited a benign clothing quarrel between women to crush completely women's movements. The way in which it was passed and the abolition of women's clubs emphasizes the gender inequalities at the time. This gender gap deprived women from rights that male revolutionaries had already achieved, such as education: many male revolutionaries were well educated, while female revolutionaries were often illiterates, even analphabets. Consequently, male revolutionaries were able to use their rhetorical skills, well acquired in French *lycées*, to manipulate women and reject their feminist demands. The gender gap also shows concerning utterances: in this report, only men's words have been completely recorded, thus glorified, while women's voices are appearing only as hearsay.

This event resulted in a paradoxical outcome: however free, the French people were still required to dress according to the fashion of each gender, just as before the Revolution. Hence, while the above law is often quoted to signify liberty of dress, it came hand in hand with women's repression, as it forbade women not only to wear trousers, but any clothing belonging to the opposite sex:

> Legislation forbidding women to wear pants was a reaction to the behavior of French feminists who had worn trousers […] during the revolution. Their clothing, their political views were unacceptable to the men who wielded power. The leaders of the revolution considered "clothing a statement of freedom and an expression of individuality" but not for women.[6]

During the French Revolution, some women joined the revolutionary army. Although their number is difficult to assess, they did take part in real combats, dressed in parts of men's uniforms, including trousers. On April 30, 1793, a decree passed that ordered all women to leave the army, but only one woman obeyed.[7] However, these female soldiers were not numerous, and over time left the army entirely. Thus, to conclude the issue of clothing and feminism during the French Revolution, it can be said that revolutionary women, with their demands for equality, symbolized by their new demands for equal clothes, represented a threat to the masculinity of the revolutionary males. As Annie Geffroy explains: "the woman with red cap is, in man's imaginary thinking, with trousers and arms, threatening, phallic."[8] We can also conclude that revolutionary males were to a certain degree revolutionary, but when it came to their masculinity and the code of masculine dressing, they stood on guard. As much as the French Revolution generated many radical changes, it did not grant any civil rights for women.[9] Albeit unsuccessful, the feminist struggle introduced the idea for further women's clothing demands; in 1800 a new French decree permitted women to wear trousers under the police prefect authorization.[10]

Clothing and feminist activism during the nineteenth century

The French feminist movement rose again in the Romantic generation, in particular among Saint-Simonians, in Paris:

> The first autonomous women's movement evolved out of the Saint-Simonian movement in the early 1830s. The feminists Flora Tristan, Jeanne Deroin, and Pauline Roland remain most strongly associated with this era, at the same time that the first feminist newspapers and journals tried to link the plight of the working class with the struggle for women's rights.[11]

At this occasion, the relationship between feminism and fashion again surfaced, as some women dared to wear men's clothes not for work purposes, as some already did, but to express a more liberated way of life:

> The most notorious woman to wear trousers […] was the novelist George Sand, who was also famous for her love affairs. Although she normally wore dresses, Sand was known to go out disguised as a man. In this way, for example, she could accompany male friends into the pit of the theater. […] Later in the century, the actress Sarah Bernhardt was frequently photographed wearing men's clothing, both for some of her performances and in private life. As these examples indicate, the practice was associated with bluestockings and actresses.[12]

Some of these women went further: they called themselves *Lionnes* (lionesses in French) and adopted an entirely masculine way of life, wearing complete masculine outfits, riding horses, participating in hunts, smoking cigars, and betting at races, although, as states Diana Crane "[i]n various ways, these women were atypical or marginal."[13] Nonetheless, this new behavior planted the seed for the idea of a legitimate change in women's fashion.

Moreover, in 1848, following the overthrow of French King Louis-Philippe, the newly formed Second Republic made possible a proliferation of new parties, including feminist ones. The *Vésuviennes*, the most radical of these feminist factions, wished to promote various reforms, including women's right to dress in the same way as men.[14] At this point, George Sand was a disappointment: the Saint-Simonians invited her to run for election, but she rejected their suggestion, on the grounds that women should first gain extended civil rights before being in a position to demand suffrage. Sand's reaction proved difficult to understand for those French feminists who were in favor of female suffrage. Very quickly, during the Second Republic, women were put aside, and once again did not gain any civil rights.

In America, by the middle of the nineteenth century, dress had become an issue for the Women's Rights Movement. In 1851, Mrs. Amelia Bloomer proposed a new feminine costume that consisted of a short skirt/dress over a pair of full Turkish trousers. Bloomer, a women's activist, and a few of her fellow activists wore the costume because it was "comfortable, convenient, safe and tidy."[15] According to Mary E. Corey, reviewing Sylvia D. Hoffert's *When Hens Crow: The Woman's Rights Movement in Antebellum America*,

> The Bloomer costume became the symbol of a woman's personal politics and a good deal of pressure was exerted on individual women to adopt it. When, for example Elizabeth Oakes Smith attended the Syracuse convention in 1852 wearing conventional dress, Susan B. Anthony objected to her nomination as president of the convention. Stanton is overheard remarking that a speech by Lydia Fowler would have been more convincing "if she had not appeared before her audience with her 'waist lined with whale-bones.'"
>
> Wearing reform dress was a powerful non-verbal way of announcing one's individual politics, but it came with a price. As each woman soon discovered, the reform dress gave them freedom of movement that conventional dress did not, but it also restricted their public movement and privacy. Strangers reacted to it as an invitation to intrude upon, ridicule, and harass anyone brave enough to wear it in public. Reform dress was never widely adopted and the last holdouts had resumed conventional dress by 1855, amid a flurry of debate about its continued worth as a political symbol and visual metaphor.[16]

Thus, at the time, there were different feminist views on the political effect of fashion. According to Margaret Finnegan, some suffragists embraced fashion as a sign of gentility: "Accounts of woman suffrage conventions repeatedly describe women 'elaborately gowned in the height of the fashion', and some suffragists obsessively followed the latest styles."[17] Others, such as Susan B. Anthony and Elizabeth Cady Stanton, advocated various forms of dress reform, mainly the above-mentioned bloomers. However, even Mrs. Bloomer abandoned trousers in 1857, when she admitted she found the cage crinoline comfortable compared to the weight of petticoats.

Feminist movements did not act in a vacuum, but influenced each other. According to Bonnie Anderson, strong ties developed between different feminist movements, namely between France, Britain, the German States, and the US.[18] As fashion historian James Laver writes:

> The formidable Mrs. Bloomer came to England in 1851 to spread her gospel and to try to induce women to adopt her sensible and certainly not unfeminine costume. […] This very modest attempt to reform female dress provoked an almost unbelievable outburst of excitement, ridicule and vituperation. What might be called the trouser complex came into full play. Women were endeavouring, it seemed, to "wear the trousers", and the mid-Victorian man regarded this as an outrageous attack on his own privileged position. *Punch*, that faithful mirror of middle-class opinion in the nineteenth century, brought out dozens of cartoons emphasizing the consequences of a possible sexual revolution, a world in which timid men were in complete subjection to their bloomered spouses.[19]

Male opposition to women's trousers has also to be understood as a threat to man's identity. Wearing male trousers was viewed as an expression of masculinity: if women were to wear trousers as well, how would men express *their* identity? The association between trousers and masculinity has a long history in the West. Men wore bifurcated garments, such as breeches and trousers, from the fourteenth century onwards, thus "[a]n important consequence of the bifurcation of male dress was that it made it appear that only the male half of the population were possessed of the means of locomotion, rendering the sight of female legs in motion […] seem indelicate or indecent."[20] Hence, male clothing symbolizes activity, while women's clothing, namely dresses, symbolizes passivity. By being willing to wear pants, women undermined one of the most important visual signs of men's power over them. However, as Laver goes on to explain: "as an attempt to influence contemporary fashion, the Bloomer Movement was a complete failure. […] Mrs. Bloomer had to wait for almost fifty years before she had her revenge in the adoption of 'bloomers' for cycling."[21]

Indeed, by the 1890s, trousers called bloomers were adopted all over Europe as suitable cycling wear for ladies. Moreover, even before that time, the Rational Dress Society, formed in 1881 in London, approved of Mrs. Bloomer's ideas on practical fashions. This society was formed by Viscountess Harberton and Mrs. King, who drew attention to restrictive clothes of the time and promoted alternative fashions that would not deform the female body. Moreover, the Rational Dress Society thought no woman should wear more than seven pounds of underwear, as every layer of undergarments made their movements more and more restricted. Rational dress as a fashion was finally adopted in 1895 by a handful of privileged women, but was not universally worn.[22]

In the meantime, in France, during the *Commune*, which followed the collapse of the Second Empire in 1870, women tried once more to gain power through clothing activism, including the right to wear trousers. However, their feminist demands were crushed, alongside all *Commune*'s movements, in 1871.

Female clothing change around the First World War

It was only by the beginning of the twentieth century that a real change in women's fashion began to be felt and the cumulative efforts of political women's rights movements had a real impact on women's fashions. Female clothes changed and became more relaxed: *haute couture* designer Paul Poiret advocated not using corsets anymore, designing instead female pantaloons and non-fitted clothing. Coco Chanel had already introduced softer fabrics for easier feminine clothing.

However, the greatest female fashion revolution occurred after the First World War, when fashions changed alongside women's roles in modern society. Women got new rights, penetrated universities, and entered the workforce in numbers.[23] First and foremost, underwear, whose purpose had been for centuries to design the female body, was left to promote a "natural" body: the corset was discarded and replaced by a chemise or camisole and bloomers. For the first time, women's legs were seen, with hemlines rising to the knee as dresses became shorter and more fitted. A kind of masculine look, including flattened breasts and hips and short hairstyles, such as the bob cut, was adopted. Thus, abstract feminist ideas of freedom and equality of rights were translated into concrete forms and objects, as women first liberated themselves from constricting fashions and began to wear comfortable clothes.

After-war feminism's attention to fashion

After the Second World War, feminists' views on fashion moved forward, as many feminists began to perceive it as an oppressive tool used against woman. "Since woman is an object," wrote Simone de Beauvoir, "it is quite understandable that her intrinsic value is affected by her style of dress and adornment."[24] According to Elizabeth Wilson:

> It was during the early part of the post-war epoch that Simone de Beauvoir wrote feelingly about the bondage of elegance: "Elegance is really just like housework: by means of it the woman who is deprived of *doing* anything

feels that she expresses what she *is*. To care for her beauty, to dress up, is a kind of work that enables her to take possession of her person as she takes possession of her home through housework; her ego then seems chosen and recreated by herself."[25]

Fashion in second-wave feminism

Dress was also important during the second wave of feminism. One famous event, the 1968 protest against the Miss America beauty pageant, on the Atlantic City boardwalk, witnessed participants crowning a live sheep Miss America and throwing "instruments of oppression" like bras, girdles, curlers, false eyelashes, wigs, and copies of *Cosmopolitan* and *Ladies' Home Journal*, into a "freedom trashcan." Activists also distributed a brochure entitled *No More Miss America*, later canonized into feminist scholarship.[26] This leaflet was divided into ten points explaining the ways in which the pageant valued female bodies over minds and presented an objectified version of female bodies for a voyeuristic male gaze. Thus, women who participated in the Women's Liberation Movement were labeled "bra-burners" in mainstream media publications.

During the late 1960s and the 1970s women's skirts shortened to miniskirts, abandonment of the bra was advocated, and tight clothing, sometimes even transparent clothing, was worn. These styles progressed to women undressing, so far as exposing their naked bodies. Thus, the question arises: can this undressing style—which meant an about-turn in controlling women's bodies, from dressing to undressing—also be termed *freedom*? Feminists such as Orbach (1978), Chernin (1983), Baker (1884), and Coward (1984) drew attention to the new pressures brought on women by the advent of almost-nakedness as well as body-shaping techniques such as plastic surgery, diet, and exercise.

> While female dress became less restrictive, this did not indicate that it had become more liberated since there were now more effective ways of molding the body in accordance with the ideas of feminine beauty. These new techniques for fashioning the female body operated in an insidious way. For though women were now encouraged to participate in exercise and to eat wisely ostensibly to improve their health and fitness, the real *raison d'être* for these activities was to attain the body shape deemed desirable by patriarchal society—a body shape which was becoming increasingly thinner.[27]

Towards the end of the twentieth century, feminists also began to point to the fashion industry as deeply harmful to women. Chapter 8 of Susan Faludi's *Backlash: The Undeclared War against American Women* (1991) discusses the beauty industry's destructive presence in women's lives by encouraging unnecessary plastic surgery as well as the purchase of unnecessary cosmetics. Faludi believes it also set unachievable standards of femininity for American women.

In a similar way, Naomi Wolf, in her book *The Beauty Myth: How Images of Beauty Are Used against Women* (first published 1991), argues that "the gaunt, youthful model [has] supplanted the happy housewife as the arbiter of successful womanhood."[28] Beauty standards spread by the beauty industry and the press are used as a political weapon against women's advancement.

Susan Bordo, in her book *Unbearable Weight: Feminism, Western Culture, and the Body* (1993), wishes to emphasize the destructive ways in which Western culture monopolizes and hurts women's bodies. Accordingly, eating disorders such as anorexia nervosa and/or bulimia, which mainly affect women, cannot simply be defined from medical and/or psychological perspectives, but must be apprehended from within our cultural context.

Feminist new struggle following Muslim migration

Following Islamic immigration to Europe, a new debate developed: the controversy surrounding the burka worn by female migrants from Arab countries. Although many feminists targeted the burka issue in Afghanistan, the debate really took off when female Muslim migrants decided to dress in an all-covering garment, which is now often referred to as a burka. For some, the veil—or the burka—is a means for individuals to express publicly their deepest religious, philosophical, and cultural commitments.[29] Most feminists perceive it differently. According to Fadela Amara, founder and leader of the French feminist organization *Ni Putes Ni Soumises*, the garment "represents not a piece of fabric but the political manipulation of a religion that enslaves women and disputes the principle of equality between men and women." She describes the headscarf as "the visible symbol of the subjugation of women." Moreover, Amara also says that there is no difference between the headscarf (the *hijab*) and the burka in terms of political oppression. Both garments, she claims, represent "a political project that aspires for gender inequality." In fact, Amara's standpoint represents most French people's positions. From March 2, 2011, new laws forbidding burka wearing were implemented in France.

Criticism of feminist attitudes to fashion

Alongside feminist demands arrived opposition, which included attacks on feminists' clothing and bodies. Some French male revolutionaries argued that

demanding civil rights made women ugly, as their counterparts from Anglophone
countries asserted. According to Marian Sawer:

> *Punch* magazine, whether in the UK or its colonial namesakes, promoted
> both visually and verbally the message that "women who wanted women's
> rights also wanted women's charms" (Eveline & Booth 1999). [...]
>
> The suggestion that campaigning for equality made women sexually
> unattractive was a useful way of discouraging them from joining the cause.
> John Stuart Mill acknowledged the effectiveness of this tactic when he wrote
> of the value of countering it by having pretty women as suffrage lecturers.
> This he thought would help persuade young women that joining the suffrage
> movement would not unsex them or cost them a husband (Caine 1979: 64).
> The suggestion that equality seeking makes women unattractive is a hardy
> perennial and closely linked to another—the suggestion that women who
> take up the cause do so because they have failed to attract a man and want
> revenge.[30]

We see that, either way, the male position concerns sexualization and
femininity when the issue of clothing arises. Moreover, throughout the entire
nineteenth century, the press attacked feminist efforts through depictions of
ugly women through caricatures. During the French Second Republic (1848–
51), and afterwards,

> Daumier and others played upon the theme of role inversion, depicting
> political women as ugly, comical, funny-looking, masculine imitators. There
> were manly wives rejecting marital authority on the advice of Mme Deroin;
> children left in the arms of despairing fathers while their mothers played at
> politics; women with monocles, cigars, and beards; and men in skirts.[31]

Furthermore, the image of a young woman in culottes came to represent all
feminists, as can be seen in nineteenth-century French caricatures, which
satirized feminists' efforts in the popular press.[32] For example, during the
Commune events, following the fall of the Second Empire in France, the
appearance of the *Pétroleuse* in the press was artificially portrayed as wild and
antithetic to the bourgeois "natural" female figure.

> But no matter what men did to the women, the *pétroleuse* remained a
> frightening but compelling figure, a fury with unbound, flying hair; a defiant
> madwoman, captured but wild; sometimes ugly and sometimes beautiful;
> often seductive; and always more powerful than her cowed male counterpart,
> who once arrested, became serious and unnaturally passive, while she
> remained unnaturally aggressive.[33]

The same can be said about the English-speaking world, where anti-suffragist articles as well as caricatures abounded in the popular press.[34]

Moreover, many do not share critical views on beauty, fashion, and the beauty industry, as expressed by Second-Wave feminists. Nancy Etcoff, in her book *The Survival of the Prettiest*, maintains that beauty holds a survival value, and that sensitivity to beauty is a biological adaptation, shaped by natural selection:

> The argument is a simple one: that beauty is a universal part of human experience, and that it provokes pleasure, rivets attention, and impels actions that help ensure the survival of our genes. Our extreme sensitivity to beauty is hard-wired, that is, governed by circuits in the brain shaped by natural selection. We love to look at smooth skin, thick shiny hair, curved waists, and symmetrical bodies because in the course of evolution the people who noticed these signals and desired their possessors had more reproductive success. We are their descendants.[35]

Indeed, according to Louis Tietje and Steven Cresap:

> Most of the time, beauty signals health, both physical and mental; health signals reproductive success. Ugliness, on the other hand, sometimes signals disease, hence reproductive failure. What could be more essential to the human project than desire for pleasure, disgust with pain, and, determining everything else, the need to reproduce? In such contexts it makes sense to say that we are naturally inclined against ugly people and in favor of beautiful people, however those categories may be interpreted. Paying attention to aesthetics in these contexts is discrimination in the positive sense, akin to prudence.[36]

Moreover, disagreement about fashion is another quarrel factor between feminists; Linda M. Scott, for example, in her book *Fresh Lipstick: Redressing Fashion and Feminism* (first published in 2004), maintains that the anti-beauty ideology of Second-Wave feminists is self-serving and elitist. Reversing the argument that mainstream imagery promotes normative beauty standards, Scott says this feminist bias is "a compulsion to enforce homogeneity."[37]

Conclusion

Debates about clothing are a field in which conflicts and feminist struggles repeatedly occur. The French Revolution, nineteenth-century political events, the World Wars, and contemporary Islamic presence in Europe show that whenever a gender struggle arises, fashion and clothing are involved. Clothing was and still is employed to express one's individual opinion, sometimes instead of using words. Conforming or resisting to dress codes is one of the immediate forms of social statements expressing consent or objection to the social order. Indeed, when observing the last 200 years' "big events," it is impossible not to see that clothing, and feminine clothing in particular, cause public discussion to erupt and stir up significant public storms.

In a very consistent manner, feminist struggle used clothing in order to promote its agenda. Often mixing practical arguments with symbolic ones in the demand for clothing change, feminists always understood that visual appearance cannot be detached from ideological struggle.

Most interestingly, the real revolution in feminine dress came after more than a century of feminist struggle: by the beginning of the 20th century, feminine clothing became shorter, easier, and, most importantly, women began losing the under-garments that for centuries had constricted their movements. Although most histories of costume consider the First World War to be the catalyst in women's dress changes,[38] this could not have been so without the fashion changes intro-duced before the war itself. This means that although female fashion changed enormously after the war, the beginning of the change preceded it. Furthermore, though women activists were and still are a noisy minority, adoption of new clothing by the majority shows that women are attentive to changes. Women understand easily where their interests are, but can introduce them into their lives only when they feel secure enough to do so. Indeed, by the beginning of that century, and mostly after the Great War, new opportunities opened up for women in education, work, and politics. These new possibilities were symbolized as well as made possible through feminine fashion. Clothes are not only symbols, but also a way to live, to move, to run, to work, to sit, and so on.

However, even in the West, feminist achievements are not definitively secure. Nowadays, new feminine struggles burst out in Europe. In some neighborhoods, mainly in France and Germany, where most inhabitants are Muslim, women's clothing is a constant topic of contention. In male-dominated spaces, women, mainly young women, are ordered to be "decent," and to do so by covering their bodies. Thus, skirts are now considered to be much too attractive, and conse-quently forbidden. Women's oppression in these neighborhoods has inspired a French movie (2008) entitled *La journée de la jupe*, translated as *Skirt Day*. The dominant protagonist, played by Isabelle Adjani, demands that one day a year will be called "Skirt Day," during which women would be allowed to wear skirts freely. Another female movie character then asks: "We fought to wear pants for 200 years, and now, we'll be drawn back to wear skirts?!" Sometimes, fiction meets reality: prominent leader of Maghrebian origin Fadela Amara (mentioned earlier) had declared on October 25, 2011, that every October 25 from now on would be *La journée de la jupe* (*Skirt Day*) as a protest day against violence against women.

Notes

1   Julia Kristeva, *New Maladies of the Soul*, New York: Columbia University Press, 1995; Luce Irigaray, *This Sex Which Is Not One*, Catherine Porter, trans., New York: Cornell University Press, 1985; Luce Irigaray, *Speculum of the Other Woman*, Gillian C. Gill (trans.), Ithaca: Cornell University Press, 1985.

2   In original French: "Celui qui sera trouvé déguisé en femme sera également puni de mort." A. Ray, *Réimpression de l'ancien Moniteur: Convention nationale*, H. Plon: 1793, online at http://books.google.co.il/books?id=IJMMAQAAMAAJ&dq=%22Cel ui+qui+sera+trouv%C3%A9+d%C3%A9guis%C3%A9+en+femme+sera%22&hl=e n&source=gbs_navlinks_s (accessed June 21, 2014).

3   Quoted from the site Liberty, Equality, Fraternity: Exploring the French Revolution, website by Lynn Hunt of UCLA and Jack Censer of George Mason University, http://chnm.gmu.edu/revolution/d/294/ (accessed June 21, 2014) (our emphasis).

4   In original French: Art. 1er. "Nulle personne de l'un et de l'autre sexe ne pourra contraindre aucun citoyen ni citoyenne à se vêtir d'une manière particulière sous peine d'être considérée et traitée comme suspecte et poursuivie comme perturbateur du repos public. Chacun est libre de porter tel vêtement et ajustement de son sexe que bon lui semble."

5   The site Liberty, Equality, Fraternity.

6   Diana Crane, *Fashion and its Social Agendas: Class, Gender, and Identity in Clothing*, Chicago: University of Chicago Press, 2001, p. 113, quoting Aileen Ribeiro, *Fashion in the French Revolution*, London: Batsford, 1988, p. 141.

7   Dominique Godineau, *The Women of Paris and their French Revolution*, Berkeley: University of California Press, 1998, pp. 242–7.

8   In French: "la femme en bonnet rouge est, dans l'imaginaire masculin, dotée de pantalons et d'armes, menaçante, phallique." Annie Geffroy, "'A bas le bonnet rouge des femmes!' (Octobre–Novembre 1793)," *Les femmes et la Révolution française*, Toulouse: Presses Universitaires du Mirail, 1990, pp. 345–51, quoted in Claude Guillon, "Pauline Léon, une républicaine révolutionnaire," *Annales historiques de la Révolution française* [En ligne], 344. Avril–Juin 2006, mis en ligne le 01 juin 2009, consulté le 01 août 2011. URL: http://ahrf.revues.org/6213 (accessed June 21, 2014).

9   For a useful summary of this topic, see Jean-Clément Martin, *La Révolution française*, Paris: Le Cavalier Bleu, 2007, pp. 35–6.

10 In order to permit women to work on sites where trousers were needed. Philippe Perrot, *Fashioning the Bourgeoisie: A History of Clothing in the Nineteenth Century*, Princeton: Princeton University Press, 1994, p. 20.

11 Sandra Reineke, *Beauvoir and Her Sisters: The Politics of Women's Bodies in France*, Urbana: University of Illinois Press, 2011, p. 8.

12 Valerie Steele, *Paris Fashion: A Cultural History*, Oxford: Berg, 2006, p. 164.

13 Diana Crane, *Fashion and its Social Agendas: Class, Gender, and Identity in Clothing*, Chicago: University of Chicago Press, 2001, p. 114.

14 Claire Goldberg Moses, *French Feminism in the Nineteenth Century*, New York: SUNY Press, 1984. pp. 123–30.

15   Crane, *Fashion and its Social Agenda*, p. 112.

16   Mary E. Corey, reviewing Sylvia D. Hoffert, *When Hens Crow: The Woman's Rights Movement in Antebellum America*, Bloomington and Indianapolis: Indiana University Press, 1995, at http://www.h-net.org/reviews/showrev.php?id=6735 (accessed June 21, 2014).

17   Margaret Finnegan, *Selling Suffrage: Consumer Culture and Votes for Women*, New York: Columbia University Press, 1999, p. 18.

18   Bonnie S. Anderson, "The lid comes off: international radical feminism and the revolutions of 1848," *NWSA Journal* (*The National Women's Studies Association Journal*), 10, 2 (Summer 1998): 1–12. See also Gerda Lerner and Linda K. Kerber, *The Majority Finds its Past: Placing Women in History*, Chapel Hill: UNC Press Books, 2005, p. 41.

19   James Laver, *Costume and Fashion: A Concise History*, New York: Thames & Hudson, 1995, pp. 180–3.

20   Steven Connor, *Men in Skirts*, http://www.bbk.ac.uk/english/skc/skirts/MenInSkirts. pdf (accessed June 21, 2014).

21   Laver, *Costume and Fashion*.

22   Pauline Weston Thomas and Guy Thomas, fashion history site: http://www. fashion-era.com/rational_dress.htm (accessed June 21, 2014).

23   Lerner and Kerber, *The Majority Finds its Past*, p. 45.

24   Simone de Beauvoir, *The Second Sex*, London: Jonathan Cape, 1953, p. 534.

25   Elizabeth Wilson, *Adorned in Dreams: Fashion and Modernity*, New Brunswick: Rutgers University Press, 1985, p. 125, quoting de Beauvoir. Italics in the original.

26   Carole Ruth McCann and Seung-Kyung Kim eds, "No More Miss America," in *Feminist Theory Reader: Local and Global Perspectives*, New York: Routledge, 2003, pp. 80–2.

27   Llewellyn Negrin, "The self as image: a critical appraisal of postmodern theories of fashion," *Theory Culture Society*, 16, 99 (1999), p. 104.

28   Naomi Wolf, *The Beauty Myth: How Images of Beauty are Used Against Women*, New York: Anchor, 1991, p. 10.

29   Josh Corngold, "A paradigm of an intractable dilemma," *Philosophy of Education*, 1 (2006): 106–14.

30   Marian Sawer, "Cartoons for the Cause: Cartooning for Equality in Australia," Ejournalist—*Australian Media Traditions Conference 2001*, http://www.ejournalist. com.au/v1n2/SAWER.pdf

31   Joan Wallach Scott, *Only Paradoxes to Offer: French Feminists and the Rights of Man*, Cambridge: Harvard University Press, 1997, p. 80.

32   Laura Strumingher Schor, "Politics and political satire: the struggle for the right to vote in Paris, 1848–1849," *The European Legacy*, 1, 3 (May 1996): 1037–44; Barbara Caine and Glenda Sluga, *Gendering European History 1780–1920*, London: Continuum, 2002, p. 76.

33   Gay L. Gullickson, *Unruly Women of Paris: Images of the Commune*, Ithaca: Cornell University Press, 1996, p. 181.

34   Laver, *Costume and Fashion,* p. 182. See also Susan E. Marshall, *Splintered*

Sisterhood: Gender and Class in the Campaign against Woman Suffrage, Madison: University of Wisconsin Press, 1997, pp. 93–140.

35   Nancy Etcoff, *Survival of the Prettiest*, New York: Anchor, 1999, p. 24.

36   Louis Tietje and Steven Cresap, "Is lookism unjust? the ethics of aesthetics and public policy implications," *Journal of Libertarian Studies*, 19, 2 (Spring 2005): 38.

37   Review by Jeanine Plant of Linda M. Scott, *Fresh Lipstick:, Redressing Fashion and Feminism*, New York: Macmillan, 2004, http://feministreview.blogspot.com/2006/12/fresh-lipstick-redressing-fashion-and.html.

38   See for example Katina Bill, "Attitudes towards women's trousers: Britain in the 1930s," *Journal of Design History*, 6, 1 (1993): 45–54.

Bibliography

Anderson, Bonnie S., "The lid comes off: international radical feminism and the revolutions of 1848," *NWSA Journal* (*The National Women's Studies Association Journal*), 10, 2 (Summer 1998): 1–12.

Beauvoir, Simone de, *The Second Sex*, London: Jonathan Cape, 1953.

Bill, Katina, "Attitudes towards women's trousers: Britain in the 1930s," *Journal of Design History*, 6, 1 (1993): 45–54.

Bordo, Susan, *Unbearable Weight: Feminism, Western Culture, and the Body*, Berkeley: University of California Press, 1993.

Caine, Barbara and Glenda Sluga, *Gendering European History 1780–1920*, London: Continuum, 2002.

Corey, Mary E., reviewing Sylvia D. Hoffert, *When Hens Crow: The Woman's Rights Movement in Antebellum America*, Bloomington and Indianapolis: Indiana University Press, 1995, at http://www.h-net.org/reviews/showrev.php?id=6735 (accessed June 21, 2014).

Connor, Steven, *Men in Skirts*, http://www.bbk.ac.uk/english/skc/skirts/MenInSkirts.pdf (accessed June 21, 2014).

Corngold, Josh, "A Paradigm of an Intractable Dilemma," *Philosophy of Education*, 1 (2006), pp. 106–14.

Crane, Diana, *Fashion and its Social Agendas: Class, Gender, and Identity in Clothing*, Chicago: University of Chicago Press, 2001.

Etcoff, Nancy, *Survival of the Prettiest*, New York: Anchor, 1999.

Finnegan, Margaret, *Selling Suffrage: Consumer Culture and Votes for Women*, New York: Columbia University Press, 1999.

Geffroy, Annie, "'A bas le bonnet rouge des femmes!' (Octobre–Novembre 1793)," *Les femmes et la Révolution française*, Toulouse: Presses Universitaires du Mirail, 1990.

Godineau, Dominique, *The Women of Paris and their French Revolution*, Berkeley: University of California Press, 1998. Avril–Juin 2006, mis en ligne le 01 juin 2009, consulté le 01 août 2011. URL: http://ahrf.revues.org/6213 (accessed June 21, 2014).

Goldberg Moses, Claire, *French Feminism in the Nineteenth Century*, New York: SUNY Press, 1984.

Guillon, Claude, "Pauline Léon, une républicaine révolutionnaire," *Annales historiques de la Révolution française* [En ligne], 344. Avril–Juin 2006, mis en ligne le 01 juin 2009, consulté le 01 août 2011. URL: http://ahrf.revues.org/6213 (accessed June 21, 2014).

Gullickson, Gay L., *Unruly Women of Paris: Images of the Commune*, Ithaca: Cornell University Press, 1996.

Hoffert, Sylvia D., *When Hens Crow: The Woman's Rights Movement in Antebellum America*, Bloomington: Indiana University Press, 1995.

Irigaray, Luce, *This Sex Which Is Not One*, Catherine Porter (trans.) ,New York: Cornell University Press, 1985.

—*Speculum of the Other Woman*, Gillian C. Gill (trans.), Ithaca: Cornell University Press, 1985.

Kristeva Julia, *New Maladies of the Soul*, New York: Columbia University Press, 1995.

Laver, James, *Costume and Fashion: A Concise History*, New York: Thames & Hudson, 1995.

Lerner, Gerda, and Linda K. Kerber, *The Majority Finds its Past: Placing Women in History*, Chapel Hill: UNC Press Books, 2005.

Liberty, Equality, Fraternity: Exploring the French Revolution, website by Lynn Hunt of UCLA and Jack Censer of George Mason University, http://chnm.gmu.edu/revolution/d/294/ (accessed June 21, 2014).

Marshall, Susan E., *Splintered Sisterhood: Gender and Class in the Campaign against Woman Suffrage*, Madison: University of Wisconsin Press, 1997.

Martin, Jean-Clément, *La Révolution française*, Paris: Le Cavalier Bleu, 2007.

McCann, Carole Ruth and Seung-Kyung Kim eds, "No More Miss America," in *Feminist Theory Reader: Local and Global Perspectives*, New York: Routledge, 2003, pp. 80–2.

Negrin, Llewellyn, "The self as image: a critical appraisal of postmodern theories of fashion," *Theory Culture Society*, 16, 99 (1999): 9–118.

Perrot, Philippe, *Fashioning the Bourgeoisie: A History of Clothing in the Nineteenth Century*, Princeton: Princeton University Press, 1994.

Plant, Jeanine, review of Linda M. Scott, *Fresh Lipstick: Redressing Fashion and Feminism*, New York: Macmillan, 2004, http://feministreview.blogspot.com/2006/12/fresh-lipstick-redressing-fashion-and.html

Ray, A., *Réimpression de l'ancien Moniteur: Convention nationale*, H. Plon: 1793, online at http://books.google.co.il/books?id=IJMMAQAAMAAJ&dq=%22Celui+qui+sera+trouv%C3%A9+d%C3%A9guis%C3%A9+en+femme+sera%22&hl=en&source=gbs_navlinks_s . (accessed June 21, 2014).

Reineke, Sandra, *Beauvoir and Her Sisters: The Politics of Women's Bodies in France*, Urbana: University of Illinois Press, 2011.

Aileen Ribeiro, *Fashion in the French Revolution*, London: Batsford, 1988.

Sawer, Marian, "Cartoons for the Cause: Cartooning for Equality in Australia," Ejournalist—*Australian Media Traditions Conference 2001*, http://www.ejournalist.com.au/v1n2/SAWER.pdf

Scott, Joan Wallach, *Only Paradoxes to Offer: French Feminists and the Rights of Man*, Cambridge: Harvard University Press, 1997.

Steele, Valerie, *Paris Fashion: A Cultural History*, Oxford: Berg, 2006.

Struminger Schor, Laura, "Politics and political satire: the struggle for the right to vote in Paris, 1848–1849," *The European Legacy*, 1, 3 (May 1996): 1037–44.

Tietje, Louis and Steven Cresap, "Is lookism unjust? the ethics of aesthetics and public policy implications," *Journal of Libertarian Studies*, 19, 2 (Spring 2005): 31–50.

Weston Thomas, Pauline and Guy Thomas, fashion history site: http://www.fashion-era. com/rational_dress.htm (accessed June 21, 2014).
Wilson, Elizabeth, *Adorned in Dreams: Fashion and Modernity*, New Brunswick: Rutgers University Press, 1985.
Wolf, Naomi, *The Beauty Myth: How Images of Beauty are Used Against Women*, New York: Anchor, 1991.

10

FASHION POLITICS AND PRACTICE: INDIAN COTTONS AND CONSUMER INNOVATION IN TOKUGAWA JAPAN AND EARLY MODERN ENGLAND, C. 1600–1800[1]

BEVERLY LEMIRE

Introduction

The historical characteristics of consumer behavior have been the subject of intensive study for a generation.[2] While researchers initially focused on Western Europe and colonial America, questions surrounding consumerism are now central to the analysis of economic, political, and cultural history across the world.[3] Debates on issues of luxury and consumption shifted from a focus on elites to plebeians, addressing as well the repercussions of the global commodity trade. When the cost and availability of such merchandise expanded, this produced profound social and cultural affects. Fashion took root as part of wider economic and social changes, a vital component of what Kenneth Pomeranz terms "the appearance of culturally based economic difference."[4] Indeed, the emergence of fashion among non-elites signaled the alterations underway and was a barometer of social change. From my perspective, fashion is a symptom of social, cultural, and economic transformation, arising in various cultures in conjunction with urbanization, dynamic commerce, and (usually) the stimulus of foreign goods injected into existing systems of material exchange. In general, pre-modern governments aimed to contain and constrain consumption, as economic systems evolved. Nonetheless, expanding commerce and rising consumption generated social forces that undercut material stability, despite the multiplication of legal injunctions during the era.[5]

Clothing is political. It is perhaps the most contentious of commodities, in large part because of its ability to make the wearer, "to mould and shape them both physically and socially, [and] to constitute subjects through their power."[6] From the 1500s to 1700s, a growing volume of new fabrics gradually redefined clothing and encouraged wider participation in fashion. In total, these events enhanced plebeian capacity to model their appearance in accordance with shifting tastes. Urban men and women, outside the elites, embraced this cultural project. As self-fashioning became more widely accepted as a cultural value it challenged the socio-political status quo, sparking official reaction. In many quarters of the world, the growing flow of commerce, and the growth of vibrant cities provided a context for the spreading fashion impulse. Historians have recently produced important new comparative studies of the world in this era, identifying notable parallels in economic development, urbanization and commercial growth in certain parts of Asia and Europe, before what Kenneth Pomeranz calls "The Great Divergence" after 1800.[7] Much of this work led to debates about the meanings of quantitative data arising from different institutional sources. Anne McCants recently proposed the development of "alternative yardsticks of economic success" finding the existing quantitative measures less than fully satisfactory in the context of Western Europe. Similarly, Susan Hanley, a historian of Tokugawa Japan, argues that a study of "the standard of living alone is insufficient as an indicator of how well people live, insufficient for analysing the preconditions of industrialization, and certainly insufficient for making cross-cultural comparison." She proposes instead a close study of material culture and the processes of consumption.[8]

The reception of Indian cotton textiles is at the heart of this work. In the two regions under review, cottons from India represented fresh new additions. The agency of "things" is now a widely accepted premise, a concept pioneered by Alfred Gell among others. Gell challenged scholars to rethink the power of objects (through physical, social, and symbolic properties) to initiate change and pointed to the dynamic potential as objects and societies interacted. His influence now extends across a range of disciplines, what Chris Gosden describes as "part of an emerging attempt to take the material world seriously in terms of how it affects human relations."[9] Indian cottons arrived in the largest volumes in both Europe and Japan in the later seventeenth and eighteenth centuries, although the quantities of imports differed significantly. This period likewise coincided with dynamic economic growth and urbanization in both locales. City streets showcased material innovations, their pavements a stage for the unruly performance of fashion by non-elites, generating a creative social friction. As Fernand Braudel noted, the affects of early modern cities were to "increase tension, accelerate the rhythm of exchange and ceaselessly stir up lives."[10] In the cities of Tokugawa Japan and early modern England, Indian cottons animated fashion cultures and the material qualities of these textiles presented unique challenges to the existing social order.

Cotton in Tokugawa Japan: "communication and performance"

Indian cotton was a catalyst commodity. The unique features of these textiles made them among the first global consumer commodities before and after 1500. Cotton's mutable appearance defied easy categorization as either luxurious or mundane. India's artisans were unrivalled in the spinning, weaving and dyeing of this fiber, producing innumerable forms. Most importantly, Indian artisans devised colorfast dyeing impervious to the rigors of laundering. Wood block printing on cloth represented an exceptional contribution to world material culture. These printed and painted fabrics facilitated iconographic interactions in a largely unlettered world, where signs and designs resonated with diverse peoples steeped in symbolic literacy, even if formally unschooled.[11] This material discourse enriched many societies, part of what Andrew Sherratt termed, "consumption as communication and performance."[12]

Indian cottons sustained social practices and fed fashion initiatives in various parts of the globe, although not all demand for cotton was driven by fashion. India provided fabrics for many peoples who demanded traditional and innovative wares. In commercially advanced societies with vibrant city cultures fashion preferences increasingly defined material practices. The presence of fashion is well documented in China, Japan, and Europe in this era, although a full chronology has not yet been mapped.[13] Thriving cities and international trade were typically godparents to fashion, which might unsettle hierarchies. Governments did not welcome fashion displays outside designated lordly ranks and the elite complained about the material innovations they witnessed among commoners.[14] Governments legislated their response.

Beginning in Japan, how did cotton textiles figure in this contest? During the fifteenth and sixteenth centuries, cotton cloth and thread began to be imported into Japan in small quantities, initially sold to the nobility and elite clergy. Cultivation of cotton followed after seeds were brought to Japan in the sixteenth century. Thereafter the growth of cotton culture in Japan followed a two-pronged process combining the importation of cloth from India, plus local production and manufacture. But India remained a fundamental influence on the evolution of Japanese cotton culture in the Tokugawa period. Japanese folklorists have traced the response of people to the introduction of this cloth—the physical properties of this fiber captivated. The texture, weight and touch of the textiles compared very favorably to local hemp and ramie fabrics and, practically, cotton was also more easily processed and dyed.[15] As cities grew and populations expanded, the demand for cotton accelerated in the 1600s from city-dwellers in Edo, Osaka, and Kyoto. Fujita Kayoko writes of "Japan Indianized."[16] These cotton textiles were able to navigate the maze of sumptuary laws extant in that era, as they carried none of the injunctions assigned to silk. Only nobles, samurai, and clergy were permitted to wear silk. Cotton was approved for non-elites, and in some cities regulations specifically authorized cottons for commoners.[17] As Kayoko observes, "cotton textiles brought revolutionary changes in the material culture of non-elite Japanese [with] … unprecedented changes in the design of their daily clothes."[18]

Indian cottons poured into the port of Nagasaki in unequalled volumes in the later 1600s, brought in by the Dutch East India Company, which constituted the principal importer of these products.[19] Cotton textiles epitomize what Jan de Vries terms "New Luxury." De Vries defines "Old Luxury" items like jewels, furs, and precious metals as marking hierarchies of "exquisite refinement," associated with the nobility and social elites, serving as signs of status. In contrast, "New Luxury" emphasized "comfort and pleasure, [and] lent itself to multiplication and diffusion."[20] De Vries notes the capacities of these products "to communicate cultural meaning, permitting reciprocal relations—a kind of sociability—among participants in consumption."[21] He bases his appraisal on early modern European societies. But this important analysis should also be applied to "New Luxuries" in other societies undergoing similar transformations, like Japan.

The social hierarchy of Tokugawa Japan was highly formalized, with the emperor and nobles, shogun plus the samurai military holding inherited positions. Over the seventeenth century, the economy flourished and the effects of this growth were evident in the rising wealth of mercantile sectors.[22] Indeed, Pomeranz suggests that demand for consumer goods in Japan was "probably less geographically uneven than it was in Europe."[23] Court politics inadvertently contributed to the integration of national markets, as regional lords were required to report to the capital regularly. These routine journeys by locally prominent men and their entourage encouraged the development of transport networks, with the same roads carrying people, news and products.[24] An English East India Company captain, Captain John Saris observed the lively traffic on the roads, while the urban Surunga he described as "full as bigge as London, with all the Suburbs." But Edo exceeded even the wonders of that provincial city, making "a very glorious appearance," containing about one million residents by about 1700.[25]

Eiko Ikegami describes a society in transition, pushing against legislated restraints, where, as she contends: "A series of developments in the Japanese economy and urban culture ... led to a remarkable and unexpected phenomenon: the rise of popular fashion."[26] Ikegami argues for the vital importance of aesthetic networks in Japan, as alliances were forged among like-minded individuals outside formally mandated social structures. Such networks provided their members with alternate forms of self-expression and even discreet defiance of the political status quo. In Japan, this sensibility was manifested by what is termed *iki*, epitomized by an elegant urbane civility, combined with a sophisticated and a sometimes-insubordinate wit. *Iki* was an urban aesthetic, especially evident in the city of Edo, outside the ruling elites.[27] *Iki* likewise thrived in Edo's licensed pleasure centers termed the "floating world." In these districts courtesans, artists and actors mixed with men of all backgrounds and experimental styles were launched for receptive audiences.

Ikegami's identification of aesthetic networks reveals the economic and social changes at work, changes that sparked new patterns of consumerism and new attention to the play of fashion [Fig 10.1]. Such networks of interest diffused the spirit of *iki* widely.[28] Jay Keister describes the "two sides of *iki*—refinement and resistance"[29] conveyed in fashionable forms. Silk might be forbidden; but fashion

Figure 10.1   "Perspective Picture of Famous Places of Japan: Nakanocho in Shin-Yoshiwara," Toyhuaru Utagawa, c. 1775. People enjoying the pleasure district of Tokyo on Nakanocho Boulevard at night. FP 2-JPD, no. 1701. Library of Congress Prints and Photographs Division, Washington, DC.

could still be manifest through the combination of textile patterns on cotton that also carried the exotic connotations of distant Asian locales. Cotton's foreign origin held a distinctive cachet, epitomized in the names of the fabrics, *bengara* [Bengal] and *matafû* [Madras] being just two. In addition, all of these cotton appellations included the suffix *shima*. The term *shima* itself meant "island" but after the Portuguese began bringing Indian cottons to Japan, it meant "a distant island," and was directly associated with the striped textiles.[30] Kenneth Pomeranz assessed the role of fashion in the expanding markets for consumer goods in Europe, China, and Japan, noting the passion for foreign manufactures in early modern Europe. Did the taste for foreign goods shape economies and societies in different ways at the two ends of the Eurasian continent? China remains Pomeranz's principal comparative focus and he identifies a different scale of fashion-driven consumption in Europe and China, positing that this "seems attributable to a difference in the degree to which exotic goods, especially exotic *manufactured* goods, became prestigious."[31] However, the example of Indian cottons in Japan does not support this hypothesis. The exotic associations embedded in cotton textiles captivated Japanese of many ranks and encouraged both overseas trade and the local manufacture of facsimiles of Indian cottons.

Ulinka Rublack recently re-assessed the culture of dress in sixteenth- and seventeenth-century Europe, identifying an enhanced visuality in that age, noting the rising prominence of a "whole set of visual practices, [including] … a greater status given to visual perception."[32] She argues that such cultural expressions increased the centrality of clothing in social and political discourse. This augmented visuality can also be discerned in the greater production of published prints in Europe, showcasing the apparel of men and women from various ranks and countries. It is intriguing to note the proliferation of visual print media in Japan in this same period, illustrating the practices of *iki* "with detailed illustrations how to look, dress, and act for both men and women."[33] The societal parallels are suggestive. Printed images drove fashion. Simultaneously, cotton textiles skirted the sumptuary regulations that multiplied from the late 1600s onward.[34]

Sumptuary laws sought to control the most potentially unruly social groups— the commercial classes.[35] Regulations could have teeth. In 1728, the sight of a beautifully dressed woman and her attendants charmed the Shogun Tsunayoshi during his progress into Edo. He later enquired about this woman, only to discover that she was a merchant's wife and not a noble woman as he had assumed. The Shogun was deeply offended by this material insubordination and both husband and wife were charged with "ostentatiousness beyond their station"; their property was seized and they were banished from the city.[36] The fact that it was a merchant's wife who so offended is hardly accidental. Merchants epitomized the inconstancy of the material world, revealed in their collective and individual aspirations, often at odds with those in inherited positions. Additionally, women were routinely sanctioned more frequently by sumptuary regimes.[37] Wearing more discreet cottons might help avoid such incidents. That was certainly part of the attraction of patterned cottons in this era. Thus, as *iki*-inspired kimono grew in popularity, carefully chosen cotton fabrics could still mark membership in an "aesthetic networks" but avoid official censure. Cottons embellished with outlandish embroidery and "unusual weaving and dyeing" were officially precluded.[38] But a subtly subversive challenge might escape notice, if crafted with the clever counterpoint of stripes, checks and discreet accents of printed floral cotton.[39] There was a widening participation in this cultural performance, a phenomenon captured in many printed images from this period. Popular figures such as actors and sumo wrestlers and popular locales, like teahouses, were the subjects of innumerable prints over this period—most of the figures attired in garments and accessories with the look of printed cotton deftly deployed for optimum impact [see Fig. 10.2].

As Ikegami writes, the spread of cotton "allowed ordinary Japanese to enjoy wearing attractively coloured kimono for the first time in the country's history."[40] Sumptuary laws did not stop material change. Rather, innovation took a more oblique path, ultimately building local industrial capacity as the taste for cotton

Figure 10.2 "A View of Nakazu," Toyaharu Utagawa, c. 1772–3. Pedestrians crossing a bridge. FP 2-JPD, no. 1935. Library of Congress Prints and Photographs Division, Washington DC.

textiles took hold. The agency of this commodity is evident in several ways. Cotton textiles elicited a strong reaction from the outset, as a result of their tactile and functional qualities. From that point onwards, *patterned* cotton fabrics became emblematic of the social changes at work throughout Japan. The fashion politics of Tokugawa Japan involved an artful resistance, reflected in part in the widespread use of foreign fabrics (or foreign-inspired designs). Importantly, these associations with foreignness were welcomed by consumers and tolerated by the authorities, as local manufacturing capacity grew.

There are intriguing parallels in the Japanese and European experiences most particularly in the sometimes-fraught practices of fashion, consumerism and sumptuary regulation. However, cotton textiles' less-opulent characteristics did not assuage all critics and in Europe the "foreignness" of this commodity produced both positive and negative reactions. The claim by Pomeranz that Europe embraced all foreign manufactured goods with alacrity (while Asia did not) needs more careful parsing, noting the histories of individual commodities.

Indian textiles flowed into northwest Europe after 1500, initially in quantities too small to excite many opponents, becoming increasingly common over the 1600s. As in Japan, the 1680s marked the high tide of cotton imports, though with much higher volumes imported into Europe. About a million and a half pieces arrived from India through the English East India Company in 1684, while the Dutch East India Company also expanded their importation of textiles. Simultaneously, more men and women incorporated Indian wares into their domestic furnishing and their wardrobes.[41] Equally important, European embroiderers responded to the designs found on Indian cotton and augmented their design repertoires from these models.[42] The result was a cross-cultural dialogue in stitchery. Peter Burke writes of "cultural translation" as "a double process of decontextualization and recontextualization."[43] Women of many social classes translated Indian textiles into new embroidered forms—curtains, cushions, hangings and coverlets—interpreting the devices to fit with their imaginative priorities.[44] The significance of their work lies in the hybrid Indian motifs revised and integrated into seventeenth-century European material life.[45] This distinctive female practice also had other implications, not least that it shaped the context for the anti-calico political campaigns that followed, that aimed at barring all Indian textiles from the continent. Female consumers were particular targets in these campaigns.

Sheilagh Ogilvie observes that the imposition of social discipline on the population of early modern Europe was a central tenet of European governments, intending to regulate "people's private lives."[46] Ogilvie advocates a rigorous comparison of regulatory regimes for insights into early modern European societies and points to the differing consumption and legal sumptuary regimes, with significant ramifications for material life and regional development.[47] Women's dress was always a matter of public debate and most frequently censured by authorities.[48] Unusually, in England all formal sumptuary legislation was repealed in 1604 and no legal mechanisms existed to enforce such restriction, even if some wished for those laws. Indeed, the notable absence of this category of law in England cannot be equated with a disinterest in the moral regulation of common people. The authorities were highly attuned to the politics of consumption.

Imported goods carried political baggage. They could produce a backlash because of the country of origin, the impact on local manufactures, or because a new commodity blurred traditional hierarchies or challenged notions of national character. Indian cottons were declared guilty on all counts by European critics. Still, men and women experimented liberally in their dress. But, by the 1680s, wearing Indian textiles in public became a contentious act for women. Throughout Europe, anti-calico activists fulminated and plotted, instigating repeated public crusades against Indian cottons and all those seen wearing such items in city streets. The most inflammatory charges were aimed at female consumers. The anti-calico campaign is well known in economic history, presented as an example of protectionism and studied as well in political history.[49] In England, opponents included a commanding alliance of wool merchants, weavers, and landowners, who blamed their uncertain economic state on the competition with imported Indian cottons. Elsewhere in Europe other interest groups also sought to ban all Indian textiles and return once again to the customary regimes of wool, worsted, linen, and silk.

I have briefly described women's singular connection to needlework designs inspired by Indian imports. By about 1700 there was a higher percent of unmarried women in England than in previous generations and they needed to work. Their jobs took many forms, including domestic service, and their growing numbers were very evident in major cities like London. In Western Europe in particular, women dominated the new consumer trades, whether stitching cheap ready-made garments, or making buttons, pins, and ribbons. They staffed the rising numbers of urban shops and served in coffee houses and market stalls or hawked goods in the streets.[50] The earnings of increased numbers of single and married women contributing to what Jan de Vries calls "the industrious revolution." De Vries observes "[t]he industrious revolution has as its social pendant female earning power."[51] Wearing a printed cotton gown or petticoat signaled allegiance to fashionable aesthetics and demonstrated the creative independence of women consumers [see Fig. 10.3]. But such choices left women open to charges of indulgence and even treason. Women's taste for patterned cotton apparel was very evident by the late 1600s, spreading from the "Common-Garden Bitch [to the] Town-bred Miss," as one detractor wrote.[52] The question confronting opponents of Indian imports was how to contain women's material desires.

France opened the attack on Indian cottons in the 1680s, banning them from the country, beginning an offensive that rippled across Europe. French

Figure 10.3 There was an immediate visual impact from this printed garment. Caraco and petticoat, printed cotton made on the Coromandel Coast, India, c. 1770–80. T.229&A-1927, given by Sir Luke Fildes KC. © Victoria and Albert Museum, London.

consumers declined to follow this law and further edicts followed. In response to their fashion insurgency, in 1695 a Parisian merchant ruminated on more dramatic tactics, proposing to offer 500 *livres* to men willing "to strip … in the street, any woman wearing Indian fabrics," in a scenario blending punishment and ridicule.[53] This scheme was not the only expression of mercantile misogyny. In England, the opposition to foreign textiles was not adjudicated solely in the Parliament, but played out in the streets of London.[54] An Act was ultimately passed in 1700, but it excluded only printed cottons and allowed plain goods to enter the country to be printed by local artisans. This law was a practical failure. A 1703 verse exemplifies the rage campaigners directed at women consumers, naming those wearing calicoes as "Jilts," "Satyrs," and "Patched, painted powder'd Drury Whores." The author proposed to "tear your Gawdy Cloaths, and pay your Backs."[55] This doggerel, one of many, equated women's choices in the marketplace with sexual misconduct deserving the lash, the penalty for common prostitutes. The anti-calico campaign intensified, defending a social and material hierarchy: a landed, commercial, political, and artisanal coalition based on the wool trade. This cross-class alliance of weavers, merchants and landowners marked one of the most potent constituencies in the nation.

By 1719 tensions were at their peak, as the English Parliament considered a second bill to bar Indian textiles. Politics took a physical turn one June evening as about 4,000 angry weavers and their supporters directed their rage against printed cottons and women dressed in these fabrics. They poured through London streets, tearing "the English and Foreign Callicoes from off the Backs of all the Women they met."[56] This marked the beginning of a violent extra-Parliamentary campaign against female consumers, a project of unprecedented scale and duration. Week after week, women attired in calico (or fabrics that looked like calico) were mobbed and beaten and their clothes ripped from their bodies. All women in public were open to attack, like the alewife that ran a tavern in Whitechapel, east London. When an anti-calico activist saw the landlady in a printed gown he "pulled out his Knife to cut it to pieces, but being prevented and turned out of Doors, he whetted his Knife upon his Shoe, and swore he would either cut the Callicoes, or stab her to the Heart." What one newspaper described as "Fighting and Mischief" ensued as husbands and male friends fought to defend women under attack.[57] In one case a butcher, shielding his wife from crowds of assailants, killed one man with his cleaver.[58]

Weavers employed an array of well-known rituals of protest; looters wrapped fabrics round their waists and waved the cloth like banners seized in combat as they raced down city streets after hit-and-run attacks on shops. Shreds of calico torn from women's gowns were nailed on a gibbet in a London thoroughfare. Nailing torn fragments of cloth to a London gibbet sought to transform these fabrics from objects of desire into emblems of shame and derision. Such a result was not easily achieved. Violence continued throughout the summer and reports of acid throwing next appeared in London papers.[59] *Aqua fortis*, or nitric acid, was hurled at women seen wearing calico "in Houses or Coaches." The targets were genteel women usually safe from plebeian insults in sedan chairs, coaches, and their homes.

Why did women keep wearing such perilous garments? We have no direct record of plebeian women's thoughts on this question. We can assume that some could not afford to replace a valued piece of their wardrobe. But women's embroidery of Indian-inspired designs also reflects their distinctive engagement with Indian goods. This connection may have impelled some to defy the attempted censorship. Or, the persistence of this fashion may be a sign of a deeply felt entitlement to self-expression. Among the hundreds of pamphlets printed during this dispute there are fleeting references to the ideal of women having "Liberty" in dress, including "Wearing what we please, and Thinking or Believing what we please."[60] This was a contentious claim. Fighting spread through the winter and spring of 1720, even as a new anti-calico bill was debated in Parliament.[61] The port of Bristol experienced at least one heated encounter that led to a weaver's death and the trial of his suspected assailant.[62]

Sumptuary laws were no longer part of the English legal environment. But the premise of such legislation retained a tenacious hold on elite sensibilities. The vilification of women reflected a broad-based effort to enforce a collective material discipline and to impose a traditional moral economy over a largely female consumer group. How could printed cotton generate such discursive dissonance? It is important to recall that printing on cloth was *not* a European practice. Traditional European techniques of textile embellishment involved patterning in the loom or embroidery, both of which were more costly and time-consuming than printing. Textile printing was an Indian innovation and adding color and design even to cheap cloth was an ideal technique for a burgeoning consumer society [see Fig. 10.4]. Thus, printed textiles signaled a radical departure from past European norms. Regardless of the origins of this cloth, they symbolized the new fashion-driven economy abhorrent to those dependent on time-honored materials and time-honored sectors. In this circumstance, *any* printed garment embodied the implacable rivalry between old and new moral economies. Eventually the wool interests achieved their political aim. An Act was passed in March 1721 banning most Indian textiles from English soil after Christmas 1722, similar to laws elsewhere in Europe.[63] Weavers celebrated with a great bonfire.[64] At the climax of this celebration an effigy of "an old Woman drest in Calicoe" was thrown on the flames.[65] As the effigy burned the customary social balance seemed restored, with crowds cheering the burning form.

Indian calicoes (plain and printed) were barred from English markets. But the political tensions surrounding this fashion remained. Women wearing any kind of printed garment, including locally made printed linen, continued to be harassed. Persecutions continued through much of the 1720s and revived

Figure 10.4   Indian printed cotton on coarse fabric, eighteenth century. This printed textiles was designed for the lower end of the European fashion market. Accession number 20. 1951, Denman Waldo Ross Collection, Museum of Fine Arts, Boston ©.

again in the 1730s in several regions of Britain and Ireland. Dublin newspapers report in 1735 the renewed "Gang" activity, with men "squirting Aqua-Fortis" on unlucky "Ladies," while the "meaner Sort" of women endured beatings and ripped clothing.[66] These outbreaks did not subside until later in the 1730s, when Parliament specifically approved British-made printed linens for the British market. The gradual *domestication* of a once exclusively "foreign" commodity ultimately altered the political equation, as British manufacturers struggled to replicate Indian technologies.

Conclusion

In both Japan and northwest Europe, Indian cottons challenged normative structures. Writing about nineteenth-century Europe, Gilles Lipovetsky notes that: "Fashion … [became] the permanent theatre of ephemeral metamorphoses because the individualization of appearance … won a new status of social legitimacy."[67] This point is well taken. However, adjustment to this regime was a multi-generational process. Japanese consumers welcomed foreign cotton imports. They incorporated these fabrics into the strict sumptuary environment of Tokugawa Japan, employing these fabrics in some instances to push the legal limits of this material regime. The association with the "foreign" continued in the nomenclature assigned these textiles, even as more of these goods were made in Japan. This case study of fashion politics provides an important illustration of the adaptable, generative history of fashion in Asia. For, despite the Pomeranz hypothesis, regions of Asia displayed a keen interest in "exotic *manufactured* goods."[68] Furthermore, extant Japanese sumptuary laws may inadvertently have assisted in the cotton/fashion evolution.

Sheilagh Ogilvie posits a sharp differentiation between the relative openness of Western European societies (England in particular) and the highly prescriptive sumptuary environment of Central Europe. She notes that for regions of Germany "women faced a huge array of institutional constraints on their work and consumption choices."[69] Her evidence of such regional constraints is convincing. However, claims for English "openness" must be carefully weighed given this case study. Formal sumptuary laws were absent in England, such as Ogilvie describes for early modern Germany, interventions that appear to have reduced material options for marginal consumers in Germany.[70] However, such systems might also have had other results. They may also have dampened social tensions surrounding the diffusion of "new luxuries," or channeled material defiance into other tracks, as in Japan. This was a transitional period when societies were called upon to weather profound social and economic changes. Were the constraining processes of sumptuary regulation an inadvertent means of mediating social friction, in the face of new commodities and new fashion norms? Certainly this was not the intent of legislators. Change in the material culture of England is well documented. But did the absence of formal sumptuary laws in England shape the environment for the widespread, vitriolic anti-calico campaign, driven as it was by a commanding alliance? Without these legal structures, and in the face of powerful factions strongly defending a material status quo, social discipline was deployed outside legal channels. Rather than navigating around well-established sumptuary laws, as was common in almost all early modern societies, English consumers faced a coalition of *ad hoc* opponents attempting to enforce *de facto* sumptuary standards. Thus, social discipline passed not through the courts but through co-ordinated groups insti-gating brutal attacks over years, and women's bodies were the battleground.

A fashion economy accepts the push and pull of competing commodities; it can absorb the disruptions occasioned by new goods and will tolerate plebeian expressions of style. The shattering of stable material hierarchies and the gradual acceptance of individual rights in dress took different routes in different developing societies. Individual rights in dress did not come readily in any community. Infractions against real and symbolic regulatory systems were penalized. In some instances the process of adjustment came with violent outbursts against distinctive fashion actors; while other cases were charac-terized by lower-level clashes and a gradual, subtle defiance of legal norms and prescribed materiality. The flourishing of *iki*-inspired styles in Tokugawa Japan reveals this other path. The systematic violence against calico-wearing women reflects how ruthlessly traditional materials could be defended, particularly when innovations were symbolized by female agency. The battles over the fashion meanings of Indian cottons are a vital part of this history and an important distinguishing marker of the development processes underway in the world communities. Indian cottons came to epitomize a fashionable collectivity, a growing individualism and a new materiality. The women and men navigating these rough waters defined the evolving characteristics of a fashion-driven consumer economy.

Notes

1   Another version of this chapter was published as "Le goût du coton: culture matérielle, politique et consommation dans le Japon des Tokugawa et l'Angleterre moderne," *Revue d'histoire moderne et contemporaine,* 2013/1 (n° 60–1), pp. 71–106.

2   Among the pioneer studies see: Jan De Vries "Peasant Demand and Economic Development: Friesland 1559–1700," in William Parker and E. L. Jones eds, *European Peasants and their Markets*, Princeton: Princeton University Press, 1975; *Economic Policy and Projects: The Development of a Consumer Society in Early Modern England*, Oxford: Clarendon Press, 1978; McKendrick, Neil, John Brewer, and J. H. Plumb, *The Birth of a Consumer Society: The Commercialization of Eighteenth-Century England*, London: Hutchinson, 1982; Lorna Weatherill, *Consumer Behaviour and Material Culture in Britain, 1660–1760*, London: Routledge, 1988.

3   For example, Kenneth Pomeranz, *The Great Divergence: Europe, China, and the Making of the Modern World Economy*, Princeton: Princeton University Press, 2000, pp. 114–65; Antonia Finnane, *Changing Clothes in China: Fashion, History, Nation.* New York: Columbia University Press, 2008; Janet Hunter and Penelope Francks eds, *The Historical Consumer: Consumption and Everyday Life in Japan, 1850–2000*, London: Palgrave, 2012.

4   Pomeranz, *The Great Divergence*, p. 152.

5   See, for example, Alan Hunt, *Governance of Consuming Passions: A History of Sumptuary Law*, Basingstoke: Macmillan, 1996, pp. 22–34; Robert Ross, *Clothing, A Global History: Or, the Imperialists' New Clothes*, Cambridge: Polity Press, 2008, pp. 12–25.

6   Ann Rosalind Jones and Peter Stallybrass, *Renaissance Clothing and the Materials of Memory*, Cambridge: Cambridge University Press, 2000, p. 2.

7   Jack Goldstone, "Efflorescences and economic growth in world history: rethinking the 'rise of the west' and the industrial revolution," *Journal of World History*, 13, 2 (2002): 330–2); S. A. M. Adshead, *Material Culture in Europe and China, 1400–1800*, New York: St Martin's Press, 1997; Pomeranz, *The Great Divergence*.

8   Anne McCants, "Exotic goods, popular consumption, and the standard of living: thinking about globalization in the early modern world," *Journal of World History*, 18, 4 (2007): 435; Susan B. Hanley, *Everyday Things in Premodern Japan: The Hidden Legacy of Material Culture*, Berkeley: University of California Press, 1997, p. 5.

9   Chris Gosden, "What do objects want?" *Journal of Archaeological Method and Theory*, 12, 3 (2005): 196.

10   Quoted in Catherine Richardson, "Introduction" in Catherine Richardson ed., *Clothing Culture, 1350–1650*, Aldershot: Ashgate, 2004, p. 19.

11   Beverly Lemire, *Cotton*, Oxford: Berg, 2011, pp. 26–30.

12   Andrew Sherratt "Reviving the grand narrative: archaeology and long-term change," *Journal of European Archaeology*, 3, 1 (1995): 14.

13   Pomeranz, *The Great Divergence*, pp. 127–33.

14   Samurai made such complaints. Hanley, *Everyday Things in Premodern Japan*, p. 2.

15   Masayuki Tanimoto, "Cotton and the Peasant Economy: A Foreign Fibre in Early Modern Japan," in Giorgio Riello and Prasannan Parthasarathi, *The Spinning World: A Global History of Cotton Textiles, 1200–1850*, Oxford: Oxford University Press, 2009, pp. 368–9.

16   Fujita Kayoko, "Japan Indianized: The Material Culture of Imported Textiles in Japan, 1550–1850," in Riello and Parthasarathi eds, *The Spinning World*, pp. 181–204.

17   John Whitney Hall, *The Cambridge History of Japan: Early Modern Japan*, vol. 4, Cambridge: Cambridge University Press, 1991, pp. 510–13; Toby Slade, *Japanese Fashion: A Cultural History*, Oxford: Berg, 2009, p. 53; Tonimoto, "Cotton and the Peasant Economy," p. 369; Yoshiko Iwamoto Wada, Mary Kellogg Rice, and Jane Barton, *Shibori: The Inventive Art of Japanese Shaped Resist Dyeing*, Tokyo: Kodansha International Ltd., 1999, p. 275.

18   Kayoko, "Japan Indianized," pp. 189–90.

19   Ibid., p. 184.

20   Jan de Vries, *The Industrious Revolution: Consumer Behavior and the Household Economy, 1650 to the Present*, Cambridge: Cambridge University Press, 2008, p. 44.

21 Ibid., p. 45.

22 Hall, *The Cambridge History of Japan*, pp. 510–13.

23 Pomeranz, *The Great Divergence*, p. 149.

24 Kaoru Sugihara, "London School of Economics, Working Papers," Global Economic History Network. 02 2004. http://eprints.lse.ac.uk/22490/1/wp02.pdf (accessed July 10, 2011).

25 *The Eight Voyages set forth by the East-Indian Societie, wherein were imployed three Ship*s ... London: 1625, pp, 372, 374.

26 Eido Ikegami, *Bonds of Civility: Aesthetic Networks and the Political Origins of Japanese Culture*, Cambridge: Cambridge University Press, 2005, p. 245.

27 See, for example, Mitsutoshi Nakano, "The Role of Traditional Aesthetics," in Andrew D. Gerstle eds., *18th Century Japan: Culture and Society*, Richmond: Curzon Press, 1989.

28 Teruoka Yasutaka, "The Pleasure Quarters and Tokugawa Culture," in Andrew C. Gerstle ed., *18th-Century Japan: Culture and Society*, Richmond: Curzon Press, 1989, pp. 3–32.

29 Jay Keister, "Urban style, sexuality, resistance, and refinement in the Japanese Dance Sukeroku," *Asian Theatre Journal*, 26, 2 (2009), p. 216.

30 Kayoko, "Japan Indianized," pp. 190–1.

31 Pomeranz, *The Great Divergence*, p. 157, original italics.

32 Ulinka Rublack, *Dressing Up: Cultural Identity in Renaissance Europe*, Oxford: Oxford University Press, 2010, p. 21.

33 Keister, "Urban Style," p. 221.

34 Donald H. Shively, "Sumptuary regulation and status in early Tokugawa Japan," *Harvard Journal of Asiatic Studies*, 25 (1964–5): 123–6.

35 Hunt, *Governance of Consuming Passions*, p. 23.

36 Shively, "Sumptuary Regulation," p. 128.

37 Sheila Ogilvie, "Consumption, social capital, and the 'industrious revolution' in early modern Germany," *Journal of Economic History*, 70, 2 (2010): 308–9.

38 Shively, "Sumptuary Regulation," pp. 126–30.

39 Kayoko, "Japan Indianized."

40 Ikegami, *Bonds of Civility*, p. 253.

41 Lemire, *Cotton*, pp. 26–30, 48–9; Om Prakash, "The Dutch and the Indian Ocean Textile Trade," in Riello and Parthasarathi eds, *The Spinning World*, pp.150–3.

42 Therle Hughes, *English Domestic Needlework, 1600–1860*, London: Abbey Fine Arts Press, 1961.

43 Peter Burke, "Cultures of Translation in Early Modern Europe," in Peter Burke and R. Po-Chia Hsia eds, *Cultural Translation in Early Modern Europe*, Cambridge: Cambridge University Press, 2007, p. 10.

44 Hughes, *English Domestic Needlework*, p. 34. Maria Jose de Mendonça, "Some Kinds of Indo-Portuguese Quilts in the Collection of the Museu de Arte Antiga" in *Embroidered Quits From the Museu Nacional de Arte Antiga, Lisboa*, London: Kensington Palace, 1978, pp. 13–14.

45　Beverly Lemire, "Domesticating the exotic: floral culture and the East India calico trade with England, c. 1600–1800," *Textile: Journal of Cloth and Culture*, 1, 1 (2003): 65–85.

46　Sheilagh Ogilvie, "'So that every subject knows how to behave': social disciplining in early modern Bohemia," *Comparative Studies in Society and History*, 48, 1 (2006): 38–78.

47　Ogilvie, "Consumption, social capital, and the 'industrious revolution.'"

48　Ibid., p. 308.

49　For example, Natalie Rothstein, "The calico campaign of 1719–1721," *East London Papers*, 10 (1964): 3–21; N. B. Harte, "The Rise of Protection and the English Linen Trade, 1690–1790," in N. B. Harte and K. G. Ponting eds, *Textile History and Economic History: Essays in Honour of Miss Julia de Lacy Mann*. Manchester: Manchester University Press, 1973, pp. 74–112; P. K. O'Brien, T. Griffiths, and P. Hunt, "Political Components of the industrial revolution: parliament and the English cotton textile industry, 1660–1774," *Economic History Review*, 44, 3 (1991): 395–423.

50　Beverly Lemire, *Dress, Culture and Commerce: The English Clothing Trade Before the Factory*, Basingstoke: Macmillan, 1997.

51　De Vries, *Industrious Revolution*, p. 179. For discussion of the involvement of women and girls in key consumer industries see Maxine Berg, *The Age of Manufactures, 1700–1820*, 2nd edn, London: Routledge, 1994, ch. 7; Lemire, *Dress, Culture and Commerce*, chs 1 and 2; and Elizabeth Sanderson, *Women and Work in Eighteenth-Century Edinburgh*, Basingstoke: Macmillan, 1996, Chs 1 and 2.

52　R. L., *Pride's Exchange Broke Up: or Indian Calicoes and Silks Expos'd*, London, 1703.

53　Fernand Braudel, *Civilization and Capitalism 15th–18th Century: The Wheels of Commerce*, Sian Reynolds (trans.), vol. 2, New York: Harper & Row, 1982, p. 178.

54　*Old Bailey Proceedings Online* (www.oldbaileyonline.org, version 6.0, September 15, 2011), February 1697, trial of William Norman (t16970224-34).

55　R. L., *Pride's Exchange Broke Up*.

56　*Weekly Journal or British Gazetteer*, June 20, 1719.

57　*Weekly Packet*, August 8, 1719–August 15, 1719.

58　*Weekly Journal or Saturday's Post*, June 13, 1719.

59　*Weekly Journal or British Gazetteer* (London, England), Saturday, June 13, 1719; *Post Boy* (1695) (London, England), September 8, 1719–September 10, 1719.

60　Daniel Defoe, *The Just Complaints of the Poor Weavers Truly Represented …* London, 1719.

61　*Weekly Journal or Saturday's Post*, September 12, 1719; *Original Weekly Journal*, January 2. 1720; *Daily Post*, May 5. 1720; *Weekly Journal or Saturday's Post*, May 7, 1720, May 4, 1720, May 21, 1720.

62　*Weekly Packet*, July 16, 1720; *Applebee's Original Weekly Journal*, August 13, 1720.

63　Beverly Lemire and Giorgio Riello, "East and West: Textiles and fashion in early modern Europe," *Journal of Social History*, 41, 4 (2008): 898.

64 For example, David Cressy, *Bonfires and Bells: National Memory and the Protestant Calendar in Elizabethan and Stuart England*, London: Weidenfeld & Nicolson, 1989.

65 *Weekly Journal or Saturday's Post*, April 1, 1721.

66 *General Evening Post*, May 31, 1735.

67 Lipovetsky, *Empire of Fashion*, p. 47.

68 Pomeranz, *The Great Divergence*, p. 157.

69 Ogilvie, "Consumption, Social Capital, and the 'Industrious Revolution,'" p. 289.

70 Ibid., pp. 287–325.

Bibliography

Applebee's Original Weekly Journal, London, August 13, 1720.
Daily Post, London, May 5, 1720.
General Evening Post, 31 May 1735.
Original Weekly Journal, London, January 2, 1720.
Post Boy, London, September 8–10, 1719.
Post Boy, London, December 1722.
Weekly Journal or British Gazetteer, June 20, 1719.
Weekly Packet, London, August 8–15, 1719.
Weekly Journal or Saturday's Post, London, June 27, 1719.
Weekly Journal or Saturday's Post, London, 1721.

The Eight Voyages set forth by the East-Indian Societie, wherein were imployed three Ships ... London: 1625.
The Female Manufacturers Complaints: Being the Humble Petition of Dorothy Distaff ... London: 1720.
Old Bailey Proceedings Online, www.oldbaileyonline.org (accessed September 15, 2011).
Adhead, S. A. M., *Material Culture in Europe and China, 1400–1800*, New York: St Martin's Press, 1997.
Berg, Maxine, *The Age of Manufactures, 1700–1820*, 2nd edn., London: Routledge, 1994.
Blanch, John, *An Abstract of the Grievances of Trade which Oppresses Our Poor*, London: 1694.
Braudel, Fernand, *Civilization and Capitalism 15th–18th Century: The Wheels of Commerce*, Sian Reynolds (trans.), vol. 2, New York: Harper & Row, 1982.
Burke, Peter, "Cultures of Translation in Early Modern Europe," in Peter Burke and R. Po-Chia Hsia eds, *Cultural Translation in Early Modern Europe*, Cambridge: Cambridge University Press, 2007.
Cressy, David, *Bonfires and Bells: National Memory and the Protestant Calendar in Elizabethan and Stuart England*, London: Weidenfeld & Nicolson, 1989.
Defoe, Daniel, *The Just Complaints of the Poor Weavers Truly Represented, with as Much Answer as it Deserves*, London: 1719.
De Mendonca, Maria Jose, "Some Kinds of Indo-Portuguese Quilts in the collection of the Museu de Arte Antiga," in *Embroidered Quilts From the Museu Nacional de Arte Antiga, Lisboa*, London: Kensington Palace, 1978.

De Vries, Jan, "Peasant Demand and Economic Development: Friesland 1559–1700," in William Parker and E. L. Jones eds, *European Peasants and their Markets*, Princeton: Princeton University Press, 1975.

De Vries, Jan, *The Industrious Revolution: Consumer Behavior and the Household Economy, 1650 to the Present*, Cambridge: Cambridge University Press, 2008.

Finnane, Antonia, *Changing Clothes in China: Fashion, History, Nation.* New York: Columbia University Press, 2008.

Goldstone, Jack, "Efflorescences and economic growth in world history: rethinking the 'rise of the west' and the industrial revolution," *Journal of World History*, 13, 2 (2002): 323–89.

Gosden, Chris, "What Do Objects Want?" *Journal of Archaeological Method and Theory*, 12, 3 (2005), pp. 193–211.

Hall, John Whitney, *The Cambridge History of Japan: Early Modern Japan*, vol. 4, Cambridge: Cambridge University Press, 1991.

Hanley, Susan B., *Everyday Things in Premodern Japan: The Hidden Legacy of Material Culture*, Berkeley: University of California Press, 1997.

Harte, N. B., "The Rise of Protection and the English Linen Trade, 1690–1790," in N. B. Harte and K. G. Ponting eds, *Textile History and Economic History: Essays in Honour of Miss Julia de Lacy Mann*. Manchester: Manchester University Press, 1973.

Horwitz, Henry, "The East India trade, the politicians, and the constitution: 1689–1702," *Journal of British Studies*, 17, 2 (1978): 1–18.

Hughes, Therle, *English Domestic Needlework, 1600–1860*, London: Abbey Fine Arts Press, 1961.

Hunt, Alan, *Governance of Consuming Passions: A History of Sumptuary Law*, Basingstoke: Macmillan, 1996.

Hunter, Janet and Penelope Francks eds, *The Historical Consumer: Consumption and Everyday Life in Japan, 1850–2000*, London: Palgrave, 2012.

Ikegami, Eido, *Bonds of Civility: Aesthetic Networks and the Political Origins of Japanese Culture*, Cambridge: Cambridge University Press, 2005.

Iwamoto Wada, Yoshiko, Mary Kellogg Rice, and Jane Barton, *Shibori: The Inventive Art of Japanese Shaped Resist Dyeing*, Tokyo: Kodansha International Ltd, 1999.

Jones, Ann Rosalind and Peter Stallybrass, *Renaissance Clothing and the Materials of Memory*, Cambridge: Cambridge University Press, 2000.

Kayoko, Fujita, "Japan Indianized: The Material Culture of Imported Textiles in Japan, 1550–1850," in Giorgio Riello and Prasannan Parthasarathi eds, *The Spinning World: A Global History of Cotton Textiles, 1200–1850*, Oxford: Oxford University Press, 2009.

Keister, Jay, "Urban style, sexuality, resistance, and refinement in the Japanese dance Sukeroku," *Asian Theatre Journal*, 26, 2 (2009): 215–49.

Lemire, Beverly, *Cotton*, Oxford: Berg, 2011.

—"Domesticating the exotic: floral culture and the east India calico trade with England, c. 1600–1800," *Textile: Journal of Cloth and Culture*, 1, 1 (2003), pp. 65–85.

—*Dress, Culture and Commerce: The English Clothing Trade Before the Factory*, Basingstoke: Macmillan, 1997.

Lemire, Beverly and Giorgio Riello, "East and West: textiles and fashion in early modern Europe," *Journal of Social History*, 41, 4 (2008): 887–916.

Lipovetsky, Gilles, *The Empire of Fashion: Dressing Modern Democracy*, Catherine Porter, trans., Princeton: Princeton University Press, 1994.

McCants, Anne, "Exotic Goods, popular consumption, and the standard of living: thinking about globalization in the early modern world," *Journal of World History*, 18, 4 (2007), pp. 433–62.

McKendrick, Neil, John Brewer, and J. H. Plumb, *The Birth of a Consumer Society: The Commercialization of Eighteenth-Century England*, London: Hutchinson, 1982.

Nakano, Mitsutoshi, "The Role of Traditional Aesthetics," in Andrew D. Gerstle eds., *18th Century Japan: Culture and Society*, Richmond: Curzon Press, 1989.

O'Brien, P. K., T. Griffiths, and P. Hunt, "Political Components of the Industrial Revolution: Parliament and the English Cotton Textile Industry, 1660–1774," *Economic History Review*, 44, 3 (1991): 395–423.

Ogilvie, Sheilagh, "Consumption, social capital, and the 'industrious revolution' in early modern Germany," *Journal of Economic History*, 70, 2 (2010), pp. 287–325.

Ogilvie, Sheilagh, "'So that every subject knows how to behave': social disciplining in early modern Bohemia," *Comparative Studies in Society and History*, 48, 1 (2006), pp. 38–78.

Pomeranz, Kenneth, *The Great Divergence: Europe, China, and the Making of the Modern World Economy*, Princeton: Princeton University Press, 2000.

Prakash, Om, "The Dutch and the Indian Ocean Textile Trade," in Giorgio Riello and Prasannan Parasarathi eds, *The Spinning World: A Global History of Cotton Textiles, 1200–1850*, Oxford: Oxford University Press, 2009.

Ramseyer, J. Mark, "Thrift and Diligence. House Codes of Tokugawa Merchant Families," *Monumenta Nipponica*, 34, 2 (1979), pp. 209–30.

Richardson, Catherine, "Introduction" in Catherine Richardson ed., *Clothing Culture, 1350–1650*, Aldershot: Ashgate, 2004.

R. L., *Pride's Exchange Broke Up: or Indian Calicoes and Silks Expos'd*, London: 1703.

Ross, Robert, *Clothing, A Global History: Or, the Imperialists' New Clothes*, Cambridge: Polity Press, 2008.

Rothstein, Natalie, "The Calico Campaign of 1719–1721," *East London Papers* 10 (1964), pp. 3–21.

Rublack, Ulinka, *Dressing Up: Cultural Identity in Renaissance Europe*, Oxford: Oxford University Press, 2010.

Sanderson, Elizabeth, *Women and Work in Eighteenth-Century Edinburgh*, Basingstoke: Macmillan, 1996.

Sherratt, Andrew, "Reviving the grand narrative: archaeology and long-term change," *Journal of European Archaeology*, 3, 1 (1995): 1–32.

Shively, Donald H., "Sumptuary Regulation and Status in Early Tokugawa Japan," *Harvard Journal of Asiatic Studies*, 25 (1964–1965): 123–64.

Slade, Toby, *Japanese Fashion: A Cultural History*, Oxford: Berg, 2009.

Sugihara, Kaoru, "London School of Economics, Working Papers," Global Economic History Network. 02 2004. http://eprints.lse.ac.uk/22490/1/wp02.pdf (accessed July 10, 2011).

Tanimoto, Masayuki, "Cotton and the Peasant Economy: A Foreign Fibre in Early Modern Japan," in Giorgio Riello and Prasannan Parthasarathi, *The Spinning World: A Global History of Cotton Textiles, 1200–1850*, Oxford: Oxford University Press, 2009.

Thirsk, Joan, *Economic Policy and Projects: The Development of a Consumer Society in Early Modern England*, Oxford: Clarendon Press, 1978.

Thomas, Keith, *The Ends of Life: Roads to Fulfillment in Early Modern England*, Oxford: Oxford University Press, 2009.

Thompson, E. P., "The Moral Economy of the English Crowd," in *Customs in Common: Studies in Traditional Popular Culture*, New York: W. W. Norton & Co., 1993.

Trentmann, Frank, "Materiality in the future of history: things, practices, and politics," *Journal of British Studies*, 48 (2009), pp. 283–307.

Van Damme, Ilja, "Middlemen and the Creation of a 'Fashion Revolution': The Experience of Antwerp in the Late Seventeenth and Eighteenth Centuries," in Beverly Lemire ed., *The Force of Fashion in Politics and Society: Global Perspectives from the Early Modern to Contemporary Times*, Aldershot: Ashgate, 2010.

Wrightson, Keith, *Earthly Necessities: Economic Lives in Early Modern Britain*, New Haven: Yale University Press, 2000.

Yasutaka, Teruoka, "The Pleasure Quarters and Tokugawa Culture," in Andrew C. Gerstle ed., *18th-Century Japan: Culture and Society*, Richmond: Curzon Press, 1989.

11
BREASTFEEDING, IDEOLOGY AND CLOTHING IN NINETEENTH-CENTURY FRANCE

GAL VENTURA

In the last decades, the maternal body has been a target for fashion designers, who are constantly inventing new cloths for both pregnant women and nursing mothers. However, is nursing fashion a new, contemporary development? What did the mothers of the past do when they wanted to nurse? Could they enjoy the benefits of the public sphere while nursing? Who was allowed to uncover her breast, and where and when? Could women be both nursing and fashionable at the same time?

This chapter will answer these questions in detail, while focusing on nursing clothing in France during the nineteenth century. My data include pictorial art as well as medical literature, commercial catalogues, etc. This chapter will thus connect nursing fashion to socio-political ideologies concerning maternal breastfeeding.

Nursing garments through Western history

The human species has always been dependent on breastfeeding, at least until the last third of the nineteenth century, when Louis Pasteur (1822–1895) invented the pasteurization of animal milk to be used to feed infants. Indeed, while examining artistic depictions of infant feeding through Western history, bottle-feeding was extremely rare in comparison to nursing women.[1] These

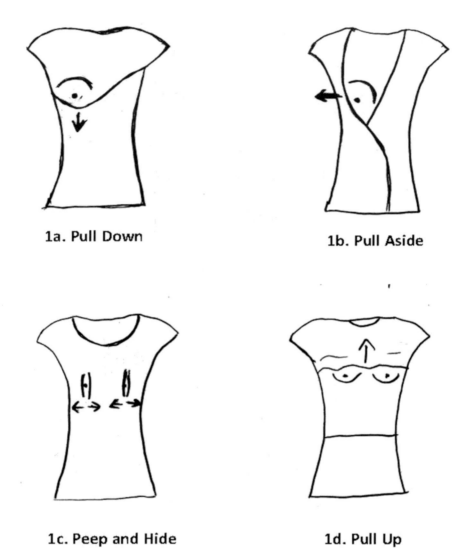

1a. Pull Down   1b. Pull Aside

1c. Peep and Hide   1d. Pull Up

Figure 11.1 Four main breastfeeding garments (G.V.).

depictions allow us to identify three major types of breastfeeding clothes, which enabled women to nurse without undressing completely: "pull down," "pull aside," and "peep and hide" [Figure 11.1, a–c]. A fourth type, "pull up" [Figure 11.1d]— which is the most easily preformed, since it only requires pulling up the shirt in order to lactate—does not appear in art, since it almost entirely covers both breast and baby, thus is less appealing for an artist who wishes to depict breastfeeding.

The first type—"pull down" [Figure 11.1a]—was generally accepted in the West, as clearly manifested through Roman depictions of Isis breastfeeding Harpocrates, or the Madonna nursing Christ in late medieval and renaissance art.[2] This type enables nursing through the dress's wide cleavage, which was pulled down in order to uncover the lactating breast. Although convenient, its disadvantages are clear: it exposes the bare shoulder, and even occasionally both breasts.[3]

The second type—"pull aside" [Figure 11.1b]—was only available through dresses that could be opened from the front. The majority of these dresses or tops included frontal buttons, which have gained popularity in the West ever since the 14th century in order to protect the body from cold weather. The main disadvantage of this method is that, much like the "pull down" mode, it uncovers the whole breast.[4] Consequently, numerous paintings depict an alternate model: "pull aside with an upper scarf," which enabled women to cover their body while nursing.

The third type—"peep and hide" [Figure 11.1c], which was the only method especially designed for nursing women—allowed them to nurse through two long slits cut in the dress's facade. This method was popular in artistic depictions from the renaissance until the end of the nineteenth century,[5] but clothing could open widely also when not nursing, thus needlessly exposing the breasts. This hazard is well illustrated in *The Fashionable Mamma or the Convenience of Modern Dress* by the British caricaturist James Gillray (1756/57–1815) from 1796 [Figure 11.2]. This caricature illustrates a trendy mother who is reluctantly nursing her baby before going to a ball through the two noticeable slits exposing her nipples, which are amusingly echoing the pattern of her dress. Indeed, this method mainly characterizes religious or allegorical women, such as the Virgin Mary or the Caritas figure. Nevertheless, the "peep-and-hide" unwanted exposure disadvantage was resolved in nineteenth-century high-collar dresses that included frontal buttons which could be open gradually on top of the breast, hence modestly covering the rest of the body while breastfeeding.

Nonetheless, despite the new nineteenth-century "peep and hide through buttons" evident advantages, most women used the "pull down" and "pull aside" systems, which enabled breastfeeding, but were not especially designed for this practice. Two different causes can explain this omission: financial status and social status that are highly linked to the possibility of exposing the breast in public. Indeed, women from lower classes, such as working-class mothers, who could not afford to buy a dress for every occasion, or to hire a wet-nurse, did not use special garments for breastfeeding. Nonetheless, they used the "pull down" and "pull aside" systems, nursing in the privacy of their shabby homes, thus avoiding the exposure of their body in public.[6] Additionally, they used the "pull up" system, which was only suitable for women who did not wear dresses.

Figure 11.2   James Gillray, *The Fashionable Mamma or The Convenience of Modern Dress*, 1796, etching, hand colored. London, Wellcome Institute and Library for the History of Medicine. Wellcome Library, London.

Beggars, on the other hand, breastfed in the public sphere and evidently uncovered their breast occasionally while nursing. This was also the case with peasant women, who occasionally nursed their children in the fields.[7] Allegedly, artistic depictions reflected the social differences in French society that enabled lower-class women to breastfeed in the public sphere, as opposed to bourgeois women, who were prevented from doing so. As a result, the only two populations that could afford unique nursing clothes were either professional wet-nurses or wealthy bourgeois women who nursed their babies themselves. However, their opposed social status, which undoubtedly influenced their nursing habits, as well as the place where they could uncover their breasts, are crucial factors in deciphering their breastfeeding garments.

La mère de lait et la mère de sang: wet-nurses *vs.* mothers

Wet-nurses have been employed since antiquity, most of them by bourgeois couples, their numbers increasing greatly in Western Europe from the 11th century on, despite strong medical opposition—doctors and moralists have throughout history strongly opposed wet-nursing.[8] Medics claimed that maternal milk is the food best suited for babies, while also establishing a strong emotional bond between the mother and her child. Several claimed that maternal breast-feeding is required by the laws of nature and her obligation towards God's commandment. At the same time, they maintained that sending a baby to a distant wet-nurse is likely to create a bond of love between baby and nurse instead of between the baby and its biological mother, although others claimed that a wet-nurse could never love the child she nourishes. In addition, numerous writers claimed that a nurse's milk can transfer the physical and moral traits of the nurse to the baby she feeds. They also warned the parents against neglect, poor hygiene and/or bad treatment by the nurse, which could endanger their baby's life.[9] Nevertheless, wet-nursing was widely accepted in France from the seventeenth century to the beginning of the twentieth among the middle and upper classes, and even among working women belonging to the urban prole-tariat in nineteenth-century France.[10]

Changing attitude towards wet-nursing during the nineteenth century

Although all nineteenth-century medical literature expressed a clear preference for maternal nursing, this evolved through three phases, which manifest the changing attitudes towards breastfeeding over time.

1) The first is exemplified by the book written by Dr. Jean-François Verdier-Heurtin in 1804.[11] He strongly opposed wet-nursing and stressed the high infant mortality resulting from this practice. The book opens with a severe criticism of mothers who refuse to breastfeed, as maternal neglect condemns entire generations to untimely death. German mothers did start breastfeeding in the eighteenth century, thus contributing to the steady growth of the German population. Verdier-Heurtin called on French mothers to give up their superficial pleasures and act according to the laws of nature.

2) The second phase shows in books written between 1820 and 1860 that stressed maternal nursing while also accepting, albeit unhappily, the alter-native. In a work published in 1827, Dr. Thomas D. Haden wrote: "Wet-nurses are sadly a necessary evil. In their absence, the upper class babies will suffer greatly."[12] The same approach emerges from a housewife's manual written by Marie Gacon-Dufour in 1826 and republished in 1834.[13] Initially, her attitude seems to resemble that of Verdier-Heurtin, as indeed she claims that nursing mothers are much more attentive to their children.[14] However, the rest of Gacon-Dufour's book casts doubt on the emphasis on maternal breastfeeding. First,

she presents several examples of the medical use of cow's milk that testify to its quality and superiority. Second, she argues that artificial feeding guarantees that the baby will get the exact amount it needs. Third, she discourses at length on nations that are known to have raised sturdy children solely on animal milk.[15] In addition, Gacon-Dufour tells the tale of an abandoned baby left on her threshold, suckled on goat's milk at her initiative, and who thrived on it. The author concludes that if she had babies herself, she would feed them in exactly the same way.[16] In contrast to Verier-Heurtin, who unambiguously supported maternal nursing, Gacon-Dufour illustrates the change that maternal nursing underwent in the early nineteenth century, when wet-nursing regained its popularity.

3) However, from the 1860s to the end of the century, such doctors as Charles Monot (1834–1914) and Jean Baptiste Victor Théophile Roussel (1816–1903)—who authored the third type of medical literature—again strongly opposed wet-nursing. In a period of awareness of France's declining population, they attributed the high mortality among infants to the practice of sending them to distant wet-nurses.[17]

Following medical recommendations, in December 1874 the Roussel Law was legislated, designed to protect babies; it obliged parents and wet-nurses to register each child that was nursed outside its home and insisted on medical examinations for both baby and wet-nurse.[18] Although the Roussel Law demonstrated a clear preference for maternal breastfeeding, it did not prevent mercenary nursing but legalized it.

From sanctity to promiscuity: live-in wet-nurses and breastfeeding uniforms

Wet-nurses' conditions

The live-in wet-nurse practice gradually became customary among the French upper and middle classes.[19] Respectively, these nurses earned five times more than their fellow workers in the country: approximately 100 francs a month instead of only 20.[20] The live-in nurses were the most important servants of the house: they were prevented from strenuous domestic tasks, and achieved improved sustenance and dwellings in comparison to all the other servants who lived in the bourgeois urban domicile. Furthermore, they received special clothing that included dresses with frontal buttons to facilitate nursing, a wide cloak, a light-colored hat decorated with two long ribbons, an apron, and a parasol to shield them from the sun.[21] These unique uniforms attracted numerous artists, who concentrated on their "peep and hide" dresses and their ribbon-decorated hats, which appeared in dozens of paintings and lithographs from the last quarter of the nineteenth century.[22]

These special outfits reflected two different issues simultaneously: practical and symbolic. On the one hand, the special "peep and hide through buttons" dresses facilitated breastfeeding in the public domain, since they enabled nurses to expose their breasts without revealing the rest of their body. In addition, the wide cloak enabled them to hide their body while nursing, whereas the umbrella protected them from the sun. On the other hand, the "peep and hide through buttons" system detached their lactating breast from the rest of their body, thus turned it into an isolated, separated organ. This symbolic detachment was a well-known visual technique, chiefly used in late medieval and renaissance images of the *Madonna Lactans* (lactating virgin), who was portrayed nursing from a singular breast, peculiarly attached to her thoroughly covered body.[23] Margaret Miles claims that this method distanced Maria's breast from erotic implications, and confirmed her asexual nature. The resemblance between the nurses' detached breast and the singular Madonna breast heightened the maternal function of this organ, while disregarding the rest of her body. By focusing on the bare breast, the "peep and hide" method concentrated on her professional attribute, while desexualizing her as a woman and dehumanizing her as a person.

Furthermore, the special attention given to their unique head-gear—which had nothing to do with breastfeeding—symbolized wet-nurses' distinctive position, thus serving as visual evidence of their occupation. At the same time, it also symbolized the elevated financial and social rank of their employers.[24]

Positive depictions of wet-nurses

These aspects are demonstrated in Edgar Degas's *At the Races in the Country* (*Aux courses en province*) from 1869 [Figure 11.3], depicting the Valpiçon family's nurse and their son Henri in their carriage at the races.[25] The wet-nurse, at the center of the composition next to Mme Valpiçon, is recognizable thanks to her special attributes: her head-gear, her parasol, her white apron, her "peep and hide" dress, and her exposed breast. According to Linda Nochlin, Degas's emphasis on the wet-nurse reflects the alienation that commonly characterizes Degas's families.[26] However, her claim doesn't fit with this particular painting as, on the contrary, Degas concentrates on the harmonious relationship between the two women, united under the parasol with the sleeping baby. Moreover, the wet-nurse here is a unifying figure, enabling the bourgeois mother, who cannot bare her breasts in public, to enjoy the family outing, while allowing the baby to benefit from the fresh air.[27] The resemblance between the nurse and one of Degas's early drawings of the Madonna[28] is further evidence of his positive and non-critical approach.

The likeness to *Maria Lactans* exists also in Degas's painting *A Wet-Nurse in the Luxembourg Gardens* from 1875, depicting a wet-nurse, identified by her

Figure 11.3 Edgar Degas, *Aux cours en province*, c. 1869, oil on canvas, 36.5 x 55.9 cm. © Museum of Fine Arts, Boston.

exposed breast and her unique uniform. In contrast to earlier representations of the wet-nurse inside her house,[29] during the second half of the nineteenth century, she was now often located in an urban park or garden. This shift reflects the medical literature, recommending daily excursions, in all weather, for both baby and wet-nurse, as well as the enormous change towards urban nature in the Second Empire: under Louis-Napoléon' reign (1852–1870), new gardens were created in Paris.[30]

Degradation of wet-nurses' depictions

A similar subject appears in Wilhio's engraving *The Wet-Nurse* from *c.* 1901. In visual homage to Degas's *At the Races in the Country* [Figure 11.13], it depicts the nurse in the new family car, along with the baby's parents. Much like Degas's painting, the print illustrates the harmonious relations between the two "mothers." The whole family is engrossed in the nursing baby, including the father, who almost runs over two frightened pigs. The sign on the left clarifies the event; it features the name of the French car company, Automobiles Dion-Bouton of Puteaux, in Western Paris, the largest car manufacturer in the world at the beginning of the twentieth century.[31] It seems that the family is just returning from the factory in their new car, which further explains the father's reckless driving. At the same time, the combination of the wet-nurse and the new family car—which has replaced Degas's carriage—creates a double status symbol clearly testifying to this bourgeois family's socioeconomic status.

Yet, the wet-nurse in Wilho's engraving differs greatly from Degas's nurses, since instead of the "peep and hide" dress, she is using the "pull aside" system, thus uncovering her whole breast and shoulder. Consequently, one cannot avoid wondering if the fascinated gaze of the father is in fact directed to his baby, or to the young nurse's attractive revealed body.

Unlike the positive depictions of the live-in nurse in high art, during the last decades of nineteenth century and the beginning of the twentieth century, popular art was depicting her in a derogatory light. This attitude is expressed in Eugène Gluck's *At the Luxembourg Gardens*. The painting is full of visual manifestations of courtship: two elegant bourgeois women on the right are glancing towards men standing near them; behind them, two other women are in conversation with men, while on the right the man on the bench is talking to the young lady sitting by his side. On the left, two soldiers are whispering next to the group of young wet-nurses, hoping to catch a glimpse of their bared breasts, much like the bourgeois man sitting to their right, who is raising his head from his newspaper in anticipation.

The eroticization of the nurse is demonstrated even more clearly in the lithograph by Louis Legrand entitled *The First Heat Wave* (*Premières Chaleurs*) from c. 1900,[32] where a pretty young nurse is sitting on a park bench with uncovered breasts and a passing soldier eyes her with great interest. The baby's calmness shows that he is not hungry, highlighting the lack of modesty and loose morals of the nurse. The soldier's own open tunic and his restraint on the sexual urges of his dog further accentuate the erotic insinuation.

According to Achard's *The French Painted by Themselves*, these hazards were mostly associated with the live-in nurses' new clothing. He stresses their demand for expensive garments: "since we are wet-nurses, are we obliged to renounce our rights for stylishness, this feminine soul's nourishment?" he mockingly asks. "All dolled-up, they stroll in Paris's gardens, allegedly to expose the baby to fresh air, but essentially to attract admirers. [...] She thrones on a bench or two chairs and receives homage from her vassals [...] The circle of her admirers grows or diminishes according to the variety of Parisian military garrison [...] each suitor in uniform is disputing for the privilege."[33]

A question arises: why did the attitude towards wet-nurses change under the Third Republic? What brought about this negative attitude towards wet-nursing in the last decades of the nineteenth century? One could argue that this was part of a wider negative attitude towards lower-class female workers, who were highly eroticized in popular art.[34] Eunice Lipton claims that milliners were especially prey to sexual attentions; they were constantly in the company of wealthy clients which made them aspire to a life of luxury and therefore inclined them to prostitution.[35] The same can be said of live-in nurses; they resided in wealthy homes, amid affluence, and might therefore have been tempted to try to improve their future economic condition. As opposed to other women workers, they were likely to have had prior sexual experience, and by exposing their breasts in public, they could be expected to attract more sexual attention than others. However, these caricatures depicted simple soldiers who could not elevate the nurse's living standards and pairing of the nurse with the infantryman hinted at the nurse's sexual laxity. It is noteworthy that this connection characterized the wet-nurse alone and not other working women.

Wet-nurses contradicted the glorification of motherhood in the Third Republic. Indeed, the growing eroticization of the wet-nurse paralleled the reemergence of depictions of maternal breastfeeding in art, exemplified in dozens of paintings, by Pierre Auguste Renoir (1841–1919), Mary Cassatt (1844–1926), Eugène Carrière (1849–1906), Maurice Denis (1870–1943), and many others. Portrayals of the maternal act of breastfeeding demonstrated the sharp contrast between the "dignified mother" and the wet-nurse, who sells her body like a prostitute, thereby endangering the baby.

A woman's virtue: bourgeois mothers' breastfeeding garments

This viewpoint culminated after the Franco-Prussian war (1870–1871), when womanly duties have been fully combined with maternal obligations. Indeed, during the second half of the nineteenth century numerous writers embraced a conservative approach, claiming that women's chief obligation was motherhood.[36] This approach, which strengthened in the Third Republic, is clearly evident in Simon's 1892 *Woman of the Twentieth Century* (*La Femme du vingtième siècle*):

> The body is not the sole object of a mother's care and predilection. She is a schoolteacher as well as a wet-nurse […] in education, they are everything. In our days, when religious influence is partially ruined […] women are almost the last hope for morality [....] I am a great supporter of maternal breastfeeding and […] nursing in domicile […] I have already opposed babysitters elsewhere […] Breastfeeding (for wealthy women) is a heavy burden […] the wet-nurse becomes a necessity, but the wet-nurse diminishes the mother […] Ladies, you can be in charge of your children's education […] your husband will aid you at need. You will not miss leisure activities, nor money. Leisure time? You merely have too much of it.[37]

The same approach was reinforced by the Catholic establishment. The religious "feminization" of the period, which was manifested through the risen number of women engaged in religious activities, facilitated the transference of such messages. Catholic and republican ideologies joined together to demand women to stay at home and educate their children with love and care.[38]

Thus, the combination of this new motherly ideal and the campaign against wet-nurses in the last decades of the nineteenth century contributed to a rise in maternal nursing that reached 59 percent[39] and promoted the return of the bourgeois breastfeeding mother to visual art after many years of absence. Nonetheless, 41 per cent of French mothers still renounced breastfeeding, for several different reasons. The most reluctant population was the bourgeois mother, whose only excuse, according to moralists and doctors, was her selfish pleasures. "The mother," according to Dr. Talbert's 1888 article, "in what is conventionally called the *high society*, is practically always sociable [...] She prefers the ball's orchestra over her baby's smiles."[40] This approach is manifested in Achard's *The French Painted by Themselves*, claiming that mothers refuse to nurse due to two different impediments: "the husband and the ball."[41] Indeed, the ball could prevent or withdraw maternal breastfeeding, due to three different factors. Firstly, cultural modesty codes, which prevented bourgeois mothers from exposing their breasts in public (unlike women from lower classes), denied any attempt to nurse outside the privacy of their home. Secondly, all-evening entertainments excluded children, thus disabling "nursing on demand," since the baby might be hungry while his mother is absent. Furthermore, the corset—which was a mandatory garment for upper class women at all times—prevented any attempt to breastfeed. This was one of the reasons why doctors strongly opposed this fashionable accessory, which according to Bertall was regarded as the major cause for all French nuisances, including the decline in the population's height as well as the defeat in the Franco-Prussian war.[42]

The Corset Controversy

Opposition to the corset is evident throughout the century. In *The Ladies' Dentist, Work Dedicated to the Fair Sex* (*Le Dentiste des dames, ouvrage dédié au beau sexe*), published in several editions since 1812, the well-known French surgeon Dr. Joseph-Jean-François Lemaire (1782–1834) describes the corset as ridiculously splitting the body to two parts:

> this corset [...] operates on health, a dangerous influence which should have been banished a long time ago. [...] This pressure underneath the breasts, deforms them, increase their volume, and forces their hemispheres closer together. We saw women imprisoned in their corset so as to seem less powerful, experiencing spasms, convulsions and fainting.[43]

Nevertheless, women refused to abandon the corset. According to Bertall, women will never accept to abolish this flattering, hornet's-waist providing, obligatory item. "Without a corset, one must admit, a wardrobe is impossible [...] The sole objective of corsets of a high-quality entrepreneur is to repair certain imperfections, either of nature, either of age, or of situation [...] what is the damage?"[44]

However, one of the main damages of the corset regarded maternal nursing, which was impossible while wearing one. Indeed, what could fashionable bourgeois mothers, who decided to follow the new end-of-the-century vigorous campaign against wet-nursing, wear in order to breastfeed? Furthermore, apart from the corset, the "peep and hide" method mostly symbolized professional wet-nurses by detaching their lactating breast from the rest of their body, thus affirming their unique profession. This symbolic detachment, which desexualized and dehumanized the mercenary nurse, was not suitable for bourgeois mothers, who were elevated as wives, mothers, and educators.

New corset invention

The invention of a new corset came to the rescue, thus reconciling doctors' instructions with feminine fashion's desires. At the end of the century a new corset was invented, which enabled women to breastfeed while remaining fashionable. This new device is mentioned in Dr. Alphonse Dumas's 1902 manual for pregnant women, which begins with a critique against the traditional corset.[45] Subsequently, he describes the new corset as soft, flexible, and looser that the conventional pressuring device. It could also be altered according to different shapes and figures, and most importantly "[it] liberates the breasts completely. [...]. Thus accomplished, it ceases being dangerous."[46]

This special corset had several advantages: it opened from the front, hence could be unbolted through the dress's frontal buttons without undressing completely. Additionally, it required no help from a servant, and thus allowed women to nurse freely whenever they sought.

The Breast by Paul César Helleu (1859–1927) from 1897 [Figure 11.4] shows such a corset. This engraving depicts the artist's graceful upper-class wife Alice Louis-Guérin nursing their third daughter, Alice, in their luxurious apartment. Her perceptible wedding ring clearly reveals her conjugal status while her fashionable look reflects her social status. Although she is nursing, her breast is modestly hidden by her daughter's head, thus providing her with the privacy her social status requires. Helleu is focusing on the loving gaze between the mother and her daughter, thus reflecting their symbiotic relationship. The painting behind her head, which was part of their large art collection, bears a resemblance to the rectangular halos that characterize living saints in Christian iconography,[47] thus reflects her sanctity and holiness as an iconic representation of maternal love.

Figure 11.4 Paul César Helleu, *Le Sein*, c. 1897, drypoint on paper, 57 x 41 cm. Private collection.

The same clothing solution is also shown in Édouard Debat-Ponsan's (1847–1913) *Before the Ball* from 1886, which, similarly to Helleu, located the bourgeois nursing scene inside the family's luxuriant home [Figure 11.5]. The painting depicts a young woman dressed in a beautiful satin ball gown. Her appearance, as well as her elegantly dressed husband, indicates that the are going to a ball. Yet, before leaving, she is breastfeeding from her opened "pull aside" dress. Her

Figure 11.5 Édouard Debat-Ponsan, *Avant le Bal*, 1886, oil on canvas, 87 x 65.5 cm. Tours, Musée des Beaux-Arts. © 2013. White Images/Scala, Florence.

fitted, elegant dress clearly indicates a corset, but the "pull aside" system reveals its novel, mother-friendly type. A young maid is standing behind her, waiting to take the baby to sleep after nursing, thus enabling the elegant couple to depart for their evening entertainments. Although the painting's title doesn't indicate the couple's identity, the father is actually a self-portrait of the artist; the mother is his wife, Marguerite Gernier (1856–1933). The presence of the artist—as a caring, proud father—highlights the familial aspect of breastfeeding that is no longer a distinctive feminine private activity. Contrary to nineteenth-century criticisms regarding the husband and the ball, Debat-Ponsan confirms that evening entertainments and maternal nursing are not antagonistic situations. It was only possible through the invention of the new corset.

Additional nursing inventions

The new corset was only one of the innovations that enabled maternal breastfeeding towards the end of the century. The first was the invention of breast-pumps that facilitated maternal absence. In a 1905 medical equipment catalogue, several breast-pumps are available in a variety of prices, ranging from 2.50 francs up to 15.[48] They enable women to pump milk with no assistance, while the fluid is drawn into a crystal vessel that prevents it from spoiling.[49] The same catalogue also offers rubber nipples that are worn beneath the dress, and avoid soreness or unnecessary milk leaks.[50]

An additional development was accomplished through Pasteur's end-of-the-century discoveries, which caused several doctors to recommend mixed-feeding: human milk with additional bottle-feeding.

Pasteur's scientific discoveries enabled the final control of medicine over infant-feeding that eventually abolished mercenary nursing. However, the growing use of feeding bottles did not signify a sudden learned respect for medical opinion, but rather stemmed from their suitability to the mothers' needs. In a century lacking women's rights, this new feeding method enabled women at last to assert a certain degree of freedom while enjoying both worlds—keeping their babies at home while participating in the pleasures outside their home.

Notes

1 See for example: Hubert Robert, *Jeune femme tenant un biberon à un bébé*, 1773, oil on canvas, 22 x 27 cm, Valence, Musée des Beaux-Arts.

2 See for example *Isis breastfeeding Harpocrates*, fourth century, marble, h: 150 cm., Rome, Vatican, Pio Clementino Museum; Dirck Bouts, *Madonna and Child*, 1465, oil on panel, 37.1 x 27.6 cm. London, National Gallery.

3 See for example Honoré Daumier, *La République*, 1848, sketch, oil on canvas, 73 x 60 cm. Paris, Musée d'Orsay.

4 See for example Federico Barocci, *The Holy Family with a Cat*, 1574–1577, oil on canvas, 112 x 102 cm., Chantilly, Musée Condé; Nicolas Verkolje, *Woman Breastfeeding her Child*, c. 1720, oil on canvas, 58 x 51 cm., Paris, Musée du Louvre.

5   See for example Giovanni Pisano, *Ecclesia Lactans* (detail of the pulpit), 1302–1312, marble, Pisa, Cathedral.

6   See for example Alexandre Antigna, *L'Éclair*, 1848 (Salon 1848), oil on canvas, 222 x 170 cm., Paris, Musée d'Orsay; Eugène Lacoste, *La Reprise du travail après les journées de Juin*, 1848, oil on canvas, 270 x 366 cm., Marseille, Musée des Beaux-Arts; Honoré Daumier, *La Soupe, c.* 1862–1865, black ink, watercolor and pencil on paper, 30 x 49.5 cm., Paris, Musée du Louvre, Département des Arts Graphiques.

7   See for example Edmond Herlin, *Le Battage de colza dans la plaine de Lille*, 1861 (Salon 1861), oil on canvas, 120 x 210 cm, Lille, Musée des Beaux-Arts.

8   Valerie A. Fildes, *Wet Nursing: A History from Antiquity to the Present*, Oxford: Basil Blackwell, 1988, pp. 1–78; Valerie A. Fildes, *Breasts, Bottles and Babies: A History of Infant Feeding*, Edinburgh: Edinburgh University Press, 1986, pp. 6–58; Carlo A. Corsini and Sara F. Matthews-Grieco, *Historical Perspectives on Breastfeeding*, Florence: UNICEF, International Child Development Centre, 1991, p. 16; R. Etienne, "La conscience médicale antique et la vie des enfants," *Annales de Démographie Historique*, 1973, pp. 15–46.

9   Corsini and Matthews, *Historical Perspectives*, pp. 22, 24, 27, 30–2, 36, 42, 52; Fildes, *Breasts, Bottles and Babies*, pp. 27, 85, 112, 202; Fildes, *Wet-Nursing*, pp. 70–2, 96–7, 100; Derrick B. Jelliffe and E. F. Patrice Jelliffe, *Human Milk in the Modern World: Psychological, Nutritional and Economic Significance*, Oxford: Oxford University Press, 1978, p. 134; Claude Thomasset, "The Nature of Woman," in Christiane Klapisch-Zuber ed., *A History of Women in the West: Silence of the Middle Ages*, Cambridge: Harvard University Press, 1992, vol. 2, p. 54.

10 George D. Sussman, *Selling Mothers' Milk: The Wet-Nursing Business in France, 1715–1914*, Urbana: University of Illinois Press, 1982, pp. 5–7, 19, 171–4; François Lebrun, *La Vie Conjugale sous l'Ancien Régime*, Paris, 1975, p. 126; Badinter, *L'Amour en plus. Histoire de l'amour maternel XVIIe–XXe siècle*, Paris, 1984, p. 57.

11 Jean-François Verdier-Heurtin, *Discours et essai aphoristiques sur l'allaitement et l'éducation physique des enfants*, Lyon, 1804.

12 Quoted in Fildes, *Wet-Nursing*, p. 190. See also Nicolas Philibert Adelon, et al., Nourrice, *Dictionnaire des sciences médicales*, Paris, 1819, vol. 36, pp. 287–332.

13 Mme. Marie Armande Jeanne d'Humières Gacon-Dufour, *Manuel complet de la maîtresse de maison et de la parfaite ménagère, ou guide pratique pour la gestion d'une maison à la ville et à la campagn*e, Paris, 1834.

14 Ibid., pp. 16–17.

15 Ibid., pp. 20–1.

16 Ibid., pp. 19–20.

17 Charles Monot, *De l'industrie des nourrices et de la mortalité des petits enfants*, Paris, 1867, pp. 86–9; Charles Monot, *De la mortalité excessive des enfants pendant la première année de leur existence, ses causes et des moyens de la restreindre*, Paris, 1872, pp. 23–4, 32–48, 51–63.

18 Fanny Fay-Sallois, *Les Nourrices à Paris au XIXe siècle*, Paris: Payot, 1980, p. 94.

19 Ibid., p. 6.

20 Fildes, *Wet-Nursing*, pp. 233–4.

21 Fay-Sallois, *Les Nourrices à Paris*, pp. 213–14, see photographs on pp. 208–11.

22 See for example Edgar Degas, *La Nourrice, c.* 1880–4, drawing from Notebook no. 34, p. 8, Paris, Bibliothèque Nationale.

23 See for example Ambrogio Lorenzetti, *Maria Lactans, c.* 1320–1330, tempera on panel, 90 x 45 cm.

24 Fay-Sallois, *Les Nourrices à Paris*, pp. 203, 213–14, 280.

25 Jean Sutherland Boggs ed., *Degas* [exhibition catalogue], New York: The Metropolitan Museum of Art, September 27, 1988–January 8, 1989, pp. 158–9.

26 Linda Nochlin, "A House is not a Home: Degas and the Subversion of the Family," in Richard Kendall and Griselda Pollock eds, *Dealing with Degas: Representations of Women and the Politics of Vision*, New York: Universe, 1992, p. 48.

27 A. Donné, *Conseils aux mères sur la manière d'élever les enfants nouveaux-nés, ou de l'éducation physique des enfants du premier âge*, Paris: J. B. Baillière et fils, 1842, p. 184.

28 See Edgar Degas, *Madonna and Child, sketch after a Milanese work of about 1510s, c.* 1857, pencil on paper, 29 x 22 cm., private collection (in John Rewald, *The History of Impressionism*, New York, 1973, p. 55).

29 See Pierre Duval le Camus, *La Nourrice*, 1831 (Salon 1831), oil on canvas, Paris, Musée du Louvre (collection Louis-Philippe).

30 Robert L. Herbert, *Impressionism: Art, Leisure, and Parisian Society*, New Haven: Yale University Press, 1998, pp. 141–3.

31 Jacques Chapuis, "Les Autorails de Dion-Bouton," *Chemins de fer régionaux et urbains*, 199, 1, 1987, pp. 7–10.

32 Fay-Sallois, *Les Nourrices à Paris*, p. 228.

33 Achard, "La Nourrice sur place," *Les Français peints par eux-mêmes*, vol. 1, Paris: Philippart, 1876–1878, pp. 21–3, translation by the author.

34 Eunice Lipton, *Looking into Degas: Uneasy Images of Women and Modern Life*, Berkeley: University of California Press, 1986, pp. 124–8, 151–63, figs 80–2, 99, 105.

35 Ibid., p. 161.

36 See for example Jules Michelet, *Du prêtre, de la femme, de la famille*, Paris: 1845, pp. 302–7.

37 *La Femme du vingtième siècle* [*Woman of the Twentieth Century*], Paris: Calmann Lévy, 1892, pp. 189–203, translation by the author.

38 James F. McMillan, *Housewife or Harlot: The Place of Women in French Society, 1870–1914*, Brighton: Harvester 1981, p. 10.

39 Sussman, "The Wet-Nursing Business," p. 312.

40 Quoted in ibid., pp. 69–70, translation by the author.

41 "[…] le mari et le bal" (Achard, "La Nourrice sur place," p. 17).

42 Ibid., p. 126.

43 Ibid., pp. 98–9, translation by the author.

44 Bertall, *La comédie de notre temps*, Paris: E. Plon, 1874, pp. 126–9, translation by
        the author.
45 Dr. Alphonse Dumas, *La Défense de la santé: Guide pratique de la femme
        enceinte*, Paris: J.-B. Baillière, 1902, p. 27.
46 "laissera aux seins toute leur liberté […] Ainsi confectionné, il cesse d'être
        dangereux" (ibid., p. 28).
47 James Hall, *Dictionary of Subjects and Symbols*, New York: Harper & Row (Icon
        Editions), 1979, p. 144.
48 See Léon and Jules Rainal, "Tire-laits," *Catalogue général*, Paris: Imprimerie
        Générale Lahure, 1905, p. 371, fig. 446; p. 372, figs 438, 442; p. 373, figs 443,
        1379.
49 Ibid., "Tire-laits", p. 373.
50 Ibid., "Garde-lait," p. 371, fig. 772.

Bibliography

Achard, Amédée, "La Nourrice sur place," *Les Français peints par eux-mêmes*, vol. 1,
    Paris: Philippart, 1876–1878.
Adelon, Nicolas Philibert et al., "Nourrice," *Dictionnaire des sciences médicales,* Paris,
    1819, vol. 36.
Badinter, Elisabeth, *L'Amour en plus. Histoire de l'amour maternel XVIIe–XXe siècle*,
    Paris, 1984.
Bertall, *La comédie de notre temps*, Paris: E. Plon, 1874.
Chapuis, Jacques, "Les Autorails de Dion-Bouton," *Chemins de fer régionaux et
    urbains*, 199, 1, 1987.
Corsini, Carlo A. and Sara F. Matthews-Grieco, *Historical Perspectives on
    Breastfeeding*, Florence: UNICEF, International Child Development Centre, 1991.
Donné, Alfred, *Conseils aux mères sur la manière d'élever les enfants nouveaux-nés, ou
    de l'éducation physique des enfants du premier âge*, Paris: J. B. Baillière et fils, 1842.
Dumas, Alphonse, *La Défense de la santé: Guide pratique de la femme enceinte*, Paris:
    J.-B. Baillière, 1902.
Etienne, R., "La conscience médicale antique et la vie des enfants," *Annales de
    Démographie Historique*, 1973.
Fay-Sallois, F., *Les Nourrices à Paris au XIXe siècle*, Paris: Payot, 1980.
Fildes, Valerie A., *Breasts, Bottles and Babies: A History of Infant Feeding*, Edinburgh:
    Edinburgh University Press, 1986.
—*Wet Nursing: A History from Antiquity to the Present*, Oxford: Basil Blackwell,
    1988.
Gacon-Dufour, Marie Armande Jeanne d'Humières, *Manuel complet de la maîtresse de
    maison et de la parfaite ménagère, ou guide pratique pour la gestion d'une maison à
    la ville et à la campagne*, Paris, 1834.
Hall, James, *Dictionary of Subjects and Symbols*, New York: Harper & Row (Icon
    Editions), 1979.
Herbert, Robert L., *Impressionism: Art, Leisure, and Parisian Society*, New Haven: Yale
    University Press, 1998.

Jelliffe, Derrick B. and E. F. Patrice Jelliffe, *Human Milk in the Modern World: Psychological, Nutritional and Economic Significance*, Oxford: Oxford University Press, 1978.

Lebrun, François, *La Vie Conjugale sous l'Ancien Régime*, Paris: 1975.

Lipton, Eunice, *Looking into Degas: Uneasy Images of Women and Modern Life*, Berkeley: University of California Press 1986.

McMillan, James F., *Housewife or Harlot: The Place of Women in French Society, 1870–1914*, Brighton: Harvester, 1981.

Michelet, Jules, *Du prêtre, de la femme, de la famille*, Paris: 1845.

Monot, Charles, *De l'industrie des nourrices et de la mortalité des petits enfants*, Paris, 1867.

—*De la mortalité excessive des enfants pendant la première année de leur existence, ses causes et des moyens de la restreindre*, Paris, 1872.

Nochlin, Linda, "A House is not a Home: Degas and the Subversion of the Family," in Richard Kendall and Griselda Pollock eds, *Dealing with Degas*: *Representations of Women and the Politics of Vision*, New York: Universe, 1992.

Rainal, Léon and Jules, Tire-laits," *Catalogue général*, Paris: Imprimerie Générale Lahure, 1905.

Simon, Jules, *La Femme du vingtième siècle* [*Woman of the Twentieth Century*], Paris: Calmann Lévy, 1892, pp. 189–203, translation by the author.

Sussman, George D., *Selling Mothers' Milk: The Wet-Nursing Business in France, 1715–1914*, Urbana: University of Illinois Press 1982.

Sutherland Boggs, Jean ed., *Degas* [exhibition catalogue], New York: The Metropolitan Museum of Art, September 27, 1988–January 8, 1989.

Thomasset, Claude, "The Nature of Woman," in Christiane Klapisch-Zuber ed., *A History of Women in the West*: *Silence of the Middle Ages*, Cambridge: Harvard University Press,1992, vol. 2.

Verdier-Heurtin, Jean-François, *Discours et essai aphoristiques sur l'allaitement et l'éducation physique des enfants*, Lyon, 1804.

12

DRESS AS POLITICAL IDEOLOGY IN RABELAIS AND VOLTAIRE UTOPIAS

SHOSHANA-ROSE MARZEL

The pursuit of happiness is at the heart of every utopia, since "utopia" is defined as "an ideal commonwealth whose inhabitants exist under seemingly perfect conditions. Hence *utopian* and *utopianism* are words used to denote visionary reform that tends to be impossibly idealistic."[1] Thus, either as a literary and/or a political *genre*, utopia describes an idealistic and perfect society, which includes all its satisfied members.

While proposing alternative societies, utopias also criticize existing ones; according to Maurice Tournier, "[s]ince its origins, utopia, prior to being the sign of an ideal world, presents itself as a crossing-out, as the other side of denounced unbearable realities. It is a negative word in its profoundest roots."[2] Thus, "[t]he basis of utopia's claim to be taken seriously as political theory is its critical analysis of socio-political reality, as much as its ideal vision. Social criticism is not the particular prerogative of utopians, but they conduct it in an idiosyncratic, forceful fashion, by demonstration rather than by reasoned argument."[3] Blending known elements with fantastic ones, utopia's creators invent "virtual worlds, which they locate in remote regions of the Earth, or in unexplored space (i.e. on other planets)."[4]

Basically, utopias' purpose is to deal with all of life's aspects. Yet, according to Aileen Ribeiro, the question of dress in utopias is often a problematic one: "sometimes they [utopian writers] ignore dress altogether, and at all times they play down the role of clothing, as the very notion of fashion must be inimical to a perfect and 'timeless' society."[5] Analyzing written accounts of utopias, mainly English, Aileen Ribeiro also notes that "[t]he impression created in many utopias is the desirability of the Spartan ideal of frugality and austerity."[6] Indeed, very often, utopias tend to be egalitarian political systems, where all members live a simple way of life, sometimes even an austere one—thus implying an automatic link between social equality and simplicity.

Rabelais and Voltaire, however, tread another path; Rabelais' Thélème Abbey (in *Gargantua*) and Voltaire's El Dorado (in *Candide*) propose two utopias founded on the institutionalization of civil rights as well as on wealth.[7] This chapter will show that, as important philosophers, Rabelais and Voltaire assigned clothes a wealth of significant meanings: in their utopias, dress both concretizes and symbolizes their socio-political ideologies. Indeed, Rabelais and Voltaire did not merely mention clothes in their respective utopias: as their utopias' inhabitants are richly clad, for Rabelais as well as for Voltaire, rich clothes symbolize as well as create social equality, in a just political system.

This is in contrast with many utopia writers who look to austerity as a means to achieve egalitarianism. In fact, many utopists believe that through total control—including dress—equality and happiness will be achieved, whereas Rabelais and Voltaire consider that liberty, just conditions, and opulence will bring about happiness.

Rabelais: Clothing in Thélème Abbey in Gargantua (1534)

François Rabelais (1494–1553), a major French Renaissance writer and humanist, dedicated five novels to a family of giants and their adventures. Although these books are written in an amusing and satirical vein, through them Rabelais denounces Middle Ages backwardness and promotes Renaissance values; according to David M. Posner, "[t]he comic or parodic aspects of the text are, for Rabelais, inseparable from the hermeneutic act, and are essential both to accurate reading and to a recognition of the limits of any possible interpretation."[8] In the second book of the series, *Gargantua* (1534), Rabelais introduces a utopia, the Abbey of Thélème.

This abbey is conceived in complete opposition to the formal medieval abbey: "Rabelais's […] utopian Abbey of Thélème, a humorous inversion of the monastic life depicts a monastery devoted to love, indulgence and luxury."[9] Indeed, when telling the foundation of the abbey, Rabelais stipulates expressly that

> for that the religious men and women did ordinarily make three vows, those of chastity, poverty, and obedience, it was therefore constituted and appointed that in this convent they might be honourably married, that they might be rich, and live at liberty.[10]

Poverty, chastity, and obedience, the three fundamental vows of Christian monasticism, are thus inversed in the Rabelaisian utopia. Instead of poverty, Thélèmites live in ostentatious luxury. Instead of chastity, generally achieved in monasteries by a strict separation between the sexes, with every abbey inhabited either by men or by women, in Thélème Abbey, men and women live together and enjoy each other's company on a daily basis. And instead of obedience, the Thélèmites' motto is to do whatever they want:

> All their life was spent not in laws, statutes, or rules, but according to their own free will and pleasure. They rose out of their beds when they thought good; they did eat, drink, labour, sleep, when they had a mind to it and were disposed for it. None did awake them, none did offer to constrain them to eat, drink, nor to do any other thing; for so had Gargantua established it. In all their rule and strictest tie of their order there was but this one clause to be observed,

Do What Thou Wilt;

> because men that are free, well-born, well-bred, and conversant in honest companies, have naturally an instinct and spur that prompteth them unto virtuous actions, and withdraw them from vice …[11]

Hence, liberty and personal freedom are the cornerstones of Thélème Abbey.

This utopia is described in six chapters (52–57). As material culture is of utmost importance in the Rabelaisian utopia, these chapters include numerous details on architecture, furnishing and clothing. Chapter 56 is entirely devoted to Thélème inhabitants' clothing. In doing so, Rabelais stresses the importance of Thélèmites' dress, both as a concretization of utopian goals as well as their visual representation. As such, the dress of Thélème's inhabitants is characterized by an inversion of the three fundamental ecclesiastical vows.

As opposed to the vow of poverty, Rabelais emphasizes the richness of cloth and dress, for both male and female; he indicates their wealth by mentioning rich materials, marvelous colors and jewelry. He begins his descriptions of dress with feminine underwear—first stockings, then girdle, farthingale, petticoat, etc.:

> Next to their smock they put on the pretty kirtle or vasquin of pure silk camlet: above that went the taffety or tabby farthingale, of white, red, tawny, grey, or of any other colour. Above this taffety petticoat they had another of cloth of tissue or brocade, embroidered with fine gold and interlaced with needlework …[12]

He goes to describe various pieces of feminine clothing such as dresses, tunics, and coats. In describing men's garments, Rabelais proceeds in the same manner, if somewhat more briefly:

> The men were appareled after their fashion. Their stockings were of tamine or of cloth serge, of white, black, scarlet, or some other ingrained colour. Their breeches were of velvet, of the same colour with their stockings, or very near, embroidered and cut according to their fancy. Their doublet was of cloth of gold, of cloth of silver, of velvet, satin, damask, taffeties, of the same colours, cut, embroidered, and suitably trimmed up in perfection.[13]

Through these depictions, it became obvious how important wealth was for Rabelais. Not only does it convey material richness, it also is a condition for well-being. Furthermore, elegance is a legitimate right, according to Rabelais; this view is completely opposed to monastic law, which orders that monks' and nuns' clothing should be extremely poor and simple.

As opposed to the ideal of obedience, Thélèmites decide anew, every day, what to wear:

> There was such sympathy betwixt the gallants and the ladies, that every day they were appareled in the same livery. And that they might not miss, there were certain gentlemen appointed to tell the youths every morning what vestments the ladies would on that day wear: for all was done according to the pleasure of the ladies.[14]

Thus, the choice of dress is diametrically opposed to the vow of obedience. This collective decision concerning dress may also be seen, however, as opposed to personal free will.

> What is particularly striking in the description of the Thélèmites' mode of dress is that, in spite of its colorful opulence, all wear the same garments at the same time, so that their clothes take on the aspect not of freedom [...] but of a uniform. Some critics have, quite legitimately, seen the surrender of individual will to the collective will of the community as a positive, even evangelical element in the episode and it is indeed true that the word "Thélème" is derived from a Greek word used in the New Testament to mean the will of God.[15]

Through the co-ordination of dress, Rabelais also describes harmony between the sexes. There again, as opposed to the Catholic idea that chastity is better that matrimonial life, Rabelais shows beneficial intimacy. Moreover, although there is no direct mention of eroticism, by including underwear, Rabelais indicates the importance of refined elegance in intimacy as well.

During the Middle Ages, monastic life was considered as an alternative to ordinary life for ordinary people. Thélème is constructed as an alternative to this alternative, not only through its inversion of the three fundamental vows, but also because Thélème Abbey is an elitist utopia. In the first place, Gargantua "ordained that into this religious order should be admitted no women that were not fair, well-featured, and of a sweet disposition; nor men that were not comely, personable, and well conditioned."[16] Thus, according to Max Gauna,

> the recruits of conventional monastic institutions, made up of women too ugly and senseless to find husbands and men too unhealthy, stupid, and ill-born to earn a decent living, will be replaced by the beautiful and the good-natured. Health, intelligence, and mental equilibrium are easy positive values to understand and to insist upon …[17]

Thélèmites are also busy with noble occupations such as hunting, riding horses, travelling, singing, etc., while an army of professionals (goldsmiths, lapidaries, jewelers, embroiderers, tailors, gold-drawers, velvet-weavers, tapestry-makers, and upholsterers) tend to their exceptional clothing. Thus, their expensive and magnificent dress materializes Thélèmites' elitist status. Indeed, the abbey of Thélème resembles the court of Francis I. According to Ruben Quintero, the analogy between Thélème and the court of Francis I has ideological purposes as well:

> the fact [is] that the buildings of Thélème are described in terms that recall the chateaux of the Loire valley, while the dress, activities, and general comportment of the Thélèmites are those of idealized courtiers at the court of Francis I. In this way, Rabelais' satire suggests that the opposite of monasticism is not an ideal Christian community, but an ideal royal court like the very one the king himself was then fashioning for himself. Subtly but unmistakably, Rabelais' satire maneuvers the King of France into his own corner in his battle against the dark forces of medieval reaction.[18]

Thus, "*Comment estoient vestuz les religieux et religieuses de Thélème*, features a reasonably faithful representation of the typical aristocratic wardrobe of the early Renaissance, so much so that it is rather like a contemporary fashion parade."[19] Valerie Steele's depiction of Francis I's clothing closely resembles Rabelais' account of the Thélèmites vestments:

> A true Renaissance prince, Francis wore clothing of extraordinary richness, made of luxurious and colorful fabrics—doublets of cloth of gold, cloth of silver, velvet, satin, and taffeta in crimson, azure, violet, and every other color of the rainbow. His clothes and those of his courtiers were further ornamented with lace, gold braid, and embroidery, and precious jewels.[20]

Hence, as Marian Rothstein sums it up: "The courtly setting marks the Abbey as a spiritually noble place. Its inhabitants' rich dress mirrors their spiritual and intellectual riches."[21]

Voltaire: Clothing in the El Dorado Utopia in Candide (1759)

French philosopher Voltaire (1694–1778), also called the Father of Revolution, was deeply engaged in the service of social reforms, justice, education, and civil rights. He waged his struggle mainly through writing. In his philosophical tale entitled *Candide ou l'optimisme*, published in 1759, Candide, the eponymous hero of one of Voltaire's best-known books, lives numerous adventures. Through their account, Voltaire criticizes aspects of his own day, mainly religious intolerance, obscurantism, and fanaticism, as well as French monarchy, with its nepotism, inequitable social stratification, corrupted nobility, etc.

In his peregrinations, Candide, accompanied by his valet Cacambo, arrives at a magnificent and imaginary country called El Dorado (chapters XVII and XVIII).[22] Through the depiction of El Dorado, the reader is shown the Voltairian utopia of a happy, well-ordered, and just state: comparable to a constitutional monarchy, El Dorado is led by a benevolent and just king, and his subjects live in peace, harmony, and wealth. Moreover, mixing fantastical elements with oriental ones, Voltaire invents an ideal country, where opulence materializes both happiness and justice: both the physical senses and spiritual aspirations are fulfilled.[23] El Dorado's clothes are part of this richness. Although less developed than in Thélème, clothing is an important part of El Dorado.

At first,

> He [Candide] stepped out with Cacambo towards the first village which he saw. Some children dressed in tattered brocades played at quoits on the outskirts. […] The quoits were large round pieces, yellow, red, and green, which cast a singular lustre! The travelers picked a few of them off the ground; this was of gold, that of emeralds, the other of rubies—the least of them would have been the greatest ornament on the Mogul's throne. "Without doubt," said Cacambo, "these children must be the king's sons that are playing at quoits!"[24]

Although the associations conjured up by the words "tattered brocades" seems antithetical, through them, Voltaire hints at the entire attitude to wealth in El Dorado: opulence is a right, part of normal life, but not revered. As pointed out by Robin Howells,

> the children's clothing is paradoxical. Their pastimes also, since the pieces they use are 'des émeraudes, des rubis'. When the children leave them on the ground, Candide and Cacambo intervene, assuming that these counters have the same value as in 'l'autre monde' (Chapter 17, p. 215). Here, then,

we have once more the complement and antithesis. Culturally precious stones are returned to earth. The riches pursued by adults in the other world become children's toys in Eldorado. The 'real' world is reversed and resumed as a game."[25]

Indeed, as Candide and Cacambo will learn later on, these children are not royalty.

As they proceed, Candide and Cacambo enter a public house. There, "immediately two waiters and two girls, dressed in cloth of gold, and their hair tied up with ribbons, invited them to sit down to table with the landlord."[26]

When preparing to meet the king, "twenty beautiful damsels of the King's guard received Candide and Cacambo as they alighted from the coach, conducted them to the bath, and dressed them in robes woven of the down of humming-birds."[27] Now dressed as richly as El Dorado's inhabitants, almost integrated into Eldoradian society, Candide and Cacambo are introduced to the king who lives like everyone else, looking for no special treatment, etc.

The El Dorado episode ends when Candide and Cacambo decide to leave El Dorado in order to reunite with their loved ones, far away. Voltaire, however, criticizes this decision with the ironic words "the two happy ones resolved to be no longer so, but to ask his Majesty's leave to quit the country."[28]

El Doradian opulence is a key theme in the Voltairian utopia. For Voltaire, happy and egalitarian life doesn't accord with simplicity—luxury equals happiness; it's even one of its conditions. Voltaire already expressed the idea that luxury will ensure happiness in the poem *Le Mondain* (1736), which includes the famous sentence "The superfluous is very necessary."[29] Hence, El Dorado inhabitants are richly dressed, in gold, silver, and multi-colored precious stones. However, in El Dorado, gold and diamonds are neither revered nor sold; richness is not regarded as such, but as part of ordinary life. El Dorado is an egalitarian dream, based on Enlightenment political ideals, where everyone lives honestly and richly.

Utopian dress and Egalitarianism

Wealth is a major theme in Voltaire's utopia, as in Rabelais'. For both writers, happy and utopian life does not translate into simplicity, uniformity, or austerity. On the contrary: luxury is a legitimate right for all. As important part of utopia, clothing expresses richness, and thus Thélèmites as well as Eldoradians are richly dressed.

This equation between richness and egalitarian utopia is quite unique, as many other utopians advocate the opposite; for example, as explained by Richard M. Berrong, "[u]nlike in Voltaire's El Dorado, in [More's][30] Utopia there could be no luxury, even if everyone was able to enjoy it. The inhabitants of Utopia have only very simple plain clothes, all of which look more or less the same. Nor is there any abundance of material possessions; each citizen receives a new outfit only once every two years."[31] According to J. C. Davis, More is not the only seeker of an austere utopia, in terms of dress as well: "Eberlein,[32] like so many other utopians, insisted on uniformity of dress, only the sexes being distinguished. Or again 'All men should have long beards – strictly enforced, none shall have a smooth face like a woman—all men shall have their hair trimmed short.'"[33] This feature repeats itself in Campanella's *City of the Sun*:[34] "The cenobitic characteristics of the community's administration and communal property are reinforced by the uniformity of dress and through the communal refectory that Campanella compares with those of a monastery."[35] And in Thomas Lawson's *Annus Sophiae Jubilaeus*,[36] "excess in dress [is] a punishable offence"[37](!).

Although some later utopias allowed some elegance for their inhabitants—as in Francis Bacon's *New Atlantis* (1624) and Samuel Goot's *Nova Solyma* (1648), most others continue to extol simplicity, practicality and utility: as in Mercier's *L'An deux mille quatre cents quarante* (1771), Edward Bellamy's *Looking Backward* (1888),[38] Charles Fourier's *Phalanstère* (1822–1832),[39] Etienne Cabet's *Voyage et aventures de lord William Carisdall en Icarie* (1840),[40] etc.

Even much later on, the Israeli kibbutz, another utopia amongst the few to ever be implemented, advocated (at its beginning) simplicity in dress: no kibbutz member could hold personal clothing, all clothing was very simple, was bought and shared in common, and there was no room for personal choice.[41] Interestingly, when dreamed utopias are put into practice, new functions are attributed to dress: clothing is used to distinguish between utopians and non-utopians; dress represents the abolition of private property. Thus, even if utopias wish to offer happiness to everyone, none of them achieve it through rich clothing, as Rabelais and Voltaire do, and egalitarianism is lived through (almost) poverty and always simplicity.

Is it because, often, utopia seeks a society where no hypocrisy exists? This would imply that clothing, as well as fashion, are tools used in order to cheat:[42] "Utopia lends itself to the satire of being hypocritical or useless ritual, and thus meets with the literary tradition of a simplified society with a minimum of structure, the golden age, the garden of paradise …"[43] Or is it, as Ribeiro exposes it, because "fashion, with its necessary expenditure and the elements of envy and competitiveness involved, was seen to be divisive and inimical to true equality?"[44] Or is it because property was often seen as the origin of inequality? In this perspective, erasing all materiality, including dress, could bring on equality. At any rate, Rabelais and Voltaire do not opt for any of those positions. According to Michaël Baraz, Thélème's luxury was even designed by Rabelais to intentionally oppose Plato's and More's utopias.[45]

Conclusion

Although not developed to the same length, these two utopias aspire for similar ideological goals: for Rabelais as for Voltaire, harmonious life will be achieved through liberty, civil rights, absence of religion, and richness. Moreover, the socio-political context of the writing of these utopias has to be considered: while separated by 200 years, these philosophers develop their philosophical utopias in opposition to the main political problems of their own present. If for Rabelais, excessive power by the Catholic Church still dominates, his utopia proposes an ironic alternative abbey; for Voltaire, society's political structure, held in place by a corrupt French monarchy, is the main problem demanding change; thus, his utopia describes a particular kingdom which is an almost-democratic country. These utopias also resemble each other in the idea that opulence is an integral part of happiness, which is expressed in rich dress as well. Furthermore, both located in imaginary places, these utopias also comply with one of the characteristics of the utopian *genre*.[46]

There are however, significant differences in dress between these two utopias: firstly, the topic of clothes is elaborated far more in Rabelais than in Voltaire; moreover, equality is central to Voltaire, and thus everyone is richly dressed, while in Rabelais the Thélèmites form an elitist society, all elegantly dressed while being served by others. Furthermore, Voltaire is more consistent than Rabelais: for the latter, the question of choice, of free will, is not clear: by describing new clothes chosen by the utopian leadership for everyone, personal taste is limited; whereas for Voltaire, advocating free will, choice is completely free. Another difference concerns the relationship between the clothing in the utopias and the fashion of the day: in Thélème, elaborate clothing echoes sixteenth century fashion, while in El Dorado, the clothes are described in a loose manner; in this way, Voltaire accentuates free personal choice as well as the imaginary aspect of his utopia.

From Rabelais' and Voltaire's perspective, freedom has to be the base of a just society. Thus Rabelais' Thélèmites and Voltaire's Eldoradian express their equality, happiness, and liberty through opulent, varied, and colorful dress.

Finally, Rabelais and Voltaire consider richness as part of civil rights and are opposed to many writers of utopias who extended their utopian logic so far as to imagine a cenobitic world, including uniformity in dress. Indeed, nowadays, it seems rather bizarre that for so many utopists a monastery or a quasi-military life was designed to promise liberty!

Notes

1   *Encyclopedia Britannica* Utopia entry, http://www.britannica.com/EBchecked/
topic/620755/utopia

2   Maurice Tournier, "Utopie, ce lieu de nulle part qui est à tous et à personne," *Mots*,
35 (Juin 1993), p. 115, http://www.persee.fr/web/revues/home/prescript/article/
mots_0243-6450_1993_num_35_1_1837. Translation by the author from the
original French: "Utopie, de ces origines, avant d'être le signe d'un monde idéal,
se présente d'abord comme la rature, l'envers dénoncé de réalités insupportables.
Mot négatif tout au fond de ses racines."

3   Barbara Goodwin and Keith Taylor, *The Politics of Utopia: A Study in Theory and
Practice*, Oxford: Peter Lang, 2009, p. 5.

4   Maria Béatrice Bittarello, "Another Time, Another Space: Virtual Worlds, Myths and
Imagination", *Virtual Worlds Research: Past, Present & Future*, Volume 1, Number
1 (July 2008).

5   Aileen Ribeiro, "Utopian Dress," in Juliet Ash and Elizabeth Wilson eds, *Chic Thrills:
A Fashion Reader*, Berkeley: University of California Press, 1992, p. 226. Ribeiro
does not include Rabelais and Voltaire in her analysis.

6   Ibid.

7   According to Maurice Tournier "la liberté de Thélème s'édifie sur le cimetière des
intolérances." "Utopie," p. 116.

8   David M. Posner, "The temple of reading: architectonic metaphor in Rabelais,"
Renaissance Studies, 17, 2 (2003)," pp. 257–74.

9   Goodwin and Taylor, *The Politics of Utopia*, p. 36.

10   Rabelais, François, *Gargantua and his son Pantagruel*, Thomas Urquhart
(trans.), of Cromarty & Peter Antony Motteux, Project Gutenberg (Chapter 52),
http://www.gutenberg.org/files/1200/old/orig1200-h/p2.htm.

11   Ibid.

12   Ibid.

13   Ibid.

14   Ibid.

15   Lance K. Donaldson-Evans, "Fashioning Gargantua: Rabelais and the history of
costume," *Mots Pluriels, Revue de sciences humaines et de littérature*, 1999,
http://pandora.nla.gov.au/nph-wb/19990731130000/http://www.arts.uwa.edu.au/
MotsPluriels/MP1099lde.html#fnB26

16   Rabelais, *Gargantua and his son Pantagruel*.

17   Max Gauna, *The Rabelaisian Mythologies*, Madison: Fairleigh Dickinson University
Press, 1996, p. 92.

18   Ruben Quintero, *A Companion to Satire: Ancient and Modern*, Chichester: John
Wiley & Sons, 2008, pp. 77–8.

19   Donaldson-Evans, "Fashioning Gargantua."

20   Valerie Steele, *Paris Fashion: a Cultural History*, Oxford: Berg, 2006, p. 19.

21 Marian Rothstein, "Thélème, Abbey of," entry in *The Rabelais Encyclopedia*, Elizabeth Chesney Zegura ed., New York: Greenwood Press, 2004, p. 244.

22 Catherine Alès et Michel Pouyllau,"La Conquête de l'inutile: Les géographies imaginaires de l'Eldorado," *L'Homme*, 32, 122–4 (1992), pp. 271–308: http://www.persee.fr/web/revues/home/prescript/article/hom_0439-4216_1992_num_32_122_369537

23 On the importance of happiness in 18th-century French thought, see Robert Mauzi, *L'idée du bonheur dans la littérature et la pensée françaises au XVIIIe siècle*, Geneva: Slatkine, 1960.

24 Voltaire, The Project Gutenberg EBook of *Candide*, Release Date: November 27, 2006 [EBook #19942] http://www.gutenberg.org/files/19942/19942-h/19942-h.htm.

25 R. J. Howells, "Cette Boucherie Héroïque: 'Candide' as Carnival," *The Modern Language Review*, 80, 2 (April 1985): 294.

26 Voltaire, E-Book of *Candide*.

27 Ibid.

28 Ibid.

29 English translation of the French sentence (by the author of this chapter) "Le superflu, chose très nécessaire."

30 Thomas More, *Utopia*, 1516.

31 Richard M. Berrong, *Rabelais and Bakhtin: Popular Culture in "Gargantua and Pantagruel,"* Lincoln: University of Nebraska Press, 2006, p. 115. See also "L'Utopie de Thomas More: une réponse au débat sur le nouveau monde?" *Moreana* XXVII, 101–2 (Mai 1990): 5–24.

32 Johann Eberlein von Gunsburg, *Wolfaria*, 1521.

33 J. C. Davis, *Utopia and the Ideal Society: A Study of English Utopian Writing, 1516–1700*, Cambridge: Cambridge University Press, 1983, p. 66.

34 Thomasso Campanella, *City of the Sun*, 1623.

35 Davis, *Utopia and the Ideal Society*, p. 72.

36 Thomas Lawson, *Annus Sophiae Jubilaeus*, 1700.

37 Davis, *Utopia and the Ideal Society*, p. 362.

38 Ribeiro, "Utopian Dress," pp. 227–30.

39 André Vergez, "La métaphysique de Charles Fourier," *Cahiers Charles Fourier*, 18 (Décembre 2007), pp. 97–104, disponible en ligne: http://www.charlesfourier.fr/article.php3?id_article=524

40 See on the matter Yolène Dilas-Rocherieux, "Utopie et communisme. Étienne Cabet: de la théorie à la pratique," *Revue française de science politique*, 41e année, n°5 (1991): 676–92.

41 Michael Chyutin and Bracha Chyutin, *Architecture and Utopia: The Israeli Experiment*, Aldershot, Ashgate Publishing, 2007, p. 58; Anat Helman, "Kibbutz dress in the 1950s: utopian equality, anti fashion, and change," *Fashion Theory: The Journal of Dress, Body & Culture*, 12, 3 (September 2008): 313–39.

42 Although the first line engraved on Thélème gate reads "Here enter not vile bigots, hypocrites," it has nothing to do with the topic of dress.

43 Frank Paul Bowma, "Utopie, imagination, espérance: Northrop Frye, Ernst Bloch, Judith Schlanger," *Littérature*, 21 (1976), p. 12. Translation by the author from the original French: "L'utopie se prête aussi à la satire du rituel hypocrite ou inutile, et rejoint ainsi la tradition littéraire d'une société simplifiée avec un minimum de structures, l'âge d'or, le paradis jardin …"

44 Ribeiro, "Utopian Dress," p. 225. Although mostly written about More's utopia, the idea is valid for all of these austere utopias.

45 Michael Baraz, *Rabelais et la joie de la liberté*, Librairie José Corti, 1983, p. 254.

46 Corin Braga, "Du paradis terrestre à l'utopie: avatars migrants du thème du 'lieu parfait,'" *Philologia* (Studia Universitatis Babes-Bolyai), 2 (2010): 105–13.

Bibliography

Alès, Catherine and Michel Pouyllau, "La Conquête de l'inutile: Les géographies imaginaires de l'Eldorado," *L'Homme*, 32, 122–4 (1992), pp. 271–308: http://www. persee.fr/web/revues/home/prescript/article/hom_0439-4216_1992_ num_32_122_369537

Baraz, Michaël, *Rabelais et la joie de la liberté*, Librairie José Corti, 1983.

Beretta Anguissola, Alberto, *Ombres de l'utopie: essais sur les voyages imaginaires du xvie au xviiie siècle*. Paris: Honoré Champion, 2011.

Berrong, Richard M., *Rabelais and Bakhtin: Popular Culture in "Gargantua and Pantagruel,"* Lincoln: University of Nebraska Press, 2006.

Bittarello, Maria Beatrice, "Another time, another space: virtual worlds, myths and imagination," *Virtual Worlds Research: Past, Present & Future*, 1, 1 (July 2008).

Bowman, Frank Paul, "Utopie, imagination, espérance: Northrop Frye, Ernst Bloch, Judith Schlanger," *Littérature*, 21 (1976): 10–19.

Braga, Corin, "Du paradis terrestre à l'utopie: avatars migrants du thème du 'lieu parfait,'" *Philologia* (Studia Universitatis Babes-Bolyai), 2 (2010): 105–13.

Campanella, Thomasso, *City of the Sun*, 1623.

Chyutin, Michael and Bracha Chyutin, *Architecture and Utopia: The Israeli Experiment*, Aldershot: Ashgate Publishing, 2007.

Davis, J. C., *Utopia and the Ideal Society: A Study of English Utopian Writing, 1516–1700*, Cambridge: Cambridge University Press, 1983.

Dilas-Rocherieux, Yolène, "Utopie et communisme. Étienne Cabet: de la théorie à la pratique," *Revue française de science politique*, 41e année, n°5 (1991): 676–92.

Donaldson-Evans, Lance K., "Fashioning Gargantua: Rabelais and the history of costume," *Mots Pluriels, Revue de sciences humaines et de littérature*, 1999, http://pandora.nla.gov.au/nphwb/19990731130000/http://www.arts.uwa.edu.au/ MotsPluriels/MP1099lde.html#fnB26

Encyclopedia Britannica, Utopia entry, http://www.britannica.com/EBchecked/ topic/620755/utopia

Gauna, Max, *The Rabelaisian Mythologies*, Madison: Fairleigh Dickinson University Press, 1996.

Goodwin, Barbara and Keith Taylor, *The Politics of Utopia: A Study in Theory and Practice*, Oxford: Peter Lang, 2009.

Helman, Anat, "Kibbutz dress in the 1950s: utopian equality, anti fashion, and change," *Fashion Theory: The Journal of Dress, Body & Culture*, 12, 3 (September 2008): 313–39.

Howells, R. J., "Cette Boucherie Héroïque: 'Candide' as Carnival," *The Modern Language Review*, 80, 2 (April 1985): 293–303.

Mauzi, Robert, *L'idée du bonheur dans la littérature et la pensée françaises au XVIIIe siècle*, Geneva: Slatkine, 1960.

Posner, David M., "The temple of reading: architectonic metaphor in Rabelais," *Renaissance Studies*, 17, 2 (2003): 257–74.

Quintero, Ruben, *A Companion to Satire: Ancient and Modern*, Chichester: John Wiley & Sons, 2008.

Rabelais, François, *Gargantua and his son Pantagruel*, Thomas Urquhart, trans., of Cromarty & Peter Antony Motteux, Project Gutenberg, http://www.gutenberg.org/files/1200/old/orig1200-h/p2.htm.

Ribeiro, Aileen, "Utopian Dress," in Juliet Ash and Elizabeth Wilson eds, *Chic Thrills: A Fashion Reader*, Berkeley: University of California Press, 1992.

Rothstein, Marian, "Thélème, Abbey of" entry in *The Rabelais Encyclopedia*, Elizabeth Chesney Zegura ed., New York: Greenwood Press, 2004.

Steele, Valerie, *Paris Fashion: A Cultural History*, Oxford: Berg, 2006.

Stosetzki, Christophe, "L'Utopie de Thomas More: une réponse au débat sur le nouveau monde?" *Moreana* XXVII, 101–2 (Mai 1990): 5–24.

Tournier, Maurice, "Utopie, ce lieu de nulle part qui est à tous et à personne," *Mots*, 35 (Juin 1993), p. 115, http://www.persee.fr/web/revues/home/prescript/article/mots_0243-6450_1993_num_35_1_1837.

Vergez, André, "La métaphysique de Charles Fourier," *Cahiers Charles Fourier*, 18 (Décembre 2007), pp. 97–104, disponible en ligne: http://www.charlesfourier.fr/article.php3?id_article=524.

Voltaire, *E-Book of Candide*, Project Gutenberg, Release Date: November 27, 2006, [E-Book #19942], http://www.gutenberg.org/files/19942/19942-h/19942-h.htm

INDEX